CHERRY CITY CONFIDENTIAL

12 MURDER CASES

that Rocked

OREGON'S CAPITAL CITY

CHERRY CITY CONFIDENTIAL

12 MURDER CASES

that Rocked

OREGON'S CAPITAL CITY

J. E. McCOMB

Black Lyon Publishing, LLC

CHERRY CITY CONFIDENTIAL:

12 Murder Cases that Rocked Oregon's Capital City

Copyright © 2020 by **J. E. McComb**

Our books may be ordered through your local bookstore or by
visiting the publisher:

www.BlackLyonPublishing.com

Black Lyon Publishing, LLC
PO Box 567
Baker City, OR 97814

ISBN: 978-1-934912-94-2
Library of Congress Control Number: 2020943797

Published and printed in the United States of America.

Black Lyon True Crime

Praise for this book:

"*If you listened to our podcast,* Murder in Oregon, *about the assassination of Oregon Corrections Director Michael Francke in 1989, you've probably already got an idea of just how crooked things were in Salem back in the day. But that's just for starters. If you're looking for more of the same—and not just on the Francke case but on eleven other disturbing murders that have rocked the state's capital city over the years—you won't want to miss J. E. McComb's* CHERRY CITY CONFIDENTIAL."
—Phil Stanford, author, ROSE CITY VICE,
PORTLAND CONFIDENTIAL, WHITE HOUSE
CALL GIRL, and THE PEYTON-ALLAN FILES

"*Having lived in Salem for over 50 years, I remember many of these murders and how they shook the community. Driving through town and past crime scenes, I am reminded what a rich history Salem has, of which many residents are unaware. As a former journalist, I appreciated the careful research evident throughout* CHERRY CITY CONFIDENTIAL. *Salem is a great place to live, but even the best places are scarred by tragedy.* CHERRY CITY CONFIDENTIAL *will find a home in my guest room and will make a great gift for anyone who lives—or has lived—in Salem.*"
—Chuck Bennett, Mayor of Salem

"*As vice-chair of the Senate Judiciary Committee in 1989, Michael Francke was murdered on my watch. I never bought the official story that Michael was killed interrupting a car burglary by a low-level street criminal. This was the Director of Corrections, a person who had learned of corruption within his department and had told people he was going to clean it up. Pretty convenient that he turns up dead the night before he was to testify before my committee.* CHERRY CITY CONFIDENTIAL *gives a detailed, well-researched account of both the 1986 investigation into prison corruption, the murder, and the subsequent investigation and trial. I found the chapters covering other murders interesting and enlightening as well, as some of those pre-date my Salem residence.* CHERRY CITY CONFIDENTIAL *is a must-read for Salem residents and true crime fans everywhere.*"
—Jim Hill, former Oregon State
Treasurer, senator, and author

Contents

Introduction   **9**

1. Center Street Sadist (Jerome Brudos)   **12**

2. The Butcher (Richard Marquette)   **33**

3. The Big House (Carl Panzram and Otto Hooker)   **47**

4. The Vanishings (William Scott Smith)   **66**

5. He Had It Coming (Alma Wurtzbarger)   **84**

6. The I-5 Killer (Randall Woodfield)   **102**

7. Over the Wall (Harry Tracy and David Merrill)   **126**

8. Ladies Night (Lawrence Moore)   **146**

9. The Bug House (George Nosen)   **158**

10. Obsession (Robert Wampler)   **169**

11. Despair (Lucy Jellison)   **187**

12. Snitches Get Stitches (Frank Gable)   **197**

Introduction

Salem is the anglicized form of the
Hebrew word *shalom*, meaning peace.

*"Understanding does not cure evil, but it is a definite help
inasmuch as one can cope with a comprehensible darkness."*
—Carl Jung

On January 18, 1989, I was busy preparing for another day working in the Oregon House and Senate Judiciary Committee Office when the news dropped: Our primary witness for that day, director of the Department of Corrections Michael Francke, was dead. Murdered. Activity in the capitol came to a virtual halt. There was no other conversation. People spent the day battling their disbelief and shock.

While the committees would work on many issues that session, the murder was never far from people's minds. Significant attention shifted toward the murder investigation and the Oregon Corrections system in general, and I was swept along with it. Who would kill Michael Francke? And why? People became obsessed—and I was one of them.

Murder has always fascinated. In 1838, New York newspapers went wild speculating who killed Mary Rogers, the "The Beautiful Cigar Girl," and inspired Edgar Allan Poe to try and solve the crime in his 1842 short story, *The Murder of Marie Roget*, a follow up to the *Murders in the Rue Morgue*, considered the first detective novel. *The Police Gazette* capitalized on the public's fascination with crime and debuted in 1845.

In 1847, a dismembered woman's body sparked a tabloid war between Joseph Pulitzer and William Randolph Hearst. Now, we are awash in crime, both fictional and true, and entire television networks exist to meet our need to know the answers to two of life's most vexing questions: Who dunnit and why?

Would the killer turn out to be someone shaped by his environment and his own decisions? Or was he destined by his DNA and chemistry to be on the wrong side of law and order? And most importantly, could I be the next victim?

Salem, Oregon, is a pretty good spot to ponder such questions. It's the second biggest town in Oregon, but feels like a small town—a small town with secrets.

Home to Oregon's mental hospital, the state's first prison, the legislature, youth reformatories, state agencies, an Indian boarding school, and until relatively recently, the state institution for those with intellectual disabilities, Salem is a town full of institutions with haunted histories.

Growing up, I assumed kids in all towns spent the occasional afternoon exploring the rhododendrons for escaped felons. And nothing conveyed love on Mother's Day quite like a leather key fob made by a serial killer from the local (now defunct) prison gift shop.

I might have begun to tumble to Salem's uniqueness when I was working in an office at the state mental hospital and the ten o'clock pastry cart was wheeled past my desk pushed by residents of the Sex Offenders Unit, and the sandwich wagon was staffed by those incarcerated in the Forensic Psych Ward (guilty but insane).These were daily reminders that life can go wrong slowly, with daily missteps building to tragedy or turn catastrophic in a single moment.

The town's institutions made it clear: No one was safe.

Even Hollywood recognized Salem's dark underbelly when it chose our mental hospital in which to film *One Flew over the Cuckoo's Nest*.

Mental illness. Cruelty. Abuse of power. Poverty. Corruption. As the old TV show, *The Naked City* might say, there are a thousand stories in the Cherry City.

What follows are a dozen of them: murder cases that rocked the city.

1. Center Street Sadist

3123 Center St.
March 27, 1969

Salem Student, 19, Feared Kidnapped. That was the March 29, 1969 headline of the *Capitol Journal* when both the police and the student's parents decided to appeal to the public for help.

Karen Sprinker, a bright, attractive 19-year-old college student had come home to Salem on spring break from her first year at Oregon State University. She was scheduled to meet her mother for lunch Thursday March 27 at Salem's largest and finest department store, where her mother worked. The day was the warmest Salem had seen that year and spring seemed to have finally arrived in the dark, rainy burg, giving citizens reason to hope for happy days ahead.

But better times for Salem were not in the cards that day, beginning when the reliable daughter failed to keep her lunch date.

Karen was a National Honor Society member, a National Merit Scholarship finalist, a member of the Marion County Youth Council, and a winner of an Elks leadership award. She was pre-med. She was never in trouble, despite this being the late sixties when trouble was under every rock. In short, she was the kind of daughter every parent hoped for—and not the kind who would stand up her mother without a word.

By 12:15, Karen's mother knew something was wrong. She had waited in the store's restaurant watching store mod-

Photo credit: J. E. McComb

Karen Sprinker parked her Dodge Dart on this rooftop parking lot before encountering Jerome Brudos, likely brandishing a fake gun.

els weave their way around tables modeling the latest fashions until she could wait no more. She called home. Then she went home. No Karen.

Where was she?

She called Karen's friends. She called the hospital.

Finally, she had to consider the worst. She called the police.

Police are understandably slow to panic about teenage girls blowing off lunch dates with their moms. Karen had gotten into a tiff with her boyfriend about religion sometime earlier. Police thought she might have gone somewhere to think or engage in any number of things a college coed might do.

It was two years after the Summer of Love. The number one hit on the radio that week was *Aquarius/Let the Sun Shine In*. The top-rated television show was *Laugh-In*. To the south of Oregon, Charles Manson dropped by a Cielo Drive address looking for an acquaintance but discovered he had moved out and actress Sharon Tate and Roman Polanski had moved in. (According to Beach Boy Mike Love, Terry Melcher's mother, Doris Day, had urged him to move out of the house when she heard that some crazy guy brandishing a knife had been there.)

It was a time of electric possibility, when anything could happen, good and bad. Or very bad.

Karen's father knew right away something was wrong. Karen was a serious girl, not an impulsive, drug-addled hippie. The police also took her disappearance seriously, upon its first report.

Investigators found Karen's locked car—actually her father's 1964 Dodge Dart—parked at the top level of the store's parking garage, with no signs of a struggle. Had someone lured Karen away to another vehicle after she got out and locked her car? Or confronted her in the lonely stairwell leading from the roof to the second floor? Whatever happened, it happened after Karen parked her car and before she made it into the store.

Despite reports that Karen had been seen at the railroad depot with two men, the sad truth was that only one person had seen her that afternoon: her killer.

•••••

Two months later, on Monday, May 13, a fisherman and his son threw their lines over the Bundy Bridge on the Long Tom River, some 40 miles south of Salem, when something in the water caught the older man's eye. Upon closer examination—to his horror—it appeared to be a floating body, that of a young woman. The fisherman immediately contacted the Benton County Sheriff. Police identified the body as Linda Salee of Portland. Salee had disappeared a few weeks earlier, on an April 23 shopping trip.

Police dragged the river and found a second body about 50 feet from the first.

Karen Sprinker had been found.

Both women murdered, both partially clothed, both tied

Photo credit: State Library of Oregon

The site of the Sprinker abduction, Meier & Frank in Salem first opened in Salem in 1955 with 185,000 square feet of merchandise and was a retail powerhouse in the region.

with their hands in front of them and both weighted down with car parts—Ms. Salee was tied with nylon cord and copper wire to a 1949 or 1950 Ford transmission weighing 35 to 40 pounds and Ms. Sprinker was lashed to a 60-pound Chevrolet cylinder head. Instead of the simple white cotton bras Karen wore, she was now wearing a longline black bra several sizes too big for her—even if her breasts had not been removed and replaced with paper towels.

The autopsy revealed both deaths were due to traumatic asphyxiation, the mutilation on Karen done post-mortem. The coroner could not determine whether she had been sexually assaulted due to her time in the water.

Police now knew that the same killer, or killers, had killed two women. They looked at the list of other young missing women, looking for similarities. There was no question some kind of monster was on the loose. The only question was how many other victims were out there—and how many more there would be.

Salem police detectives had followed up on the few leads of the Sprinker disappearance but had been stalled when her body was found. Despite the tragic conclusion of the search, the bodies and where they were found offered a silver lining in that they provided police a number of clues.

The cities from which the girls had been taken, and the Long Tom River site, indicated a man familiar with those places: Portland, Salem, and Corvallis. The auto parts to which the women were tied could possibly be traced. The weight of the heavy auto parts and the bodies pointed to a strong man. The rope, electrical wire, and the knots used indicated a possible electrician. The black bra could possibly be traced. With the knowledge that the two cases were related, detectives could look for commonalities between the two girls as well as other missing young women—if he could kill two, perhaps there were others.

It was not long before police *did* find other missing girls.

First, there was 19-year-old Linda Slawson, who had moved from Minnesota to Aloha, Oregon, in search of a better life. She had disappeared January 26, 1968, while out on her job selling encyclopedias door-to-door in Portland.

Next was 23-year-old Jan Whitney who had disappeared along Interstate-5 on November 26, 1968, on her way home to McMinnville from Eugene.

Police were also aware of at least two attempted abductions that could possibly be tied to the two murders.

Twenty-six-year-old Sharon Wood was in the Portland State University parking garage on April 21, 1969, at 3:30 in the afternoon. She was preoccupied and running late to an appointment. She was in the basement when she realized she was on the wrong level. She started to turn back to the isolated stairs when instinct told her she was being followed. She headed for the daylight entrance into the garage when someone tapped her on her shoulder.

A man raised a pistol and told her if she didn't scream he wouldn't shoot her. Sharon did scream and backed away. She continued to scream and kick as the man threw his arm around her neck. She grabbed at what turned out to be a toy gun. She bit his thumb and her jaw locked. He pulled her hair toward the floor and began dashing her head against the concrete trying to free his thumb. A car drove by. Her jaw relaxed. The man ran.

The next day, 15-year-old Gloria Smith reported she had nearly been abducted at 10:30 in the morning as she walked along the railroad tracks near Parrish Junior High returning from a dentist appointment. It was a month after Karen had disappeared. The man had pulled her between two houses. He showed her a gun and told her to come with him; he wouldn't hurt her and began pulling her toward his car. Gloria saw a woman she knew working in a nearby yard, broke free, and ran to her. Gloria described her would-be abductor to the police, including his large size and that he had freckles.

Linda Salee disappeared the following day. Could they all be connected? Police began working on the theory they were.

Given where the victims were snatched, police thought the killer was likely living in the Willamette Valley. Salem police visited Sprinker's Corvallis college dorm, a target-rich environment if one is looking for pretty, naïve, young women. Police interviewed dorm residents in teams, asking about anything suspicious they had noticed, focusing on Karen's dorm.

Police despaired of uncovering anything useful until a few of the girls reported being called to the dorm phone only to discover a man they had never met on the other end of the line, a "Gary Keith." He had asked for them by their first name. He chatted them up, saying he was a Vietnam veteran and had been held prisoner. He was lonely. Would they have coffee or a Coke with him? Most had turned him down, but to the joy of the detectives, one girl had met him.

The man had been much older than the typical college boy—about 30, chunky and tall, pale with freckles and losing his hair. He was a disappointment to the college girl. The small talk was forgettable, but what was memorable was when he started to massage her shoulders, squeezed, and asked her to think of something sad. When the coed said she couldn't, he asked her to think about the young women killed and found in the Long Tom River. He asked her, "What makes you want to be raped like those other girls?"[1]

It was not the kind of question that led to second dates.

Police asked the girl to agree to see the man again, should he call, and then to notify police. She agreed. Lead detective Jim Stovall remembered that the 14-year-old attempted kidnapping victim in Salem had described a similar man—those freckles—and this made police hopeful about their lead. On May 25, the man called the coed again.

Two detectives were waiting in the dorm lounge when a pale, loutish, older man wandered into the dorm lounge and took a seat, nervously looking toward the door for his date. Police moved in and began questioning him. He told them his name was Jerry Brudos, he lived in Salem on Center Street with his wife and two children, was an electrician and was in Corvallis to do yard work for a friend.

The man's story checked out and police had no cause to hold him—the lech factor of an older married man hanging around women's college dorms was (sadly) not a bookable offence. They took note of the car he was driving—a beat-up light blue 1963 Comet station wagon—and began investigating their prime suspect.

First there was his criminal history, which was a good match for their suspect. Brudos's prior addresses matched up well with the other missing girls. And he was an electrician—that matched the knots found with the bodies in the river.

A detective followed up and questioned Jerry in his home workshop in a part of the garage that connected to the house by a covered breezeway. The workshop gave the detective the creeps and he reported seeing a hook in the ceiling and lots of knotted ropes. He shared his findings and returned with three of his colleagues for a closer look. They noted the rope and knots were similar to those found with the bodies in the river. When Brudos saw the detectives had taken an interest in his ropes and knots, he volunteered a piece of rope with a knot in it to the detectives, much to their delight.

However, the station wagon Brudos owned didn't match the description of the car the junior high student had seen. When asked if he ever drove anything else, Brudos admitted to occasionally driving a friend's VW Karmann-Ghia, a car closer to the one described by the nearly-kidnapped Gloria Smith.

When the police took rope and knot samples back to the lab for comparison they found them identical to that found on the two bodies. The detectives faced a dilemma: risk arresting Brudos too soon without enough evidence to convict him or delay an arrest to gather more evidence and possibly risk another young woman's life.

They put Brudos's picture in a photo lineup and asked Gloria Smith to point out her would-be abductor. She chose Jerry. If they needed to bring him in sooner, they could do so on the attempted kidnapping charge.

Meanwhile, police watched him.

Brudos knew he was under surveillance and contacted a criminal defense attorney. Police obtained a search warrant for his two cars.

•••••

Jerome Henry Brudos was born January 31, 1939, to Henry and Eileen Brudos in South Dakota. Jerry had an older brother Larry. Jerry was five years old when he discovered his first pair of high-heeled shoes and was immediately drawn, taking them home. His mother did not support his new interest and ordered him to throw them back in the dump where he had found them. Instead, little Jerry hid them—the first of many secrets he would have

Photo credit: Marion County Sheriff's Office

30-year old Jerome Brudos was arrested May 30, 1969, and quickly confessed to the murders.

from his disapproving and critical mother.

When he later talked to psychiatrists, Brudos blamed his mother for his sexual deviancy—her displeasure at finding the shoes allegedly launched his fixation with shoes and undergarments.

Psychological studies show that the most important figure in a child's life is the mother, and from the mother the child learns what love is. If a child is unable to form attachments, these children grow up isolated, given to fantasy to cope. Sometimes those fantasies become deviant and violent.

Little Jerry Brudos began to fantasize—a lot.

The family moved to California where Jerry failed to make a good impression. The first-grader stole his teacher's high-heeled shoes. He was a sickly child and he failed the second grade. For most of his life he was plagued by headaches.

The family moved to Grants Pass, Oregon. Jerry began stealing neighbor girls' underwear and shoes. When Jerry was 13, the family moved to Salem and he began fantasizing about capturing girls while he continued his pastime of stealing shoes and underwear. The family moved again to Corvallis where he continued to steal women's things, but Jerry wanted something to help him preserve his pleasure—these Kodak moments—and he put his camera to use.

At age 12 and 13, Brudos began abducting girls his own age or younger at knife point. He would take them into the family barn, order them to disrobe and then photograph them. He'd lock them in the corn crib and leave, returning a few minutes later wearing different clothes and combing his hair in a different direction. He would tell the captive that he was Ed, Jerry's twin brother. He would ask the girls not to report his brother, as Jerry was in counseling. He would then pretend to destroy the film—no harm done.

While his family lived in Dallas, Jerry attended Dallas High School from 1954 to April 1956. He came to the attention of the police around that time. Sixteen-year-old Jerry lured a 17-year-old girl into his car and drove out to the country where he pulled her from the vehicle, began to beat her and ordered her to strip. The girl screamed and tried to protect herself from his blows. A farming couple drove by and stopped. Jerry explained that the girl had fallen out of the car and was scared. The girl shook her head and Jerry changed his story.

Actually, he corrected, some "weirdo" had attacked the girl and Jerry was driving by when he saw the fight and stopped to help. The skeptical farming couple took both of them back to their house and called police. Under police questioning, Jerry admitted to police that he was the one who had beaten the girl. He said he wanted to frighten her into taking off her clothes so he could take pictures of her. Police went to his house and searched his room. They found women's clothing, women's high-heeled shoes, and photographs of a nude girl.

Police arrested him on charges of assault and battery, and for attempting to take pornographic pictures of a teenage girl. The Polk County Juvenile Department investigated and discovered that the nude girl in the photo was a frightened neighbor. When police interviewed her, she reported she had entered the Brudos home upon Jerry's invitation but was immediately confronted by a masked man. The man put a knife to her throat and demanded she disrobe. The man took pictures, directing her to pose in different ways. The man left the room and then immediately afterward, Jerry came in and claimed that a masked man had locked him in the barn but he had managed to break free. The girl recognized the masked man as Jerry immediately but fear silenced this observation. She took off as soon as she could, too afraid—and ashamed— to report him to authorities.

Brudos was arrested for assault and battery, and for attempting to take pornographic pictures of a teenage girl, and was committed in 1956 to the Oregon State Hospital for evaluation. He spent about eight months there. During the day, he attended North Salem High School. Psychiatrists diagnosed him with an adolescent adjustment disorder and the sexual deviation of fetishism. One psychologist ventured a diagnosis of borderline schizophrenia but the hospital's disposition board did not consider the diagnosis valid. The doctor in charge of Brudos considered him a menace to the community and recommended continued institutionalization but Jerry was released on a court order.

Jerry finished high school in Corvallis in 1958, ranked 142 out of class of 202. He attended Oregon State University for a short time and then Salem Technical Vocational College for a while. He joined the Army for seven months but was discharged when a staff psychiatrist found him unfit for duty.

A failure, Jerry moved back to Corvallis with his parents, but his mother made him live in an unheated shed in the back yard when the older—and clearly preferred—brother Larry returned home for the summer. With this snub, Jerry progressed from stealing shoes and underwear to stalking women wearing high heels. In Salem, Jerry followed and then choked into unconsciousness his first victim before he stole her shoes. His second victim in Portland fought back and Jerry only scored one shoe.

Brudos worked for the U.S. Army Corps of Engineers as a laborer between April 18, 1960, and May 27, 1962. He was 21 years old and worked out of a Eugene duty station on the Long Tom Channel. He was fired for taking excessive leave. Sources said that Brudos had periodically fished off the Bundy Bridge over the Long Tom River.

In 1960, Corvallis police arrested him on charges of burglary, involving a girls' dormitory at Oregon State University. Police found 17 pairs of women's hose, one set of "false breasts," one dress, seven slips, one girdle, 17 pairs of panties, and 15 pairs of women's shoes. He had also stolen items of women's clothing from clothes lines in several parts of the city. Charges were dropped in 1963 due to a lack of interest by prosecutors.

Fetish burglaries are those breaking-and-entering cases where the items stolen are usually articles of women's clothing, usually stolen for autoerotic purposes. The most common fetish objects are shoes, underwear, and stockings or specific body parts, usually the feet. The typical fetishist is more aroused by the fetish object than the person wearing the item. During the FBI's project of interviewing serial killers in order to develop profiles of killers, special agent John Douglas found 72% of interviewees had a preoccupation with fetishism of some kind during their formative years. In cases involving murder, fetish items often become mementos used to achieve sexual arousal, reliving the crime, at a later time.

At age 22, Jerry got his FCC license and began working at a Corvallis radio station. He met 17-year-old Ralphene there and they were married a few months later when she became pregnant to overcome her parents' disapproval of her plans to marry Brudos.

In 1964, Corvallis police booked Brudos on a bad check charge. He was put on parole for a year and ordered to make restitution.

Jerry and Ralphene moved around a great deal, living in Corvallis, Portland, Tigard, and Salem; Jerry had a difficult time keeping jobs. In 1967, the family moved to Portland and Jerry found work as an electrician. They seemed to be a fairly content married couple, although some of Jerry's demands troubled young Ralphene. He urged her to do housework in the nude wearing high heels while he photographed her, at least once making her pose on their daughter's tricycle. Ralphene didn't know what to make of that. Was this something all married couples did?

Ralphene found she was pregnant again and Jerry was more enthused about this child; he had pretty much ignored his daughter. He was looking forward to seeing this child born.

FBI studies of serial killers have found that a "precipitating stressor" often occurs prior to a man escalating his crime to rape or murder. Relationship problems, losing a job, a bad financial turn—all can trigger someone on the edge to tip over it. In what became an important turning point for Jerry, Ralphene did not allow him in the delivery room when she gave birth. Ralphene did not want jealous Jerry to see her with another man—the doctor.

Hugely disappointed, Jerry began stealing women's shoes and clothes again. He broke into a house to steal shoes and when the woman awoke, he strangled her until she went limp. He then committed his first rape, stole her shoes, and fled.

Photo credit: J. E. McComb

The Brudos family rented this home on Center Street, a few blocks from the Oregon State Hospital where Brudos spent time during his teen years. He abducted his victims and took them to his "workshop" behind the house (behind the trailer in this picture).

In January 1968, Brudos encountered Linda Slawson selling encyclopedias door to door in his southeast Portland neighborhood. For Jerry, opportunity literally knocked. Brudos lured Slawson down to his basement workshop feigning an interest in her books, hit her in the head with a 2x4 and then—in his first reported killing—strangled the unconscious girl to death while his mother and daughter were upstairs.

He then sent the two out to get dinner so he could be alone with his victim. He dressed her in some of the stolen clothes and shoes from his collection. While he wanted to keep her, the house was small and the risk of his wife finding the body was great. He put Slawson's body in his car's trunk and drove to the Saint John's Bridge. He pretended to fix a flat tire and threw her body into the river, weighted down with an engine. Not being able to completely part with her, he cut off her foot as a memento before he threw her in and kept it in the freezer to model his shoe collection. The body was never found and

Brudos was not prosecuted for her death. He abandoned the foot some time later in the same manner.

A Portland neighbor complained that Brudos would park his car in the neighbor's driveway blocking him in and refused to stop doing so. The man from whom Brudos rented the Portland house said the basement looked like some kind of laboratory and Brudos seemed to be home a lot during the day. An employer reported that Brudos did very poor work.

Six months later, Portlander Stephanie Vilcko was reported missing and her body was later found in a wooded area. Brudos did not confess to her death and disposal of the body was different from his other victims. Still, she remains associated with Brudos in some texts.

When Jerry lost his Portland job, the family moved to Salem, into a little gray house on Center Street, a few blocks from the Oregon State Hospital where Brudos had lived as a teenager after his assault arrest. He stashed his shoe and clothing collection in the attic. One day Jerry surprised Ralphene by walking into the room wearing a bra, panties, girdle, stockings, and high-heeled shoes. Naïve Ralphene didn't quite know what to make of it. Later, Jerry left pictures of himself dressed as a woman lying about the house for Ralphene to find.

Jan Whitney was Brudos's next confirmed victim. Whitney had nearly earned her college degree at University of Oregon but was no longer attending full time. She lived in McMinnville. She was reported as missing November 25, 1968, after obtaining registration information from the University of Oregon. She left Eugene late in the afternoon and picked up two young male hitchhikers, not uncommon behavior for the late 1960s. Engine trouble forced her to pull the 1959 red and white Rambler over onto the shoulder of I-5 near the Jefferson interchange. Another northbound car pulled over to help. Its driver: Jerome Henry Brudos.

Brudos told Whitney he could fix her car, but he needed his tools in Salem. He picked up all three and headed north. The two hitchhikers asked to be dropped off so they could continue on their way. Brudos did so, drove home and then strangled Whitney in his driveway while she was still in his car, about 20 minutes after picking her up. He then had sex with her body. He moved her body to his workshop and then drove back to her car and towed it to the rest stop between Albany and Salem. Upon returning home, he had sex with the body again, and dressed her in some of the clothes from his collection.

Two days later, with Whitney's body still hanging in the workshop, the Brudos family left for Thanksgiving dinner with relatives. While they were gone, a passing car lost control and hit the garage-workshop. Investigating Salem police couldn't get into the locked garage, and so left a card for the residents to contact police. Jerry, upon seeing the card, told his wife he had some errands to run before he called police. He was gone for several hours. When police returned to check the damage, they saw nothing out of the ordinary.

During this time, Brudos had a job in Lebanon, just south of Salem and he regularly made the commute near where Whitney's car was found. Her body was found much later—July 27, 1969—tied to a piece of railroad iron in the Willamette River near Independence.

Karen Sprinker was his next victim. Brudos told police that she had parked and locked her car and was headed for the elevator when Brudos confronted her with his gun. He told her he wouldn't hurt her if she didn't scream and came with him. She obeyed. He drove her to his house. He raped her and made her wear clothes from his collection. The black longline bra was from a Portland clothesline. He photographed her. He put a rope around her neck and using a "come-along" pulley, lifted her from the ground. She strangled and died. He had sex with the body. He cut off her breasts to try to make molds for mementos, but failed to achieve the effect he was looking for. He got rid of the body that night.

Linda Salee was taken next, on April 23, 1969. Salee had driven from her secretarial job in west Portland to the Lloyd Center mall on the other side of town to shop for her boyfriend's birthday. A clerk recalled waiting on her. Salee returned to her car, pitched in her packages and reached for her car keys in the glove box where she regularly kept them. Brudos appeared and told her she was under arrest for shoplifting, likely flashing a phony badge. She readily followed him to his blue Comet station wagon. It's unclear what he told her, but he drove her to his Salem home and after about a half an hour, he strangled her with a leather strap.

Salee had been scheduled to meet her boyfriend at the YMCA pool that night but she never showed. When she didn't arrive for work the next day, police were called and they found her car at the Lloyd Center parking garage.

After his arrest, Brudos told psychiatrists that he had sex with the women before and after their deaths. He attempted to cast an epoxy resin mold of one of the victim's breasts, but was not happy with the result, which police found in the house he shared with his family. He took pictures of at least two of the victims while they stood nude in high heels—all while his wife and children were feet away in the house. His wife later reported that he did not allow her into his padlocked workshop very often and always made her knock before entering. This was inconvenient, as the freezer was in the workshop and Ralphene had to tell Jerry what cut of meat to bring into the kitchen, as he would not allow her to rummage about on her own.

·····

Jerome Brudos was a serial killer. The FBI defines a serial murder as the unlawful killing of two or more victims by the same offender(s), in separate events. Killers are likely created through a combination of biological, social, and psychological factors. Serial killers are categorized as either "organized" (e.g. planned crime, controlled mood, living with a partner) or "disorganized" (e.g. socially immature, unplanned crime, anxious mood, living alone, sexually incompetent), but it is not unusual for a single killer to have elements of both types. Brudos was predominately an organized killer.

Opportunity may play a pivotal role in the first killing, but as the killer relives the act, he begins to consider how it could have been better. Each successive killing allows him to improve his methods, that is why when police hunt serial killers they try to uncover the first kill to discover clues to the killer's identity; it is likely more sloppy and closer to home than the others.

Serial killers differ in many ways, including their motivations for killing and their behavior at the crime scene. However, there are traits common to serial murderers, including sensation seeking, a lack of remorse or guilt, impulsivity, the need for control, and predatory behavior. These traits and behaviors are consistent with the sociopathic personality disorder.

As a child, the future killer may lie, kill an animal, set a fire, or threaten or hurt another without be discovered or reported. (The classic childhood signs of a future serial killer: bed-wetting, animal cruelty, and fire-setting.) Very few report having friends. Distrust and a sense of entitlement dominate their thinking.

The FBI believes that all serial killers are sexually-motivated, however, some are more explicitly sexual in nature. Sex murderers fall into two categories. The first type kills their rape victim to escape detection and punishment. The second type is the sadistic killer who murders as part of a ritualized, sadistic fantasy; subjugation of the victim through cruelty is critical and the infliction of pain is a means to the subjugation. Brudos was the sadistic type, also known as a "lust murderer" or an "erotophonophile."

Lust murderers entertain violent, obsessive sexual fantasies and usually kill their victims during sex. They often mutilate their victim's sex organs. Erotophonophiles generally have a preferred victim "type" and seek out persons with that description. In a 1990 study of sexual sadists, researchers found sadists were employed white males (75%), married (50%), had a history of homosexual experience (43%), and cross-dressed (20%). Victims were unknown to the sadist (83%), typically abducted, blindfolded, gagged, and tortured. Most frequently, death results from strangulation, blunt force, or the use of a pointed sharp instrument. Ted Bundy is perhaps the most infamous lust murderer.

•••••

On Friday, May 30, 1969, just before the long Memorial Day weekend, police obtained an arrest warrant for Brudos and headed to Corvallis where Brudos and his family were visiting relatives. Before arresting police arrived, the Brudos family hit I-5 heading north. Surveilling police fell in behind. Between Corvallis and Salem, the Brudos car changed drivers, with wife Ralphene now driving and Jerry lying down on the back seat under a blanket. Instead of taking the Salem exit as expected, the Comet continued north. Fearing a run to the border, police moved in and arrested Brudos on a charge of armed assault in connection with the attempted abduction of Gloria Smith.

While changing from civies into jail garb, police noted Brudos was wearing women's panties.

What followed was hours of dogged and expert questioning by Salem detective Jim Stovall. Brudos seemed torn between remaining silent and sharing his clever ability to avoid capture. Brudos thought his IQ was 160 and that he was too smart to get caught. In the end, Brudos could not stop from bragging. With the aid of Stovall's fatherly coaxing, Brudos confessed to the killings.

From jail, Jerry called Ralphene and asked her to get rid of some boxes he had out in the workshop—just some old clothes and pictures. Somehow this didn't seem like a good idea to Ralphene. She consulted Jerry's attorney who told her not to destroy evidence. She didn't.

District Attorney Gary Gortmaker obtained a search warrant for the Brudos home. Among the items removed were women's clothing and underwear, numerous pairs of high-heels and photographs of women, both clothed and nude. Most of the photos were shot from the neck down. And in one a mirror on the floor caught the image of a leering Brudos looking at the body.

Police found other items of interest as well: a photo of Brudos wearing women's clothing; lists of women's names, addresses, and phone numbers; a list of Oregon State University sororities and living organizations; victims' keys.

Wasting no time, on Monday, June 2, District Attorney Gary Gortmaker charged Brudos with four counts of murder in the deaths of Salee, Sprinker, Whitney, and a Jane Doe later identified as Linda Slawson. Brudos was held without bail in the Salem city jail following the arraignment.

On June 5, 1969, the grand jury indicted Brudos on only one count of first-degree murder, that of Karen Sprinker, after hearing two days of testimony from four witnesses, including William Miller, a friend of Brudos who testified that Brudos had helped him change a cylinder head on his Chevy, matching the one used to weigh down Miss Sprinker's body.

Brudos pleaded innocent by reason of insanity to the killings. Judge Val Sloper ordered a psychiatric exam to determine whether Brudos was competent to assist in his own defense and whether he knew right from wrong at the time he murdered Sprinker. He was jailed with the order of no visitors except his court-appointed attorney Dale Drake. The state was ready to go to trial the next week but Brudos's attorney wanted four to six months to prepare and have his client examined by psychiatrists.

Five psychiatrists and two psychologists examined Brudos. They agreed he had sociopathic personality disorder and demonstrated sexually deviant behavior. Such individuals are selfish and impulsive, impervious to social mores.

Brudos confessed to psychiatrists that he felt no guilt or remorse about the murders. And while he found the women's clothing sexually stimulating, he was more stimulated by the actual killing. Women were objects to be used for his needs. Doctors assessed that Brudos's homicidal condition was progressive and untreatable.

Three days before he was to go on trial for Sprinker's murder, he pleaded guilty on June 27 and avoided a trial. Judge Sloper handed down three consecutive life sentences and Brudos was moved from the jail to the Oregon State Penitentiary, a few blocks from his Salem house, and became inmate #33284.

Following the Brudos trial, District Attorney Gary Gortmaker charged Brudos's 25-year-old wife, Ralphene, with first-degree murder. Gortmaker claimed she acted as her husband's accomplice. A woman visiting a neighbor of the Brudoses reported to police that she saw Ralphene open the back door of the house to Jerry who was carrying a blanket-wrapped figure, presumed to be Karen Sprinker. A trial was set September 22. Brudos's seven-year-old daughter was subpoenaed as a witness against her mother.

The witnesses fell apart on the stand. Ralphene's court-appointed attorney Charles Burt, a 40-year-old trial veteran, noted that while Ralphene wasn't an educated person, she wasn't insane or abnormal and had no reason to help her husband—and had actually preserved evidence when it was in her best interest to destroy it.

A psychiatrist had examined Ralphene under sodium amytal and found her to not be the type of person to participate in murder-mutilation, but found her rather passive and compliant. On a vote of 11-1, she was acquitted October 1. The DA took another swing at her, arresting her as an accessory-after-the-fact soon after the jury had retired to deliberate. He dropped the charges two days later and Ralphene was free, having spent 55 days in jail.

While Brudos was eligible for parole, he was never released. In 2005, he told the Oregon Parole Board that he felt more stable after 17 years of psychological treatment. He had also earned a college degree in General Sciences and a degree in Counseling. Brudos refused to explain why he committed the torture-murders. He was among those serial killers interviewed by the FBI to develop personality profiles of killers.

Sixty-seven-year-old Brudos died in prison of colon cancer March 28, 2006, at 5:10 a.m. He is buried in the prison cemetery.

•••••

Many newcomers to Salem have never heard of Jerome Brudos. His reign of terror was brief. But for a certain generation of Salemites, Brudos represents the ultimate threat—evil lurking in the shadows of a suburban parking garage on what should have been an ordinary day in the life of an ordinary person. And if it could happen to Karen Sprinker, then no one was safe.

2. The Butcher

1865 Highway Ave. NE
April 19, 1975

Most of Betty Lucille Wilson was found Saturday afternoon, April 19, 1975, in a slough near Brown's Island Sanitary Landfill.

It was about 4:00 p.m. when the fisherman first saw it—or *them*. Parts of a woman's body. The legs, arms, head, and breasts had been severed from the trunk. Items of clothing were scattered along the bank—under the bridge where Homestead Road S. crosses the slough. The fisherman led police to the site where they found the body parts floating in water about two feet deep.

State Medical Examiner Dr. William Brady was called to the scene, as were officers from the Marion County Sheriff's Office, the state police, and representatives from the District Attorney's Office. Investigators sealed off the area. District Attorney Gary Gortmaker stated that it appeared the body had been dumped from the bridge recently. Pages from the local *Capital Journal* were found near the body, the body pieces wrapped or recently wrapped in newspaper like cuts of beef from the butcher. The genitalia had been cut away, and the right nipple was also gone. And like a butcher's cuts of meat, the flesh had been opened and scored, bleeding out the pieces.

It was dusk before the all the pieces were removed from the shallow waters of the sluggish slough with the aid of flood-

Photo credit: J. E. McComb

Richard Marquette encountered Betty Wilson at a dance club on a Friday night. The next day, her dismembered body was found under this bridge over the Willamette slough off South River Road.

lights. No weapon was found.

Fingerprints could not be used to identify the victim, as the hands had likewise been sliced and flayed. Authorities described the victim as being between 30 and 40 years old, Caucasian, about 5'5", with dark curly hair and weighing about 150 pounds. The victim had a scar on her nose. One front tooth pointed out awkwardly and she was missing the other one. The autopsy determined that the woman had been strangled; a knife had been used to sever the body parts from the trunk.

Salem residents gazed past their Sunday morning pancakes to see a photo of the severed head on page one of their newspaper. Police were asking the public's help in identifying the woman. Some readers took pen in hand and complained to the editor later that week.

Still, the strategy paid off. A man came forward and said he had a hired a seamstress who resembled the photo. He had a name and a phone number. By Monday, the dismembered woman had been identified by her sister as Betty Lucille Wilson, 35, lately of Scio. Ms. Wilson had last been seen alive about 11:00 p.m. at the Pepper Tree Supper Club, 3190 Portland Road NE. Authorities believed she had been killed elsewhere and dumped in the slough.

Salem was supposed to be a safe haven for Wilson; she had recently moved to escape a sadistic husband in North Carolina. Her husband had provided for his family by parking them in an old bus with no plumbing on the edge of the Fayetteville city dump. Following one of her husband's beatings, she was blind for five days. Shortly before she fled with her sister for Salem, her husband had attacked her with a butcher knife and was indicted on a charge of attempted murder.

Hiding in her visiting sister's car, she fled the state. She had been living with her and her sister's husband in Scio since that January. Her visit to the Pepper Tree was only the second time she had ventured out at night since moving to Oregon.

Betty's sister told police that the plan for Friday night was for Betty to go to the lounge with her sister's daughter and boyfriend, but the daughter was turned away at the door for being under age. Betty, likely suffering from a bout of cabin fever, was anxious to stay, so they left her there, where she danced and forgot about her troubles. When the niece and the boyfriend returned to the club at about 11:00 p.m. to take Betty home, she waved them off, saying she wasn't ready to go home; she would meet them at the apartment.

It was a decision she would come to regret.

Investigators returned to the Pepper Tree and asked servers if they recalled seeing the victim and whether she had been with anyone. It had been a busy Friday night but the bartender remembered the woman and that she had danced and talked with a man. He didn't know his name, but the man did come into the club a couple of times a week.

Detectives returned to the landfill looking for witnesses. They discovered that cars admitted to the site were logged in with the driver's name and had to pay to dump their load. Police examined the early Saturday morning entries. Two names were regular dump visitors. The third was a stranger driving a Ford pickup camper. The man wrote out his name for the dump employees, saying they would never be able to spell it. It looked like "Marzuette."

Sgt. James Byrnes got a bad feeling, looking at that name. He had worked on a murder case more than ten years earlier and the killer had a similar name. Based on his gut, he tracked down the whereabouts of that earlier killer.

Richard Laurence Marquette, 40, was a parolee living at 1865 Highway Ave in a mobile home about half a block east of the Pepper Tree Supper Club.

Quite a coincidence—and police officers are not a breed who believe in coincidences.

It was normal police procedure to interview persons known to have committed similar crimes. Byrnes, who headed a team of six Marion County Sheriff's Department investigators on the case, went to Marquette's mobile home Monday night about 6:15 to question him. Based on that conversation and his own observations, Byrnes obtained a search warrant for the property. Investigators searched the home until about 5 a.m. Tuesday morning and found quantities of blood and hair, a fingernail, the back panel of a bra, and a silver chain later identified as the victim's.

Police were sure they had their man; now it was just a matter of collecting the evidence and bringing him to justice.

•••••

Richard Marquette was born December 2, 1934, in Portland. He lived with his parents and a brother and sister. His father left the family when Dick was 18 months old. His mother remarried when he was about six.

Likely suffering from an undiagnosed learning disability, he was grades behind in reading and math and couldn't read well when he dropped out as a sophomore.

He was left-handed, but teachers tried to turn him into a rightie. Conversion can cause multiple problems in the developing left-handed child, including learning disorders, dyslex-

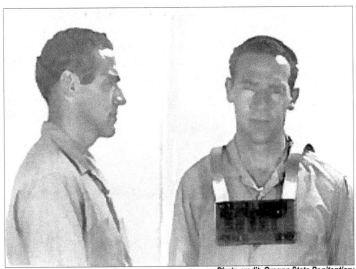

Photo credit: *Oregon State Penitentiary*

Before moving to Salem, Richard Marquette lived in Portland where another unlucky woman lost her life after a night of drinking with Marquette.

ia, stuttering, and other speech disorders. Unsure of himself, Marquette did not make many friends and often expressed himself with hostile or disruptive physical behavior.

There were reports he had a temper. At his first trial, relatives described a loving boy who had difficulty in school, was often alone, and flew into blind rages if kids called him dumb or stupid.

His mother testified that Dick had spent a lot of time alone and was always considerate to her. When Marquette was arrested, he had a tattoo of a wreath with "Mom" on his right forearm.

As a child, Marquette was evaluated by a psychiatrist from the Child Guidance Clinic of the University of Oregon's Medical School. Dr. Evans saw Dick about 13 times when Marquette was 11 and 12 years old. Evans testified that Marquette was being treated for his feelings of inferiority over his academic failures, had an aggressive behavior problem, and the feeling that he was not accepted by his mother.

In interviews with serial killers, the FBI found that most subjects' mothers had been cool, distant, unloving, and neglectful. Nearly half the killers reported that they had never had consensual sex with anyone and the lack of normal relationships fueled their aggression.

Marquette dropped out of Roosevelt High School in December of 1951 as a sophomore at age 16. When he was 17, he enlisted in the Army. He served in Alaska in the military police, re-enlisted and went to Korea for 31 more months where he drove trucks and jeeps. In 1955, he was given a general release from the Army and volunteered for the Oregon National Guard to fulfill his service requirements. He was dishonorably discharged from the Guard after 18 months when he was convicted of armed robbery. His Army records did not show a history of psychiatric disorders.

He did not re-enlist again and instead, worked a variety of odd jobs. He lived with relatives or in rooming houses, mostly alone. He lost his driver's license for driving without insurance. Co-workers described him as a hard-drinking, odd individual. Owning no car, he walked to work and bummed rides home.

His first arrest was June 20, 1956, when he was charged with attempted rape. The victim did not press the matter and police dropped the charges. On July 23, 1956, he was arrested for drunk driving. The next arrest was August 11, 1956, for assault with intent to rob. Marquette had struck a gas station attendant with an eight-inch crescent wrench wrapped in a towel. He was convicted and sentenced November 29 to 18 months in the Oregon State Penitentiary.

Parole was denied in April 1958 because the board did not feel he was a good risk.

His First Victim
June 5, 1961
214A SE 27th Avenue, Portland

The first sign that something was amiss in the southeast

Portland neighborhood on June 8, 1961—Rose Festival Week—was when Mrs. Eglah Lilly called her dog from the backyard and found him playing with something wrapped in a newspaper. She investigated and that something turned out to be a human foot—a foot with painted toenails.

She called police. Her dog led investigators to another package, this time containing a hand. The body parts were all fresh and bled dry. Detective Sgt. Tom Tennant found more body pieces next door, wrapped in paper bags and newspapers and thrown onto a brush-covered embankment separating the yards from a sidewalk.

Patrolmen were called in to search the area and they recovered two feet, a hand, and parts of an arm and a thigh. Fingerprints of the thumb and three fingers were obtained, but they would have to be checked manually against more than 150,000 local fingerprint cards.

Neighbors came forward with more body parts. On June 17, a box was found near a storage garage on Alder between 27th and 28th Avenues that contained two fingers, internal organs, flesh from the lower abdomen, and skin. The package was in plain sight of passersby and residents of the area said the box had been there at least a week. An arm was later found in Lone Fir Cemetery.

Police narrowed their search by looking at reports of missing young females and eventually matched the fingerprints to Joan Caudle, 23 years old and mother of two, who had been reported missing by her husband the night before the body pieces were discovered. Mr. Caudle said his wife had headed downtown to shop for Father's Day on Monday, June 5, at about 3:00 p.m. He had put their two children, aged three and four to bed when she did not return. She had called him around 9:00 to tell him she would be a little late. That was the last time he heard from her. The next day, Tuesday, he phoned police to report her missing and followed up Wednesday by filling out a report at the station.

Her picture was published in *The Oregonian*, asking for witnesses who might have seen her to come forward. A woman contacted detectives claiming to have seen Caudle and a man in a tavern on SW 4th and Washington. She remembered both of them from her old St. John's neighborhood. At one point the man had been engaged to one of Gloria's girlfriends. His name was Richard Marquette.

At the time, Marquette was employed at a wrecking yard and worked part-time at a grocery store on SE Powell Boulevard, where he was last seen that Thursday, June 8. Witnesses said Marquette had been acting suspiciously since the discovery of the body parts. The grocery store owners reported that while Marquette seemed a little upset that Thursday, he was a kind boy who wouldn't hurt a mouse.

On June 14, police proceeded to the address on his employee records, a little two-room house with weeds and trash threatening to overtake the hovel. Entering through the insubstantial unlocked door, they immediately noted the smell of flesh marinating in the summer heat. Police found several "packages" of Mrs. Caudle in the tiny home: the torso, a thigh, the lower portion of two legs, one mutilated hand attached to a forearm, and another section of arm. They were wrapped in newspaper, bled and butchered just like the pieces found scattered in the neighborhood. Still missing was the head and the upper portion of one arm. Women's clothing was found in a shopping bag at the foot of the bed, a woman's purse and sunglasses under the bed.

Police told the press that Mrs. Caudle had been stabbed six times in the back with a sharp, narrow instrument, the marks spaced in pairs, neatly up and down the spine.

Marquette was on the lam. Portlanders reported seeing him under every bush and were generally panicked at the idea of running into him. An all-points bulletin was teletyped to police agencies. A barber came forward and reported that he had cut Marquette's hair June 8, the day body parts were first discovered. Marquette asked the barber to leave a three-day growth of hair on his upper lip, saying he was going to grow a mustache. The barber cut Marquette's hair in a flat top style and police descriptions went out with that additional information.

Governor Hatfield appealed to J. Edgar Hoover and the

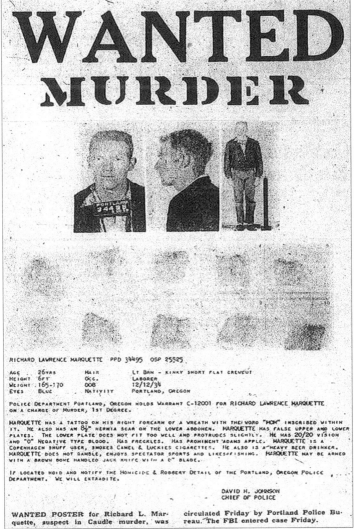

WANTED POSTER for Richard L. Marquette, suspect in Caudle murder, was circulated Friday by Portland Police Bureau. The FBI entered case Friday.

Photo credit: FBI

The FBI added Marquette to their "Ten Most Wanted" list as the 11th most wanted man in the land, the first time in their history.

FBI added Marquette to their "Ten Most Wanted" list. They did so, and Marquette became the eleventh most-wanted person for the first time in FBI history. Fliers with his face were distributed.

On June 30, one day after the release of Marquette's Wanted flyers, the manager of an employment agency in Santa Maria, California, recognized his newest client in the mug shots. The FBI was called and agents surprised Marquette at work repairing furniture for resale in a church thrift shop and he was arrested.

The prosecution's theory was that Caudle's death had occurred during rape or attempted rape, one of four felonies that qualified as first-degree murder and was eligible for the death penalty. It was the first time in Oregon history a first-degree murder charge was based on the theory of rape or attempted rape.

At his trial Marquette described his evening the night of the Caudle murder.

After work, Marquette stopped for a few beers with a friend on the way home. He had a few more when he arrived home. He headed downtown thinking he would go to a movie at the Circle Theater. Instead, he stopped in at a tavern at 7th and Sandy Blvd. and from there cabbed over to the Grand Oasis bar on SW 4th Avenue, where he encountered Mrs. Caudle who recognized him from elementary school. They talked and drank.

Marquette testified that Caudle admitted that she was married but allegedly said she wasn't living with her husband and they were planning to divorce. The pair visited half a dozen other taverns. He wasn't sure how he got home, but prosecutors found the cabbie that had driven them back to Marquette's rental.

Marquette guessed that they must have bought beer somewhere along the way because he found beer bottles at his house when he awoke. He also found something more disturbing than empties. He testified that he found Caudle dead in bed beside him. He said he didn't remember much of the night. He theorized that he had either strangled or broken her neck because he didn't want her to scream.

He dragged Caudle into the shower and used a 100-year-old, foot-long butcher knife from the kitchen to cut her up, starting with her head.

He went to work that day, but came home after a couple of hours, too hung-over to stay. He began the process of disposing of the body, wrapping up parts of the body and tossing them around the neighborhood. He returned home and tried to clean up. Later he put the victim's head in a shopping bag and walked the four or five miles to the river north of the Sellwood Bridge where he threw it into the high water in the brush.

When asked why he had dismembered her, Marquette said that one neighbor was an early riser, and he feared being seen if he carried out the body whole. As to why pieces were scattered throughout the neighborhood, Marquette said he panicked; he did not know what he was doing and thought they were hidden.

He worked a full day Wednesday and Thursday. Thursday was the day the first of the body parts were discovered.

He decided to leave town with just the clothes he had on, in part to escape the terrible smell that now permeated the house. He took an express bus to Los Angeles, then to San Diego and entered Tijuana, Mexico where he stayed about a week, passing the time with old Army buddies. He returned to California and showed his identification at the border but was not detained.

Back in California, he befriended some people who put him to work in a church salvage store repairing furniture, where he was found when the FBI came calling.

Following his arrest and transport back to Portland, Marquette led police to a plastic bag containing the decomposed head in a swamp near Oaks Park. Mrs. Caudle's dentist identified the head as belonging to his patient. The left central tooth was missing and the one next to it loosened.

Marquette was formally charged and he entered a plea of not guilty by reason of insanity. The defense was under the burden to prove by a preponderance of the evidence that Marquette was insane at the time of his crime. The court appointed two defense attorneys to Marquette.

Marquette's time on the witness stand was marked by long awkward silences when he seemed unable to respond to questions. His attorney had to yell at him at times to get him to answer. Marquette couldn't recall if the woman provoked his anger. He denied raping her.

Both sides lined up psychiatric experts. The prosecution sought to prove that Marquette knew what he was doing and knew right from wrong, making him eligible for the death penalty. The defense wanted to prove Marquette was too mentally ill to know right from wrong. Confusing matters was Marquette's conflicting stories; sometimes he said he couldn't remember what had happened, and other times he told a story. It was difficult to ascertain whether he told a story in response to pressure to do so or whether it was an actual memory.

Dr. William Thompson testified that Marquette had serious sexual conflicts. Whenever anyone brought up the subject of sex, Marquette either blocked it out, unable to remember or desired not to talk about it.

Dr. Henry Dixon diagnosed Marquette as a "simple schizophrenic." The symptoms of that disorder included marked social isolation and withdrawal; marked impairment in role functioning as wage earner, student, or homemaker; markedly peculiar behavior (talking to self in public, hoarding, collecting garbage); marked impairment in personal hygiene; blunted or inappropriate affect; digressive, vague, overly elaborate, or circumstantial speech, or poverty of content of speech; odd beliefs or magical thinking; unusual perceptual experiences; marked lack of initiative, interest, or energy. (Black and Boffeli, 1989).

Dixon stated that underlying Marquette's emotional difficulties were feelings of rejection, isolation, difference, incompetency, impotency, and fear. A psychologist's evaluation found Marquette had painful confusion, mistrust and fear of himself and the people around him and when under stress, was given to violent aggressive acts, accompanied by amnesia.

The case was tried in 12 days. In closing arguments, the

defense argued that the evidence did not support a first-degree murder charge, as there was no premeditation and as a simple schizophrenic, he was given to violent aggressive acts on occasion of great stress, accompanied by amnesia.

The prosecution argued Caudle was killed defending her chastity. Marquette was not a simple schizophrenic but an emotionally unstable personality, a person with a psychopathic adjustment.

The jury found Marquette guilty of murder in the first degree. The

Photo credit: Marion County Sheriff's Office

Marquette was picked up at his Highway Avenue trailer just down the street from the nightclub where he met Betty Wilson after her body parts were discovered in a South Salem slough.

state recommended a gas chamber death, but the jury recommended clemency. The presiding judge, who was required to follow the jury's recommendation for sentencing, gave Marquette life imprisonment. The Oregon Board of Parole and Probation voted to release him November 1, 1972, and he was released January 5, 1973.

A member of the Parole and Probation Board defended the decision to release Marquette, as he had been a model prisoner; he just had a deep psychological hatred of women that came out only under certain circumstances—circumstances that were unlikely to occur again.

1975 Trial and Prison

Marquette was charged with murder. Marquette's court-appointed public defender requested and was granted a psychiatric exam to see if Marquette was capable of assisting in his own defense and whether he had any mental defect.

Faced with the evidence, Marquette pleaded guilty.

Marquette also confessed to another murder he committed the prior year, 1974. He didn't know the victim's name. He had picked her up in a bar, took her home, and when she resisted his advances he had strangled and dismembered her. Marquette led police to where he had buried her pieces in two shallow graves at Roaring River Rest Stop near the Clackamas River. No clothing—or head—was found and the woman was never identified.

Three murders, all likely the result Marquette becoming enraged when he was unable to perform sexually in an alcoholic torpor. With three deaths on his hands, Marquette fit the FBI's definition of a serial killer of the "disorganized" type.

On May 30, 1975, he was sentenced to life imprisonment and became prisoner #1908466 at Oregon State Prison, where he remains today. Criminal psychiatrists working with Marquette came to the conclusion that he was a perfectly normal, socially adjusted individual unless women turned him down. At the time of the Wilson killing, Marquette had been nursing a broken heart, as his serious girlfriend had broken up with him a few weeks before. The sting of rejection, they concluded, set off a murderous rage.

Oh yeah. Perfectly normal. Except for that one little thing.

3. The Big House

September 27, 1915
Southern Pacific RR Tracks, two miles north of Albany

In 1915, at a time when prisoners had colorful names like Cripple Jimmy, Crowbar Kelly, and Scarface Springer, the son of one of Salem's founding pioneers crossed paths with one of America's most evil men.

One would not survive.

Harry Percy Minto was born to Salem founding pioneers John and Martha Ann Morrison Minto in 1864 at the family's south Salem farm. He and Martha Ann had eight children, three of whom died while young. Harry was the youngest who survived.

Harry married Jesse Glenn. They had no children. He served as Salem's Chief of Police from 1892 to 1896, and was employed as a prison guard in 1895 and 1896. He served as Marion County Sheriff for two terms leaving office in 1910 or 1911. Minto was recognized as one of the best detectives on the west coast and was appointed penitentiary superintendent based on his record.

Salem, with its State Institute for the Feeble-Minded, the State Insane Asylum, and the Oregon State Penitentiary—all essentially prisons where residents did not have the freedom to come go—meant that escapes leaked out into the town's neighborhoods on a regular basis. Harry Minto was kept plenty busy.

As Marion County sheriff, Harry Minto criticized Governor Oswald West in 1911 for his lax policies on crime and allowing some prisoners out in Salem during the day or cutting their sentences short.

He said, "To me it seems nothing more nor less than an injustice on a public which demands that these men be kept behind the bars, not so much as a punishment, but merely as a protection to society. Under the present conditions prison discipline can mean next to nothing, and the guards are left on their

Photo credit: State Library of Oregon

Harry Minto (pictured here in 1908) was born to one of Salem's founding families and whose farm now makes up the Minto-Brown Island area.

own resources with hundreds of men to take care of and at the same time the inside guards are prohibited the use of arms."[1]

Minto was an enthusiastic supporter of the death penalty. When the question was put before the state whether to abolish capital punishment, Minto predicted mob rule would take its place, were it to be adopted. "When a man with cold-blooded deliberation, premeditation, and wanton malice takes the life of another, the existence of that man should cease."[2]

When Democrat Governor West left office and Republican Governor Withycombe came in, the new broom swept clean the Democrat's appointees in state government. Dozens of positions needed to be filled. Withycombe needed a prison superintendent who had similar ideas about crime and punishment as himself.

In his 1915 inaugural address, Withycombe stated, "The

Photo credit: State Library of Oregon

Born in 1822, sheep rancher John Minto emigrated from England to south Salem and served in the state legislature. He and wife Martha Ann had eight children together, including John (#1) and Harry (#7). He died at age 92 early the same year Harry was cut down.

feature of the prison policy of the past which probably has most concerned the general public has been the tendency toward exaggerated leniency."[3]

Many applied for the post of prison superintendent. *The Morning Oregonian* wrote, "To read over a list of applicants for these places is like scanning a register of the ex-Sheriffs [sic] of various Oregon counties."[4]

On March 23, 1915, Governor Withycombe appointed Harry Minto to the position of Superintendent of the Oregon Penitentiary. Secretary of State Olcott thought the incumbent superintendent should have been retained, but said, "When Harry Minto starts after a man he usually gets him. I have known him since I was a boy and his great ability cannot be questioned."[5] As superintendent, Minto would receive $2,000 a year, and live in a residence at the prison.

Minto supported the Auburn system of penology, which

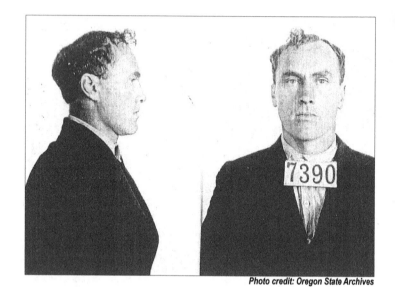

Photo credit: Oregon State Archives

When arrested and convicted in Astoria, Oregon, Carl Panzram gave his name as Jefferson Baldwin. He escaped Oregon State Penitentiary and went on to kill 22 and blaming, in part, his treatment in OSP for his murderous rage.

evolved during the 1820s at the prison in Auburn, New York. Prisoners worked during the day and were kept in solitary confinement at night; silence was enforced at all times. Prisoners wore gray clothes, sometimes with vertical black stripes.

In Oregon, prison uniforms with stripes were discontinued during Governor West's administration.

• • • • •

Carl Panzam was born June 28, 1891, on a small Minnesota farm. His east Prussian father, John Panzam, was a violent man and had fought in the Franco-Prussian war. He immigrated to America for a better life, homesteading on the frontier, in Sauk Centre, Minnesota.

Carl was the youngest of five children. His father succumbed to his yearnings to be elsewhere and eventually abandoned the family when Carl was seven. The two eldest sons left their poverty-stricken family as soon as feasible. Brother Albert quit school to help more on the farm but was lured away by the bright lights of East Grand Forks.

Carl broke into a house and burglarized it. The judge looked at Carl's record—he had been arrested for being drunk at age eight—and sent him to reform school in 1903 at age 12. Carl recalled his childhood in his autobiography, later published by Henry Lesser, a sympathetic guard, as *Killer: Journal of a Murderer,* where he recounted physical and sexual abuse at the hands of the Christians in charge, forever making him skeptical about any reports of the existence of human kindness or the benefits of religion, in general.

(Note: This book is now available as *Panzram: A Journal of Murder.* Amok Books. November 1, 2002. Also available are the Carl Panzram Papers through San Diego State University, which include his autobiographical manuscript. Many thanks to Library Dean Patrick McCarthy of San Diego State University.)

Not being able to read very well, Carl reported that he was beaten for not learning his Sunday school lessons. One place where students were corrected was called the Paint Shop because "they used to paint our bodies black and blue."[6] Children were stripped naked and bent over a large wooden block and tied, face down. A large towel was soaked in salt water and draped across the child's back to his knees. Next, a man took a strap that measured two feet long and four inches across that had holes punched through it. Every time the strap came down, the skin would come up through the punched holes. After about 25 or 30 lashes, blisters would form and burst. The salt water washing over the wounds would be the concluding torture. Panzram writes that after a week or two, the boy might be able to sit down if he didn't sit on anything harder than a feather pillow.

Carl was written up and punished for numerous infractions, including folding a napkin wrong. He began his revenge. Because his captors thought schooling would be wasted on Carl, he was put to work in the kitchen. There he took his revenge and urinated in the soup and coffee and masturbated into the ice cream. He put rat poison in the rice pudding. He burned down the Paint Shop.

The other boys told him he needed to behave and say he loved Jesus in order to get out, and Carl did that. After two years, he was deemed reformed. Privately, his reaction was something different, vowing to "rob, burn, destroy, and kill everywhere I went and everybody I could as long as I lived."[7]

Carl returned home and to school, but the other children pointed at him and yelled "reform school" after him, a provocation that led to fisticuffs. Carl then brought a gun to school. When the gun fell out of Carl's pocket during an attack, there was an uproar. The incident netted a beating and near strangulation from his older brother, and Carl was inspired to catch a freight town out of town. The 14-year-old's streak of bad luck continued however, and he was soon gang-raped by hobos.

Panzram was caught burglarizing a home in Butte, Montana, and was bounced back into reform school, this time the Montana State Reform School. He spent the year working in the shoe shop, the fields, or trying to escape. Panzram wrote that one of the officers was particularly cruel to him and Carl decided to murder him and he hit him in the head with an oak plank that had three or four pounds of iron on the end of it. While badly injured, the guard survived. Too young to be sent to prison, the reform school clamped down even harder on Carl.

After nearly a year there, Carl escaped. The 16-year-old lied about his age and joined the Sixth Infantry Regiment. Alas, he did not have the temperament for military life and did not take direction well. He was court-martialed within three months for trying to walk off the post with two stolen coats, a suit, and a pocketful of gold collar buttons. He was sentenced to three years in the aged, firetrap of a prison at Fort Leavenworth. Punishments included standing at attention through the night, beatings, running drills, and the use of a straightjacket cinched so tight as to cause unconsciousness. Those who attempted escape were forced to "carry the baby"—a heavy iron ball chained to his ankle. Naturally, Panzram was among those. He burned down the prison shops but was not caught. He was discharged in 1910, determined to make life as miserable for others as it had been for himself.

He got a job at a mule-skinner camp for a few weeks, and then took his cash into Denver. He bought a gun, got drunk, and purchased the services of a woman. He awoke to find himself robbed, beaten, and sick. A few weeks later he discovered he had the clap, as well. He promised himself to leave the ladies alone.

In 1912, he was pinched in The Dalles, Oregon, for highway robbery, assault, and sodomy. While being held, he broke out of jail. He spent the next three years in and out of various jails and prisons.

In 1915, at the age of 23, Panzram was arrested in the rough-and-tumble port town of Astoria for stealing less than 20-dollars-worth of merchandise. He gave his name as Jefferson Baldwin. Panzram made a deal with the judge and District Attorney that if he pleaded guilty and gave up his ill-gotten gain he would get a short stint on the county road gang. Instead, the judge gave him seven years in the Oregon State Penitentiary after he confessed. Panzram showed his appreciation by busting up and then setting fire to the jail.

On Baldwin's prison intake form, to the question, "In your judgment, should he be given a chance at the expiration of his minimum?" the Astoria sheriff wrote, "I think he should serve 70 years instead of seven."

Panzram (now Baldwin) was shackled to the baggage coach of the Oregon Electric Railway and freighted to Salem. The warden was Harry Minto. In his book, Panzram recounted his first meeting with Minto.

I was sent to the Oregon State Prison in 1914, and as soon as I got there I was in more trouble. I swore I would never do that seven years and defied the warden and all of his officers to make me. The warden swore I would do every damn day of those seven years or he would kill me. I haven't done it yet and I am not dead, but he is. His name is Harry Minto. If I couldn't escape, I would help everybody else that I could. I was always agitating and egging the other cons on to try to escape or raise hell in some way.[8]

·····

Until 1959, the Oregon State Prison in Salem was Oregon's only prison. Built in 1866, it was octagonal with three radiating wings. Cells were stacked in four tiers. Each cell had running water and a small sink. Men were given "soil pots" instead of toilets. There were "dark cells" or "dungeons" that were used for isolation. Men in the dungeon might be handcuffed to the door with their arms over their heads for days.

In his booklet, *The Oregon Penitentiary*, an inmate known only as Prisoner No. 6435 described the prison and said "… its management has been but a series of spasmodic and incomplete experiments."

(According to OSP files, Prisoner #6435 was Jesse Webb. Webb was convicted of murder October 21, 1910, and was sentenced to "be hanged by the neck until he is dead." He entered the prison August 5, 1911. His sentenced was commuted to life by Governor Oswald West. Webb was granted a full pardon on December 15, 1922. Upon release, he moved to Seattle.)

Ex-con Lee Duncan described the Dark Hole in his biography, *Over the Wall*.

I haven't told you about the Dark Hole as yet. It was a place that never was shown to visitors, and very few people besides the inmates released back to society, knew that such an inhuman type of confinement existed inside the Oregon State Penitentiary. It was located on the second tier of the north cell block in the back, out of sight, where it could never be ferreted out by a pair of human eyes not aware beforehand of its location. It was utterly dark inside, with the walls painted black; too small to stretch out full-length on the filth-infested, rust-imbedded steel floor, and the ceiling just barely high enough to sit up. It contained no bed, no blankets, no water, soap, towel, lights; nothing except a rusty human excrement bucket. Two thin slices of bread and a bowl of tepid water was brought up once each day.

To hamper escapes, in 1866, Warden J. C. Gardner patented the Gardner Shackle, better known as the Oregon Boot. It consisted of a heavy iron band that locked around the ankle and could weigh up to 28 pounds. Extended wear caused pain and physical damage—and could maim a man for life. As early as 1873, some had second thoughts about using the Oregon Boot. "A great wrong we are compelled to put on the prisoners for want of sufficient walls is the Gardner shackle," said then-Superintendent William Watkins. "We are necessarily compelled to iron them so they cannot scale the walls. There are prisoners who have worn this instrument of torture, known inside the prison as a man killer, until they are broken down in health and constitution … It is murder of the worst type."[10]

Photo credit: Popular Science, 1922.

The "Oregon Boot" was created to hamper escapes but could maim a man for life and added to the misery of Oregon inmates.

When moving throughout the prison, prisoners were to move in lockstep, with one hand on the shoulder of the man in front of him, eyes down. On orders of new Governor Withycombe, Minto reduced prison industries to mollify local business owners who didn't want the competition. Pay for working inmates was reduced from one dollar a day to 25 cents a day, money that had once gone to help support prisoners' families.

These changes created unrest among the prisoners and Minto hired back some of the old-line guards who had been dismissed by the prior administration for being too brutal. Cruel, sometimes fatal punishments were common. One guard—Jim "Vinegar" Cooper was known by the older prisoners as the "man of flogs." Cooper's favorite torture was to hoist a prisoner onto a pillar and lash him with a cat-o-nine-tails. A former colleague of Cooper's described it as consisting of several strands of waxed rawhide fastened to a wooden handle.

The Oregon State Pen was one of the toughest in the country. In his book, *Thirteen Years in the Oregon Penitentiary*, Joseph "Bunko" Kelley describes the treatment of one prisoner.

> *The next thing of note was the case of an Italian who could not speak English. He had his head part way out of the wicket one day when Sherwood came along the tier. Sherwood hit the Italian on the head and stunned him. Next day they wanted the Italian to come out of cell, but he was sick from the blow, so Sherwood and Leedy manacled him and then beat his head with clubs. Brofield was present and saw his assistants smothered with blood.*

•••••

Prisoner No. 6435 recounts that "tasks were extremely hard for the convicts who incurred official displeasure, and cases have known where men working in the foundry have poured molten metal in their shoe tops in order to escape the flogging sure to follow if an impossible task remained incomplete by nightfall. This would render him subject to hospital treatment and probably cripple him for life, which seemed to appease official appetite."[11]

Having heard of Panzram's assault on the Astoria jail, Panzram was put in the last cell on the bottom tier of B Block. On the first morning of Panzram's stay, he launched the contents of his soilpot at his guard. As punishment, Panzram was then handcuffed to the door of a dungeon cell for the next 30 days.

Several weeks after Panzram's arrival, Vinegar Cooper spotted Panzram chopping a hole in the roof in an escape attempt. Panzram was stripped, flogged, and thrown into the Cooler once again.

Bunko Kelley provides us with a description of one flogging of a boy who was given conflicting orders and guessed wrong. He was ordered to strip and lashed ten times. Then lashed more.

> "Lay it on, Charley," said Brofield, "and call on me for mercy. I am Jesus Christ. I am the man you've got to call on. Now crack him around the side where it hurts, from his shoulders down to his hips. Skin him. Crack him around the side on the tenderspot."
>
> When they let Delmane down his back looked like beefstake. "The next time you get flogged," said Brofield, "I'll kill you."
>
> Delmane received 120 lashes with the four-prong lash, making 500 lashes on his back. Don't faint, gentle reader; it is true. Oh to think that such a man should be placed over human beings. But Bunko Kelley isn't afraid to tell the truth.
>
> After Delmane was taken down from the post they packed him to the dungeon, where he remained 30 days, living on crusts of bread and chewing his blankets. He was a raving maniac.
>
> They knew he was going to die. The doctor at the asylum said that the lash had cut into the spine. Delmane's hands were manacled to his sides and they put on an Oregon boot to try to make the convicts believe he was a bad man. One morning Leedy, the chapel guard, came to his cell with a flunky to put on clean clothes. Delmane was so weak that he fell over his bucket and spilled it on the floor.
>
> With hellish fury, Leedy unlocked one of the brass locks on the door and taking it in his hand as a weapon, he commenced pounding Delmane on the forehead until the boy's blood and brains oozed out.

With Panzram on the premises, discipline eroded. Inmates grew surely. Guards told Minto they would no longer patrol except in pairs. Panzram set fire to the flax storehouse and cut the fire hose. He tore a pipe out of the cement floor and banged it against his cell walls, howling. Other prisoners followed suit. Vinegar Cooper suggested to Minto that troublesome prisoners be forced to wear suits of red and black stripes. Minto introduced the suits, but instead of clothes of shame, they became badges of honor. Panzram wore his "hornet suit" with a swagger.

Then Panzram met a malleable soul and went to work infecting him.

I finally met a big, tough, half-simple Hoosier kid in there and I steamed him up to escape. He done everything I told him to and some more that I didn't. He went to the warden and he asked for a job on the farm. He got it. As soon as he did he attempted to escape right under the warden's eye.[12]

The "Hoosier kid" was 21-year-old Otto Hooker, inmate #7198. He had been sent down to Salem from Umatilla County to serve an 18-month sentence. (Some sources indicate his sentence was indeterminate.) He was arrested following the conclusion of the 1914 Pendleton Roundup, armed with a revolver, a blackjack, and a long-bladed dirk, in the Roundup's deserted ticket office. Hooker had posed as a buckaroo. He had been arrested a few nights earlier on suspicion of burglary, but released for lack of evidence.

When he was found in the ticket office, he was sleeping on two stolen blankets, the keys to the John Lang grocery store which had been robbed, along with other stolen goods. He pleaded guilty to attempted burglary October 10, 1914, and was delivered to the state pen on November 6.

He was originally from Wichita, Kansas. His mother had died and he wasn't in contact with his father. He grew up in his grandmother's house, but she wasn't able to keep him out of trouble. Hooker had served several jail sentences for minor crimes and had a long police record. At age 15, he was tried on a murder charge, but was acquitted. The six-footer was physically fit, polite, walked with a slouching gait, and his nose had been broken when he was 19 by a guard.

On his prison intake form, when asked about extenuating circumstances in Hooker's criminal case, his parole officer wrote, "No, not to my knowledge, unless it is the defendant's mental condition. I think he has been reading dime novels."

Hooker was on a work gang of about 25 prisoners "grubbing" brush a mile south of the penitentiary. He was quiet and polite and not considered an escape risk. Nevertheless, Hooker slipped away from the work crew, unnoticed by the guard. When his absence was noted, the alarm was sounded and Warden Minto rushed to the scene. A posse was quickly

Otto Hooker was serving an 18-month sentence for burglary when Carl Panzram convinced the "Hoosier kid" to escape while out on a work detail. A wild gunshot of Hooker's caught Minto right between the eyes.

formed and began tracking Hooker.

The posse decided to split into two, with Minto and some men going to the nearby town of Jefferson to notify Marshal Benson there to be on the lookout for Hooker. Minto then returned to the spot where Hooker had made his escape.

Otto Hooker entered Jefferson about ten o'clock that evening. Marshal Benson spotted and recognized him, likely due to his prison garb. He ordered Hooker to surrender. Hooker made as if to comply. Benson walked up to him to make the arrest. When Benson was within arms' reach, Hooker lunged for Benson's revolver and wrested it from his grasp. The two men tumbled to the street. Hooker pressed the gun on Benson and fired. The bullet struck Benson just north of his collarbone with the bullet ranging downward. Hooker immediately ran off and witnesses reported that he was headed south, toward Albany.

Minto, upon hearing that Benson had been shot by his escapee, took some men and formed a new posse. They drove to Albany and backtracked on foot north toward Jefferson,

$50

REWARD

Escaped from the Oregon State Penitentiary

OTTO   HOOKER

Description

AGE, 21
HEIGHT, 5 feet 10 inches
WEIGHT, 186 pounds
COMPLEXION, light
HAIR, light brown
EYES, greyish blue
OCCUPATION, laundryman
CARRIAGE, erect

Finger print $\dfrac{1 \quad T}{1 \quad Rr}$19

Moles, Marks, Scars, Etc.

Large irregular scar inside left thumb; scar on left middle finger, inside; Pit scar above left eyebrow; nose turned slightly to right.

Discarded clothing will bear the number 7198.

FIFTY ($50) DOLLARS REWARD WILL BE PAID BY THE WARDEN OF THE OREGON STATE PENITENTIARY FOR THE ARREST, DETENTION AND ADVICE OF THE ABOVE, WHO WAS RECIEVED AT THE PENITENTIARY NOV. 7, 1914.

Under sentence of 1 to 2 1-2 years from Umatilla county.

Charged with attempt to commit burglary.

Escaped from Prison Farm Sept. 27, 1915.

Salem, Ore., Sept. 27, 1915   **H. P. MINTO**, Warden

Photo credit: Oregon State Penitentiary

Hooker's bid for freedom was short-lived, captured 24 hours after the fatal shooting of Minto.

hoping to cut Hooker off. Two miles out of Albany the posse

split in two, with Minto and Walt Johnson, a prison guard, following the railroad tracks. The other two followed the wagon road.

The two men heard the crunch of gravel from up ahead. Minto and Johnson left the tracks for the adjoining field. They spotted Hooker coming up the track in a "dog trot." Johnson faded into the shadows of the shrubbery and motioned for Minto to do the same. They waited for their man. It was 11:30 p.m.

When the desperado was within 30 feet, Minto stepped forward in the moonlight and called: "You, halt!" The convict's stolen revolver barked a sharp reply. Warden Minto squeezed the trigger on his double-barreled shot gun as he fell in his tracks. The desperado's bullet had found its target, but Hooker didn't stay to assess the situation. He fled. Johnson's hail of bullets chased after him in the darkness, but none found its mark. Johnson rushed to Minto only to find him dead — shot between the eyes. Johnson signaled the rest of the posse and someone found a telephone to call Salem with the news.

Over 200 men combed the countryside north and east of Albany. Three posses were formed. Emotions were running high and if law enforcement didn't find Hooker first, there was concern that mob justice would prevail. In Albany, groups of armed men walked the streets with rifles. Autos with guns sticking out the sides were seen every few minutes. Police sent for blood hounds from Portland; Walla Walla, Washington; and Weed, California.

Hooker was sighted about an hour after the fatal shooting near Millersville, south of Jefferson, heading south. Men were sent to search the railroad cars of the incoming and outgoing Southern Pacific. An Albany man reported to police that he heard a man cough, the sound coming from an unfinished house next to his at Eighth and Cleveland. The posse split up, with some remaining at the rail yards and others going into Albany to investigate the coughing.

Police came to the intersection and found the reporting neighbor leaning out of a second story window pointing a rifle at the empty house. Police found Hooker hiding under the floorboards. Guns trained on the desperado, they ordered him to crawl out and readied the handcuffs. As Hooker stuck out his hands for the steel bracelets, he abruptly pulled back a hand and reached under his body for a gun. Catching sight of the pistol and fearing an unscheduled departure into the next world, Officer A. L. Long from Portland fired into Hooker's chest. It was 11:30 p.m. — 24 hours since the fatal shooting of Minto.

Hooker was taken to St. Mary's Hospital and questioned, but refused to explain the details of his escape and seemed surprised to learn he had shot Marshal Benson.

Reporters noted that Hooker was always polite when asking for water, saying "please" and "thank you," and he begged for food, as he hadn't eaten in two days.

At one point, he seemed to be in a great deal of pain and groaned, "O, my God, kill me."

His request was accommodated. He expired at 2:05 a.m.

After Harry Minto was killed, Governor Withycombe decided that he had been too easy on prisoners. He appointed Harry's older brother John to take his place. When John Minto took over, he vowed that every inmate would remember his brother's death. He made Vinegar Cooper his assistant. Tortures that had largely been abandoned were brought back.

Minto forced inmates to build a "bull pen" — a prison within the prison and open to the elements, where eight new isolation cells were housed. Carl Panzram soon found himself within one. During the day, he and other recalcitrant prisoners were forced to walk in circles all day. Talking or looking around was forbidden. Stopping was forbidden and wandering off the circle was considered an escape attempt and guards were authorized to shoot to kill.

Guards seized on any excuse to torture and beat prisoners. One prisoner allegedly threw a rock at a guard and was shot dead. Minto would use a fire hose on handcuffed prisoners for punishment, leaving them bruised and half-dead. Not surprisingly, Panzram was among those who got the hose. Panzram writes of the experience. "This is more than ten years ago but still every time I catch an Oregonian and get him in a corner, I sure give him hell. Many a man has paid for what those men done to me that Sunday morning."[14]

While hardly soft-hearted, Governor Withycombe had specifically ordered Minto not to use the hose on prisoners. When he discovered he had been disobeyed, he had the Board of Control fire John Minto for the hosing of Jefferson Baldwin (Panzram) and James Curtis.

John Minto disagreed with the decision of the Board of Control. He said, "It was simply a case of my retaining control of things here or not, and I acted according to my best judgment. Officially, the board gave me no reason for requesting my resignation."[15]

Following the dismissal of John Minto, 200 prisoners petitioned the Governor for a superintendent who would treat them humanely and fairly and one who had not been a sheriff or police officer. The consensus was the Minto and his henchman Sherwood (who was acting superintendent until Minto was replaced) had been brutal—so brutal that the prisoners were plotting to poison the guards. "I know it is dangerous. The men are in such a temper that it would require but little to precipitate a riot," said Governor Withycombe.[16]

Whenever Panzram wasn't in the hole or the bullpen sawing on its door hinges, he would help prisoners escape. Following the foiled mass escape plan when inmates planned to put rat poison in the food, a riot ensued. Armed guards were doubled.

In a bold move, Withycombe hired a new type of warden, one who believed in books and trust, and didn't torture. When new Warden Murphy was told that Panzram had been caught cutting the bars on his cell and how punishment had not made any difference, Murphy ordered Panzram extra rations and books. Panzram was favorably impressed, but his skepticism was too ingrained for kindness to penetrate. Murphy tried to institute the honor system, where prisoners could leave the prison by day and return at night. This actually worked pretty well for months. However, Panzram became drunk in the company of a woman and stayed out too late. He broke into a house and stole food, clothes, a loaded gun, and seven dollars.

The Albany Sheriff saw and recognized Panzram and tried to arrest him. A gunfight ensued. Panzram was returned to the pen, put in the bull pen and hung by his wrists from his cell door for eight hours at a time for weeks. He escaped for good a few months later in May 1918, when he put on the white uniform of a trusty cook and walked away, and was out of gun range by the time the guards spotted him.

Panzram traveled the world leaving a trail of mayhem in his wake. He went to Chile, Panama, Peru, Scotland, England, France, Germany, Africa, and Portugal, stealing, sodomizing, and murdering men and boys. He returned to New England, where he was caught rifling through suitcases in Larchmont, New York, and arrested. He boasted that he was a wanted man back in Oregon and tried to claim the $500 reward for himself.

He was jailed in Clinton Prison, also known as Dannemora—the hell hole—where generations of brutal guards had passed down sadistic prison practices. Panzram broke both legs and his back trying to escape over the wall. He was dumped into a wheelbarrow and carted back to his cell, never receiving medical treatment for his injuries. He spent five years there, the last two and a half in solitary brooding on the injustices done to him.

Guard Henry Lesser befriended Panzram, helped him with his autobiography, and devoted himself to the cause of prison reform.

Panzram wrote to Oregon's prison superintendent and asked to be excused from serving the remaining years in his seven-year sentence. He asked that he be allowed to go to South America instead. Oregon decided that the cost of transporting him wasn't worth it, and that South America could have him.

Panzram was released from Dannemora a free man and made some effort to poison the town's water with arsenic on his way out of town, but staying alive took precedent. He was arrested a month later in Baltimore for burglaries and transferred to Washington D. C. He killed a guard in a spectacular, grisly, fashion in the prison laundry. He was sentenced to hang. He welcomed death, threatened suicide and resisted do-gooders' attempts to save his life. He confessed to 22 murders.

While writing his autobiography, Panzram still proclaimed his general evil and debauched ways and fingered the justice system. "It costs you thousands of lives and billions of dollars every year to keep on doing business with the present prison and educational systems. Don't you think it's pretty near time you woke up to the fact that you're a lot of chumps. That's the way it looks to me,"he said.[17] However, he also revealed evidence of some soul searching.

I would like to get a real sincere opinion from someone like this guy Fife who has a keen, analytical trained mind and who is able to give an unbiased opinion as to just what the hell is wrong with me. All I want is to find out the reason why I am what I am and why I act the way I do. I have been puzzled all my life about this and I would sure like to know the answer to this before I leave this world.[18]

He was hanged at 6:03 a.m. on September 5, 1930.

In 1917, the Oregon State Board of Control ordered an investigation of the prison and its practices. It recommended that toilets and heating be installed in the cells. It also had thoughts on those cases "where the sex abnormality has manifested itself in criminal tendency" as well as other crimes. "The method of castration, therefore, should be reserved as a penalty for the outspoken, habitual brutal criminal, the rapist, the confirmed inebriate, the incorrigible burglar or gunman, the gibbering idiot, or imbecile cretin with inherited tendency to crime, and the unstable erotopath."[19]

It is impossible to know if Panzram's treatment in Oregon's prison fueled the subsequent murder of innocents or whether the fate of Carl Panzram was sealed from birth as secure and heavy as an Oregon boot, but Panzram had a theory.

He wrote, "Why am I what I am? I'll tell you why. I did .not make myself what I am. Others had the making of me."[20]

4. The Vanishings

Terry Cox Monroe
February 12, 1981
2395 Front Street

It was Thursday at the Oregon Museum—Ladies Night—and 21-year-old Terry Cox Monroe stepped out of the Oregon Museum Tavern for some fresh air after an evening of dancing, leaving behind her glasses and cigarettes.

She was never seen alive again.

She had turned 21 the prior April, but this was her first venture into a tavern. She didn't drink much. She had gone out with some co-workers from Pay Less Drugstore for some dancing. Her boyfriend Mark Johnson would have tagged along, but he was only 20. Terry worked with Mark's sister Laura. They all lived together with Mark's parents. When Terry didn't come back into the tavern, her friends assumed she had gone home. When Terry didn't arrive home, Mark and his family assumed she had spent the night with one of her co-workers. When Laura went into work on Friday and saw Terry's car in the parking lot, Terry nowhere to be found, she knew something was very wrong. She called police and reported Terry missing at 9:34 a.m. Friday morning.

Police put out a description of Monroe: waist-length blonde hair, blue eyes, 5'11" and model slim at 105 pounds. Police asked anyone who was at the tavern that night to call them. Police treated the disappearance as a homicide and questioned nearly everyone who had been in the tavern that night but came up empty.

People speculated that perhaps Monroe had encountered the I-5 Killer who was running loose and terrorizing the northwest. But Randy Woodfield had an alibi tighter than an Oregon State Hospital straightjacket: he was busy robbing three different businesses in Washington that night.

Friday morning, police searched miles of the area around the tavern on foot, by boat, and by plane. The waterfront near the tavern was covered with gravel and overgrown brush, making footprints and tire tracks less likely to be found. What they did find that morning was not encouraging: Monroe's clothing and pieces of her identification along the bank of the Willamette River, about a half-block from the bar.

Police estimated that if her body was in the river, it would surface in five to seven days. But her loved ones tried not to let their thoughts drift in that direction.

With each passing day without news, Terry's friends' hopes ebbed.

A month after she had gone missing, a boater spotted the body of a white female wedged among pilings and debris, on March 15. She was about three miles downstream from the tavern. She was positively identified through the jewelry she was wearing. The autopsy found that she had died of homicidal asphyxiation. Police presumed her body had been in the river since shortly after she was taken.

A reward fund was set up at Commercial Bank, in hopes it would lead to additional information, and eventually, Terry's murderer.

Her family and friends would wait 31 years to discover the identity of her killer.

Sherry Eyerly
July 4, 1982
Faragate Street

It was Independence Day and a Sunday. Pastor David

Photo credit: J. E. McComb

Faragate Road is a dark, lonely stretch of road linking homes along the river to south Salem neighborhoods. It was here where Sherry's car was found, door open, lights still on.

Stark had received a late-night call from one of his flock in need of marital counseling. He had just begun his journey when he came across an eerie sight: there in the dark, on secluded Faragate Street was an empty Domino's car idling on the road, driver's door open, the headlights on and the emergency brake set. Three large boxed pizzas lay scattered on the ground. Stark immediately drove to a nearby convenience store and called police about 10:20 p.m.

Another neighbor, George Hutmacher, also came across the empty, idling car when he drove home from a fireworks display with his two sons. After checking out the vehicle brief-

Photo credit: J. E. McComb

Sherry Eyerly's family erected a memorial at her abduction site. When her killer confessed, the memorial was dismantled. Her body has never been found.

ly, he completed his journey home and phoned police.

Faragate Street is an unlit gravel road off Browns Island Road, off South River Road in South Salem. It isn't easy to find in the daytime, let alone at night.

When police arrived on the scene, they found signs of a struggle at the car. At 5'2" and 100 pounds, Sherry did not represent a defensive physical powerhouse.

Family and friends gathered at Sherry's parents' house to keep a vigil and try to keep their spirits up.

Eighteen-year-old Sherry Eyerly had just graduated from Sprague High School as an honors student and was considering her future. She planned to attend college but hadn't settled on a school yet. She had taken a part-time job delivering pizzas for Domino's and had moved in with a cousin enjoying her first taste of independence, while she mulled over her future.

Sherry had just returned to town from a week-long family vacation at Shasta Lake in California. She was called into work on July 4th, and at about 9:00, Domino's got the order that sent Eyerly out. The caller sounded middle-aged and had ordered two pizzas. It sounded like someone else was in the room, as he asked what kind of pizza they had ordered before. He gave his address as Riverhaven Drive S., near the end of Faragate Street S. The man was familiar with the Domino's menu. The only unusual aspect of the order was that he asked for a specific delivery girl, saying she had delivered pizzas to him in the past. He added she drove an orange VW.

The girl requested by the caller was not working that night, and so at 9:40 p.m., Sherry Eyerly grabbed her hat, keys, and the pizzas for a routine delivery, although the address was outside the store's usual delivery area. It was a slow night.

That was the last time Sherry was seen.

Once the police began investigating, they discovered that the call-back number given by the man ordering the pizza was for a downtown motel. The name given was fictitious. The address was fictitious.

The next day, deputies and a dozen members of the Search & Rescue Explorer Post 18 combed through the blackberries alongside the gravel road searching for Eyerly and clues. Friends and family joined the search. A private helicopter searched the area for two and a half hours. The Eyerly family hired two dowsers—people who use a divining rod—and a professional dog handler to search the area. The search continued throughout the week. Divers explored the nearby river. Other than the Domino's cap found about 500 feet from the car and a footprint, they found nothing.

Neighbors reported seeing two vehicles in the area that night: a 1973 or 1974 dark-colored Monte Carlo and a mid-1950s to mid-1960s lime green pickup truck with mag wheels and lights on the roll bar.

The next day, Domino's got a call from someone demanding a ransom for Eyerly's safe return. The kidnapper, however, never called again and made no attempt to collect money. That aspect of the crime was never publicized so police could discern false confessions.

The crime hit Salem hard. This could be anyone's daughter. Her family created a $6,000 reward fund for information leading to the arrest and conviction of those responsible for the abduction and hired a psychic. The reward was later boosted to $20,000. *Unsolved Mysteries* filmed an episode about Eyerly's disappearance and aired the episode multiple times but it never generated any leads. Eyerly's disappearance became legendary among Salem teenagers—all wondered what happened to her. All wondered if it could happen to them.

Marion County Sheriff's Office reported that several psychics had called over the first weekend to give investigators their impressions of where Eyerly was, including Mount Hood, Klamath Falls, and San Diego.

Police zeroed in on suspect Darrell J. Wilson, 30. At first he denied having met Eyerly, but eventually conceded that he did know her. Wilson drove a lime-green pickup truck similar to a vehicle seen near where Eyerly disappeared. After her vanishing, Wilson suspiciously repainted his truck brown. Wilson's alibi was that he was camping at Elkhorn Lake, 34 miles east of Salem the night Eyerly vanished. When detectives sought to confirm the alibi, they found he had been missing from the campground from 6:30 p.m. July 4 to 3:30 a.m. on July 5. Disappointingly, authorities found no physical evidence in the truck linking Wilson to Eyerly.

On August 22, 1982, Marion County Sheriff detective Will Hingston took psychic John Catchings to Wilson's house. When offered, Wilson declined the opportunity to take a polygraph but said he would talk to the psychic. Wilson kept the brochure of the psychic's that included some of the crimes he had helped solve, but didn't volunteer any information deemed useful.

Hours after being questioned, Wilson committed suicide. Many took that suicide to be a confession. While the case was never officially closed, in the minds of many, Wilson was the killer. With Wilson dead and the trail growing cold, the investigation lost momentum. Nevertheless, Salem police assigned a detective to work full time on the Eyerly case until mid-March 1984 when budget cuts forced reassignment of the deputy.

It would be 24 years before her family and the community learned the identity of her killer.

Rebecca Ann Darling
February 19, 1984
3185 River Road N.

Working the graveyard shift at a convenience store is a rough gig—those hours when the store attracts rowdies, drunks and souls unmoored to societal conventions.

Rebecca Ann Darling, 21, was working the graveyard shift at the Circle K on River Road North one Sunday until—she suddenly wasn't. She was gone. A customer had seen her as late as 3:20 a.m., but she had vanished a half hour later when another customer found the store empty. Co-workers all agreed that Darling would not have left the store unattended voluntarily.

Police found Darling's purse, car keys, and coat still in the store and her car was still in the parking lot. There was no evidence of a struggle and nothing obvious was missing. Darling had worked at the store since the prior October and was the only clerk on duty that night.

Rebecca was 5'10" tall, weighed about 160, and had long brown hair and brown eyes. She had been wearing white bib overalls, a Circle K T-shirt and tennis shoes. She had gone to McKay High School in Salem, but dropped out in her junior year, completing her high school graduation requirements at Chemeketa Community College. She lived with a boyfriend who was also working the graveyard shift, but at the Circle K across town on State Street. He had spoken to Darling at about 3:00 a.m. An hour later, the police were calling him to tell him

Photo credit: J. E. McComb

Rebecca Ann Darling was working a night shift February 1984, when she was abducted from the convenience store at this location.

his girlfriend was missing.

Darling had not been scheduled to work that night, but had traded shifts with another clerk.

The clerk who worked the prior shift reported that a man had come into the store twice, asking for Darling by name. At the time, it didn't strike her as particularly strange; regular customers got to know the clerks, and the shirts the clerks wore often had their name on them. The man who had asked after Rebecca bought beer three times from the store during the prior shift and appeared drunk.

A composite drawing was made from the clerk's description and ran in the paper the next day. He was described as white, about 26 years old, 5'7", and about 160 pounds. He had longish brown hair and brown eyes and a reddish brown mustache.

Darling's family had moved from Salem to Texas three years earlier when her father was injured doing his landscaping work. Her boyfriend described her as a strong girl but was nervous about working the late night shift and had wanted to quit, but the couple needed the two incomes. The store's clientele tended to provoke anxiety. The boyfriend recounted that a man had approached Darling on several occasions, telling her that she reminded him of his dead wife. The man had brought in pictures for Darling to see, and she had agreed there was a resemblance.

Security was lackluster and the store's only telephone was in a back room, the setup in all the stores at the time.

Salem police received more than a hundred telephone calls about the case, but none supplied a solid lead. Police continued to seek a man who had asked for Darling on the day she disappeared.

The Darling disappearance reminded many of the Eyerly disappearance two years earlier. Two young women vanished, no bodies found, and no evidence. However, Salem police did not believe the two cases were linked. On April 18, the Circle K Corporation stated that it planned to increase security at its 51 Oregon stores, in light of Darling's disappearance.

A farmer tending his cows found Darling's decomposed, partially-clothed remains March 25, mostly submerged in the Little Pudding River six miles northeast of town. The body had gotten caught up in some brush along the river about 30 yards downstream of a bridge in the 10,000 block of Kaufman Road. The body was so decomposed that authorities could not immediately tell the race, sex, or age. Nude from the waist up, she had been strangled with a piece of rope, hands bound behind her back. The State Medical Examiner found no evidence of sexual assault, and the body was wearing underwear, but the state of the body made such a finding less likely.

Katherine "Katy" Redmond
April 7, 1984
Cordon Road & State Street

The green, two-door Datsun was found at 3:50 a.m. near the intersection of State Street and Cordon Road, the engine

Photo credit: J. E. McComb

Willamette student Katy Redmond borrowed a car after a party. Her body was later found miles away off State Street, just past Cordon Road.

running, the driver's door ajar, a purse still in the car. The driver was missing. There were no signs of a struggle. The rear bumper had a small dent.

It was an eerie echo of Sherry Eyerly's disappearance.

The car belonged to a Willamette University professor. He had loaned it to his daughter to use, a Willamette student. It was Saturday night, and 18-year-old coed Katherine Ione Redmond, who roomed with the professor's daughter, was missing. Redmond had left an all-night Beta Theta Pi fraternity party in Baxter Hall, near State and 12th Street. The party featured skits, a mock debate, and kegs of beer.

The Mill Valley resident was nearing the end of her first year at Willamette. She had pledged Alpha Chi Omega and lived in the sorority house on Mill Street. The beer was flowing, but party-goers reported that Redmond did not appear drunk. She borrowed the car about 3:15 a.m. She had not asked permission but the keys were in the room she shared with three others. She didn't say where she was going.

Redmond was 5'4" with wavy medium-length brown hair and brown eyes. She was last seen wearing rust-colored knee-length shorts, a white blouse, a denim jacket and black shoes.

Salem police, Marion County Sheriff's deputies, and cadets searched the grassy, wooded area where the car was found—about five miles east of campus—until late Saturday afternoon, but found nothing helpful. They returned Sunday with Explorer Scouts and searched until nightfall, again, without finding any signs of the coed. Divers also searched a nearby creek and pond. A helicopter and light plane flew over the area.

Ominously, a shoe was found by the search team that first day about five feet off State Street and about a half-mile east of the intersection.

Word quickly spread on the small campus of 1,200, where everyone knew everyone and the mood turned somber. Requests for escorts spiked. Redmond was a popular, outgoing student who never missed a class. She was a good student, active in the model United Nations, and a member of the editorial board for a student academic journal. Another roommate worked at the search party's command center making coffee, waiting for news.

Neither the police nor the community drew a connection between Redmond's disappearance and those of other women in the community.

Two people called police to report they had seen a station wagon in a ditch off State Street around 4 a.m. on April 7 near Cordon Road. Police contacted towing companies and found a driver who had responded to a 6 a.m. call April 7 from a man who said his vehicle was stuck in a ditch. He pulled the car free and followed the man home to a Silverton address where he was paid by check.

That man was 25-year-old William Scott Smith.

Investigators determined that Redmond's shoe had been found just 40 feet from where Smith's vehicle went into the ditch.

Photo credit: Oregon State Penitentiary

A state trooper returned to the area where the car had been towed. He walked north about 400 yards and found Redmond's body at 4:00 p.m. on Wednesday, four

William Scott Smith was behind the disappearance of young women occurring over several years.

days after she had gone missing. Her nude body was found in a brushy wooded area four-tenths of a mile east of the intersection where the car was found. Her clothing was found 15-20 feet from her body. The location was secluded with substantial blackberry bushes and was not visible from the road.

The Deputy State Medical Examiner determined she had died of traumatic asphyxiation, meaning she was either strangled or smothered. There was evidence she had been raped. The finding had been withheld from the press for a day, so the scene could be studied by state police criminologists.

The body was within four miles of where Rebecca Darling had been found.

An interagency task force was formed to investigate the Redmond murder along with the unsolved slayings and disappearances of half a dozen other women over the prior three years. A 24-hour hotline was set up. The Oregon State Police assigned nine investigators. Salem Police Department and Marion County sheriff's office each contributed five detectives. Detectives from Washington checked into the death for a possible link to the Green River Killer, but local police were skeptical of a connection, with District Attorney Michael Brown dismissing the theory outright.

A Salem police officer interviewed Smith the evening they had made the tow truck call discovery. Smith made no admissions at that time. He told police that he had visited two friends' homes that night and was driving home on State Street when he overreacted to the bright lights of an oncoming vehicle and drove into the ditch. The officer noticed numerous scratch marks on Smith's arms, neck, chest, and ankles consistent with the type made by berry bushes. More damning, police saw a deep scratch mark on Smith's chest and what appeared to be two bite marks on his right arm. Smith became a prime suspect. Police put him under surveillance and sought search warrants for the home, photographs of the bite marks, Smith's teeth impressions and his fingerprints.

•••••

William Scott Smith was an unemployed high school dropout. Teachers and acquaintances described Smith as temperamental and defiant. He lived with his father and stepmother. The home was a few miles from where the two bodies were found. Smith had worked a series of odd jobs, working for trucking companies, as a truck stop cook, an apprentice carpenter in Puyallup, Washington, and as a convenience-store clerk.

Police looked at his rap sheet and saw trouble. Smith had a record of arrests and convictions for sex-related crimes and misdemeanors. As a teenager, he stole 26 cases of beer from a Silverton Safeway.

He was linked to other crimes but prosecutors lacked evidence to press charges. In 1978, he was convicted of menacing in Silverton and second-degree burglary in Salem. In 1979, he was arrested, along with another man, on a charge of second-degree sexual abuse in a sexual assault of a Salem woman following a graduation party. The jury found Smith innocent of the charge, but convicted the other man, James Andrew Sexton. In 1981, Smith was convicted in Boise of indecent exposure. In another incident, Smith pulled over a female driver on I-5 then masturbated on her windshield, leaving behind fingerprints, among other things.

On top of these prior crimes and misdemeanors, he had a charge of telephone harassment pending.

Anderson's Sporting Goods ran out of mace. Gun sales were up. Women were asking for escorts to their car. A teacher reported that her first and second graders were discussing Redmond's death. With the deaths of Darling and Redmond, Salem was looking at eight unsolved deaths of women since 1981.

On April 10, a woman reported to police that her vehicle had been bumped from behind by another car at the intersection of Lancaster Drive and Highway 22. The bumping had occurred just 20-30 minutes before Redmond's car was found. The woman was driving home from a friend's house and had stopped for a red light. The station wagon slowly rolled into her rear bumper. The woman set the hand brake and was getting ready to get out of the car to examine the damage when she noticed the man who had bumped her was already out of his car and approaching hers. When she saw his size, she decided to stay in her car.

The decision likely saved her life.

The man suggested she get out of her car to inspect the damage. Instead, she suggested that they both drive to a service station where the lighting was better. He agreed, but then drove off when she pulled into a station. He drove north on Lancaster toward State Street—where he would turn right and encounter Katy a mile or so later.

After Redmond's death, the killer got the nickname of "Bumper" in police circles because of their developing theory that the killer drove up behind cars, hit them, forcing the young female driver to pull over and exchange information when he would grab them. Detectives admitted that there was some damage to the rear of Redmond's car but they couldn't tell whether the damage was the result of a recent collision.

Police asked the public for any information concerning a battered late 1960s or early 1970s gray, blue, or green station wagon. Citizens who had seen such an older American-made station wagon in the vicinity of State Street and Lancaster Drive and Cordon Drive between midnight and 6 am Saturday were asked to contact police. Police also asked for anyone who had been bumped by a car to come forward.

Local women called police asking how they could tell whether a police car pulling them over really contained a cop and not a serial killer. Officials from the state, city, and county police advised that if a driver was uncertain about whether a police impersonator was trying to pull them over, they should proceed to a lighted, populated area before stopping.

The trail was getting hot. The task force doubled in size: 17 Oregon State Police employees, six deputies and four reserve officers from the Marion County Sheriff's Office, seven detectives and seven patrol officers from the Salem Police Department.

Police interviewed Smith's family and friends. The car driven by the suspect was impounded April 11—the same day Redmond's body was found—once a warrant had been obtained for its seizure.

An unnamed source leaked to the *Silverton Appeal-Tribune* that police had a suspect. *The Statesman Journal* published a photo of the suspect outside the Marion County Courthouse. The leaking annoyed Marion County District Attorney Michael Brown who wanted to keep a lid on the investigation and didn't see how the photo was in the public interest—he didn't want everybody in town involved in the investigation.

But in reality, everybody already was.

On Monday, April 23, 25-year-old William Scott Smith appeared for sentencing on a telephone harassment charge for which he had pleaded guilty in March. Court records indicated that Smith had made obscene phone calls to a woman. Police had tapped the line and arrested him January 31. He was indicted the same day.

Smith was accompanied to court by his pregnant girlfriend, the mother of two. She and Smith had lived together in a northeast Salem apartment, until they were evicted for nonpayment of rent. She had accused Smith of physical abuse the prior October and of criminal mischief in January. Both charges had been dismissed.

The judged gave Smith a six-month sentence and fined him $500 for the obscene telephone calls. Once taken into custody, he immediately began serving his sentence.

Police had held off questioning Smith until the misdemeanor charge was settled, since Smith was represented by legal counsel. With the case settled, police began questioning him in earnest that same day.

On April 24, Smith, in custody, met with his girlfriend and several members of his family.

At the pre-trial hearing, Smith's father, stepmother, and girlfriend testified that Smith had indicated to them that he had killed Redmond. Dwain Smith said his son was ready to talk to investigators about the Redmond murder.

On April 25, the District Attorney convened a grand jury to hear evidence in the Redmond murder case, who returned two counts of aggravated murder in the cases of Katherine Redmond and Rebecca Ann Darling against William Scott Smith.

The indictment accused Smith of killing the two women in the course of committing one or more other crimes. The indictment in Darling's cased alleged Smith had kidnapped and raped her. The indictment in Redmond's case alleged Smith had kidnapped, sexually abused, and sexually penetrated her with a foreign object. Defense attorney James Susee was assigned as Smith's legal counsel. The penalty for each aggravated murder charge was life in prison with a mandatory minimum of 20 years before parole. A simple murder charge did not have a similar requirement.

The grand jury returned an indictment against Smith the same day, April 25th.

The 300-pound Smith confessed to police that he carried Darling from the Circle K to his car without a struggle. He then drove Darling to his home on Lardon Road. His father and stepmother were out of town at the time. He bound her hands with cotton rope behind her back then raped her. He wrapped the rope around her neck three times, strangling her.

The death occurred in the driveway. He then drove her body three miles to the Kaufmann Avenue Bridge over the Little Pudding River and dumped her body.

Smith entered a plea of innocent on May 11, 1984. Without the confessions, the evidence was shaky. Circumstantial evidence linked Smith to the Redmond slaying. There was virtually no evidence linking him to Darling's death, aside from Smith's confession. Smith's attorney filed a motion to suppress the confession. Judge Val Sloper denied the motions.

A month later, Susee opted for trial by stipulation before a judge rather than a jury. In a stipulated trial, the prosecution summarizes the evidence that would be presented if witnesses were called to the stand.

Judge Val Sloper found Smith guilty July 9, 1984, following the 20-minute trial by stipulation. It was an anticlimactic conclusion to terror that enveloped the community for months. Smith never offered any motive for the slayings.

Even 20 years later, Eyerly's disappearance haunted the community. The Marion County Sheriff's Cold Case Squad decided to reinvestigate the case in 2005. William Scott Smith had been questioned following his conviction of Darling's and Redmond's murder but had an alibi. He had told police that he was on a long-haul trucking trip out of state on the day Sherry was taken. The Cold Case Squad discovered that Smith had been stopped by Silverton police the day after Eyerly went missing, proving he was in the area.

In November and December 2006, Marion County Sheriff's cold case investigators interviewed Smith who finally confessed to Eyerly's murder. Smith stated that he and accomplice Roger Noseff had planned to abduct a Domino's Pizza employee and hold her for ransom. After they took Eyerly from the area, Noseff told Smith they had grabbed the wrong girl. Smith said it was too late and strangled her along a secluded spot along the Little Pudding River and dumped her body in the river. The river has flooded many times since 1984 and Eyerly's body has never been recovered.

Smith stated that it was Noseff who made the ransom call. Because the call had not been made public, the confession was deemed authentic.

The sheriff's office spent the next year trying to confirm the confession and find Eyerly's body but lacked physical evidence and Noseff had died of cancer in 2003. However, in his confession, Smith knew details of the pizza order that had never been released; that the caller identified himself as "Dubar" and that he had ordered "Destroyers" — pizzas with all the toppings.

On October 18, 2012, William Smith confessed to strangling Terry Cox Monroe outside the Museum Tavern to Salem cold case detectives. The cold case team had reviewed the evidence and done follow-up interviews. Smith waived his right to contest the case and pleaded guilty to her murder. He was given his fourth life sentence.

Smith is serving a life sentence for the kidnapping and murder of the four women.

And a new generation of Salem women will need to learn not to get out of their car if someone bumps them from behind on dark, lonely country roads.

5. He Had It Coming

Chemawa Indian School
September 5, 1921

In the wee hours of a Sunday morning, Alma Wurtzbarger, 37, shook awake her 20-year-old nephew who was staying with her and her husband Andrew, 42.

"Well, I've killed him," she confessed.[1] Alma was already dressed and carrying a valise.

Recognizing her precarious legal situation, Alma decided she needed to consult the obvious person: her daughter. She asked nephew Eliza Miles to dress. (Miles was the nephew of Alma's second husband, and had only been in town about a week, having traveled from Douglas, Arizona.)

They then made their way down the narrow, uncarpeted steps to the first floor and out the door. Following the railroad tracks, they walked the seven miles into Salem. Her daughter, Mrs. Ralph Derrick, resided at 2355 Laurel Avenue. Once there, Alma laid out her story to her dazed daughter and son-in-law.

At 6 a.m., Alma phoned Sheriff Bower's office. "I think I've killed my husband," she told him, backpedaling a bit from her earlier declaration to Eliza.[2] Given the condition the coroner found Mr. Wurtzbarger, it is questionable whether Alma harbored any doubts on that score. Police carted Alma off to jail where she recounted the previous night's activities.

She and Andrew lived on the grounds of the Chemawa

Photo credit: State Library of Oregon

Established in 1880, the Chemawa Indian School continues to exist today. Native American boarding schools were established in the US during the late 19th and mid-20th centuries to assimilate Native American children and youth into Euro-American culture and eradicate their own.

Indian School, where Andrew was employed as a laborer. The boarding school opened on the Salem site in 1880s and was based on the U.S. Training and Industrial School founded in 1879 at Carlisle Barracks, Pennsylvania, under the philosophy of Captain Henry Pratt.

Pratt wrote, "A great general has said that the only good Indian is a dead one, and that high sanction of his destruction has been an enormous factor in promoting Indian massacres. In a sense, I agree with the sentiment, but only in this: that all the Indian there is in the race should be dead. Kill the Indian in him, and save the man."[3]

To this end, Pratt promoted boarding schools for Indian youths where children would be required to drop their Indian names, stop speaking their Native tongue, and cut their hair.

These schools emphasized vocational skills. At the time, this passed for progressive and compassionate thinking. Later, some would refer to this as cultural genocide.

The Wurtzbargers had both attended a dance on the campus Saturday night and had returned home around 9:30 p.m. They were in their shared bed by 11:00. Like a lot of recent nights, they quarreled before turning in. Alma got up a few hours later, inadvertently waking up Andrew in the process.

"What the hell are you doing," he asked his bride of three months.

"I'm fixing my asthma medicine," she replied.

"I hope it chokes you to death," the newlywed responded.[4]

Alma was matter-of-fact about her actions. "I then went downstairs. I thought it over. It was then that I came upon the hammer, and when I saw it, I knew what I would do. I took it upstairs with me, and finding him asleep, I beat him over the head several times. Eliza did not wake, because he died without a groan," she said.[5]

Mrs. H. Ayers of Los Angeles was staying in the other half of the little cottage. She was in Salem visiting her father who lived on the campus. She told police that she was awakened about three o'clock Sunday morning by a noise that sounded like a chair falling, but she thought little of it, as she had "become accustomed to disturbances of that kind."[6] She told police that she had often heard profane remarks hurled by Wurtzbarger at his wife.

Police had to smash a window to enter Wurtzbarger's little house, as Alma had locked front and back doors before setting off for her daughter's house. The upstairs hall light was still burning. Police entered the 10x10' front bedroom and found all four walls and the low ceiling spattered with blood. Only two pictures, "cheap and unattractive"[7] looked down from the white plastered walls on the scene. The body was still in the bed, although the mattress had broken through the bed to the floor from the force of the blows. Andrew's head had suffered many "crashing blows"[8] and the coroner found the skull had

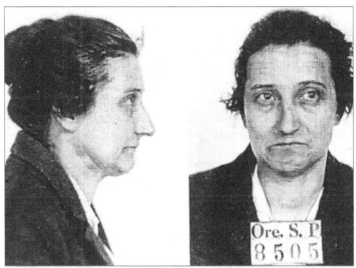

Photo credit: Oregon State Archives

Alma Wurtzbarger turned herself in to law enforcement after killing her husband following his threat to kill her that weekend. Because the murder took place on federal land, the Feds took control of her case and showed no mercy.

simply been "beaten to a pulp."[9] Alma's blood-soaked kimono and nightdress had been abandoned in an empty room next to the couple's bedroom.

The headline in Monday's *Capital Journal* was of the kind that made every husband's man-parts shrivel: *Chemawa Man Slain. Wife Using Heavy Hammer Beats Andrew Wurtzbarger To Death While He Sleeps.*

A reporter asked Mrs. Wurtzbarger how well she had rested during her first night of incarceration. "I slept fairly well," she responded.[10]

The press was skeptical. "Despite Mrs. Wurtzbarger's statement that she had not spent a sleepless night, the strain of the last few hours showed plainly in her thin, almost expressionless face. Most of the time she spends staring at the cement floor of the spacious cell in which only her narrow cot is placed."[11]

The article continued, "The murder charge which, without question, looms before Mrs. Wurtzbarger, has in no way interfered with her appetite." He went on to report she had eaten a veal steak, creamed tomatoes, a piece of pie and a cup of tea for dinner the night before, and had a fortifying breakfast of two eggs, a waffle, another piece of pie, and a cup of coffee that morning.

The newsman noted, "Mrs. Wurtzbarger showed a tendency to become angry when newspaper men put questions to her."[12]

"Had you ever considered killing him before?" she was asked. "Certainly, not," she said, with the reporter adding "disgust was evidence in the shrug which accompanied her terse reply."[13]

"You will plead self-defense?"

"I certainly will."

Alma had told police matron Myra Shank of her fear. "Mr. Wurtzbarger told me Saturday night that I'd never be here when the sun came up Monday morning."[14]

Alma's daughter emphatically defended her mother. "I am positive that mother was forced to do what she did by his actions."[15]

The Wurtzbargers reportedly had quarreled frequently and the prior Tuesday Andrew had probably broken one of Alma's ribs. *The Sunday Oregonian* reported that she would have an X-ray but failed to report the findings.

Reginald Chapman was a 15-year-old Indian boy who helped the Wurtzbargers with odd jobs and often ate meals with them. He was a witness to their frequent quarrels. He reported that he had often heard the name "Charles Gallagher" in connection with the fights.

·····

Alma Wurtzbarger was born in Alabama and had moved to Salem from Douglas, Arizona. She had lived in Salem about two years. Her first husband, Dennis Carter, had died. With her second husband, H.K. Miles, she had a daughter and son.

Son Otis worked as a clerk at the Multnomah Hotel in Portland. Alma and Miles had divorced, reconciled and married, and divorced again.

Alma moved, hoping the Oregon climate would reduce her asthma symptoms.

Alma met Charles L. Gallagher while they were both working at the state "feeble minded school."

She was a housekeeper, he was a cook.

Gallagher had a prison record. A bartender by trade, he had been convicted of embezzlement from the bartender's union in Astoria. He was given a sentence of one to ten years, and entered prison March 26, 1914. He was paroled a year later, on March 26, 1915, for good behavior. He moved to Sacramento, but got careless and quit reporting to his parole officer. "I went to California and worked 17 months," he told reporters later. "All the time I minded my own business and kept to myself." Against all odds, after three years in California he was spotted and recognized by his parole officer. He was returned to prison for violating parole on October 24, 1918. "I felt that the second stretch had been unjust," he said later. "Think of it—a year for just failing to report."[16]

He then served another year and was paroled October 24, 1919. On October 13, 1920, he was given a full pardon and restored to citizenship.

He admitted that the job at the school was not his long term plan. "I was just going to work long enough to get a 'front' and then pull some kind of a job. I didn't know what, but you learn in the penitentiary."[17]

"Everybody at the institute knew I was an ex-con and they were all against me. Well, that suited me. I was against everybody, too. Then Mrs. Wurtzbarger came to my rescue. I tell you, man, you can't know what that meant. She stood up for me against all of them. She talked to me as she would have to her own son—and she has raised two fine children. One of them is working with me right now—her 17-year-old son. She braced me up. I saw where I was wrong and I made up my mind to go straight."[18]

In recounting those days for reporters, Gallaher said,

"Mrs. Wurtzbarger has been my good angel. She raised my soul from hell, when I was full of bitterness and vindictiveness against the world.

"She married Wurtzbarger last May. I thought it was going to be us, but—well, even she wasn't entirely free of the usual prejudice against an ex-con. I knew she had made a mistake, and so did she by the end of the first week. He was a brute. He conceived an insane jealousy for me. He used to beat her constantly. I wanted to do something—but where did I get off? He was her husband, and I knew what they would say if I butted in."[19]

Alma had met Andrew J. Wurtzbarger in February 1921. He had been a member of the Hall Hibbard camp of the Spanish War Veterans. He was a member of the 18th Indiana volunteers and was honorably discharged. He had come to Salem in 1920. He had a son from a prior marriage, but the son was no longer on the scene, having been an inmate of the state training school and then joined the military and was now stationed in Honolulu.

Those who worked with Andrew said that while he was an efficient worker, he was unable to get along with the men around him. Andrew was also unable to save money. Following his death, the papers reported that he lacked the savings to pay for his own burial.

Following a brief romance, Alma and Andrew married three months later, May 28, 1921.

Charles Gallagher recounted that time. "She married Wurtzbarger, but I did not cease loving her. Her boy, Otis, came to Portland to work with me and lived with me for a while until Wurtzbarger insisted that I was not a fit man for any boy to associate with."[20]

Andrew took to quarreling with his wife almost immediately, often physically mistreating her and cursing her. Reginald Chapman reported to police that the couple was arguing over correspondence between Alma and Charles Gallagher about the time of Mr. Wurtzbarger's death.

The first episode of Mr. Wurtzbarger's jealous rage was provoked when Alma received a letter from her second husband a few weeks after she and Wurtzbarger were wed. Alma told officials that it was merely a friendly note regarding her children. Wurtzbarger flared into a jealous rage and forbade her to have further correspondence with him. She explained to Andrew that she and her ex-husband had agreed to remain on friendly terms for the sake of the children but Andrew responded that she couldn't fool him; he knew the ex was trying to get Alma to return to him. He would see her dead before he would give her up to another man.

The next explosion of anger was occasioned when Alma received a letter from Charles Gallagher. Mrs. Wurtzbarger explained to police that she had never considered Gallagher as more than a friend (a story she would later amend), although he had proposed marriage to her several times. She had consistently rejected his proposals. After her marriage, she received a letter from Gallagher and she wrote him back, telling him of her marriage and asking that he cease his attentions. Gallagher responded to this letter, and Andrew Wurtzbarger saw it and unleashed his bad temper.

At gunpoint, Andrew forced her to write a "mushy" letter back to Gallagher, dictating the letter himself and inviting Gallagher to reply.[21]

Then he waited.

The response arrived on a day when Alma was out of town. Andrew met her at the Oregon Electric Train station, and as soon as they were out of earshot of others said, "Well, I got a letter from that guy."[22] Alma protested that she did not want to know what was in the letter, but Andrew "chided and abused" her all the way home and when they got home, he insisted—at gun point—that she read it.[23]

When asked by reporters whether there were "terms of endearment" in the letters between them, Charles Gallagher reported, "There were not. The letters were nothing more than what might pass between two friends. The first letter might have been a little friendlier than the last. In the last letter she explained that she had previously written while her husband threatened her life."[24]

Alma told her attorney that Andrew was principally jealous of her ex-husband. A few days before the murder, Alma suggested a separation—that they could never be happy together. Andrew replied that she would continue to live with him until she died and that he would follow her to the end of the earth and kill her if she tried to get away from him.

On the night of the murder, Alma reported that Andrew was "as nice as anyone could be" toward Alma, as they were in the company of the nephew. However, as soon as he got her alone, the abuse started again. Andrew was convinced that the nephew was there to help Alma escape him and help her return to her ex-husband. "Mrs. Wurtzbager wanted the door of the room left open to afford better ventilation in the close, stuffy room," said her attorney, a Mr. Shields. "But Wurtzbarger would not have it. He closed the door and commenced to abuse her. She says that he choked her and threatened to kill her if she attempted to get away from him, continuing the abuse until he fell asleep."[25]

Talking to a reporter on the day she surrendered herself to the sheriff, Alma described her late husband. "Mr. Wurtzbarger had an unbearable disposition. He has always been that way, but it was not until lately that he became so violent. He was jealous of every man that I spoke to, and I was allowed to have no friends. I stayed in the house most of the time, doing my housework, and I was seldom gone. He never has treated my children right, and lately he has just ignored them."[26]

When questioned about Charles Gallagher, she said, "I seldom saw him, and seldom heard from him. He was nothing more than a distant friend to me, only he was more of a friend than anyone else."[27]

Pleading insanity and self-defense, Alma argued that the continued threats so unbalanced her reason that she was not responsible for her actions. Her attorney stated, "Mrs. Wurtzbarger was convinced that either her husband or herself [sic] had to die, and she simply concluded that she would not be the one to go."[28]

Marion County District Attorney John Carson charged Alma with first degree murder, punishable by the death pen-

Copy.

Falls City,Oregon.
April 10th 1922.

Honorable Warren G.Harding,President,United States of America
        Washington,D.C.
Dear Mr.President,

We,the undersigned citizens of Falls City,Oregon;having been personaly acquainted with the late Andrew J.Wurtzberger who was killed by his wife on the night of the 4th of September 1921 at the Chemawa Indian School;Marion County,Oregon;do Depose that the said Andrew J.Wurtzberger was while living in this town a dangerously bad man.Brutal to his first wife.Dishonest.Immoral.

From our intimate knowledge of him while he resided here we cannot help but feel that his second wife Mrs.Alma L,Wurtzberger who is now confined in the Oregon State Penitentiary had every reason to feel that her life and the life of her children would be taken by him if she didnot kill him first.We make this statement knowing the brutal nature of the man.

From trustworthy reports we believe Mrs.Alma L.Wurtzberger suffered mental and physical tortures and was consumed by fear of him that she was driven to defend her own life and that of her children by kill -ing him.

Being Firmly convinced that Mrs.Alma L.Wurtzberger was in a state of mind verging on insanity through fear and bodily pain sustaind by his brutal beatings when she took the law into her own hands and killed him;we do petition you Mr.President to grant her a pardon and restore her to liberty and her children.

Mrs.Alma L.Wurtzberger is an entire stranger te us but we feel that there has been a sad miscarriage of justice and that you will be performing a humane act by extending to her Executive clemency.

Hoping our plea in her behalf will meet the kindly consideration due it at your hands;we thank you and ask God to bless you and our nation.We are
                        Very respectfully yours,

Mr.J.J.Sammonds	Mr.H.P.Bogart	Mr.M.A.Pugh
MR.Wm.Aldermen	Mr.W.C.McKoron	Mrs.J.J.Sammonds
Mr.Thos.G.Allen	Mr.C.A.Hunter	Mr.J.D.Moyer
Mr.Wallace Brown	Mr.W.R.Gardoner	Mrs.Jessie Moyer
Mrs.Grace Brown	Mr.Fred Zuver	Mr.C.G.Matheois
Mr.E.P.Brown	Mr.J.L.Hunter	Mr.F.M.Harris
Mr.E.S.Rich	Mr.Dale Gottfried	Mr.J.R.Moyer
Mr.N.A.Lunde	Mr.W.B.McKoron	Mrs Mary C.Moyer
Dins McMurphy	Mr.H.A.Montgomery	Mrs.Mead McKown
Louise Chappell	Emma Johnson	Mr.H.Wagner
Mrs H.P.Bogert	Mr.D.J.Grant	Mr.A.F.Courter
Mr.Geo.M.Tice	Mr.Gordon D,Treat	Mr.C.T.Ellison
Mr.T.D.Hallowell	Mrs.Lela M.Hubbard	Mr.A.B.Hubbard
Mr.Glen D.Furgson	Mr.D.D.Bell	Mr.W.M.Bancroft
Mr.C.R.Cochran	Mr.W.D.Bancroft	Mr.C.B.McPherson
	Mr.D.M.Chaffe	

Photo credit: Oregon State Archives

Salem residents wrote to President Harding to report that Mr. Wurtzberger was a brutal man and his wife was only defending herself when she killed him and deserved mercy.

alty. She was arraigned before Justice of the Peace Blaine Mc-Cord in Woodburn the day after the murder. Her son-in-law sat by her side. She was transported to Woodburn because Peach Unruh, the Justice of the Peace for Marion County, was out of town. *The Capitol Journal* reported that a crowd had gathered outside the Woodburn court, "in the hope of getting a look at the woman who admits that she beat to an unrecognizable pulp the head of the husband whom she had married but three months ago."[29]

Reporters described her approach to the courtroom as "leisurely," and "as she strolled along she stopped twice—once to arrange her hair and the second time to tuck in a shoestring whose flopping apparently annoyed her. There was no indication that her approaching arraignment on the gravest charge the courts offer was worrying her in the least."[30]

The crowd was such that officers needed to clear a path for Mrs. Wurtzbarger to enter the courtroom. The papers reported on her appearance:

> *She was clad in the same brown dress that she wore on Sunday morning when she gave herself up to Sheriff O. D. Bower, and she had given the same meticulous attention to her appearance that had caused comment in the past. Over her dress she wore a heavy cloak. She was wearing no hat.*[31]

She was held without bail. Eliza Miles was picked up and held as a material witness with a $1,000 bail, later reduced to $500.

Coroner Lloyd Rigdon's formal inquest reported that the jury had found "that Andrew J. Wurtzbarger had come to his death on the 4th of September by being struck on the head by a hammer in the hands of one Alma Louise Wurtzbarger, wife of said Andrew J. , in such a manner as to be the murder of him."[32] Dr. John Mott, who examined the body, hypothesized that death could have been the result of a fractured skull, laceration of the brain tissue, or from loss of blood.

Rigdon reported that he and his associate morticians had been besieged by scores of curious persons who had called at the morgue at all hours in the hope of getting a glimpse of the corpse, including several women, noted the newspaper. All requests were denied unless the person claimed to be acquainted with the dead man.

The question of police jurisdiction arose almost immediately. While the Marion County Sheriff was already involved, the crime had occurred on federal property. Yet those involved in the crime were not Indians. The wheels of justice stopped turning while lawyers sorted out the situation.

Attorney General J. H. Van Winkle weighed in. "I am of the opinion that pursuant to the said provision of the constitution and the consent of the state of Oregon to the purchase of the land where the said school is located the courts of the United States have exclusive jurisdiction of a crime committed in a building of the said industrial school," he said.[33]

With the presumption that the Feds had jurisdiction, U.S. Marshal John D. Mann, accompanied by his wife, took Mrs. Wurtzbarger to Portland to face a grand jury September 25.

Local law enforcement continued to gather evidence to assist federal prosecution and because the jurisdiction had not been officially determined. The murder weapon was brought to Portland. It was a blacksmith's hammer and weighed about ten pounds. The face was about two inches in diameter and the other end was a rounded knob. The handle was about 14 inches long and covered with blood.

The jurisdictional issue was decided in *United States v. Wurtzbarger* that November. The Federal District Court held that under Constitution article 1, section 8, Congress had authority "over all places purchased by the consent of the Legislature of the state in which the same shall be, for the erection of forts * * * and other needful buildings."[34]

The charge was murder in the first degree, filed before United States Commissioner Kenneth Frazer in Portland by U.S. Attorney Lester W. Humphreys. The penalty in the federal code was death. Mrs. Wurtzbarger was moved to Multnomah County Jail to await trial.

Once in federal custody, the September 11 *Sunday Oregonian* reported that Alma "sat silent in the county jail here, a federal prisoner, brooding over her trouble and talking neither to her jail mates nor the matron in charge." When a reporter asked her why her husband had been so abusive, "she replied in a voice scarcely audible that she did not want to talk about it anymore and turned away from her questioner."

Her jail caretakers reported that Alma had spoken to no one since coming to the jail, "spending her time brooding and staring out the window with an occasional spell of silent weeping."[35]

Federal authorities believed that Alma was the first woman in Oregon to be tried on a charge of first-degree murder in the United States court, and it was believed to be the first case of its kind presented.

Alma's attorney Roy Shields stated that her defense would be based on the contention that cruel and inhuman treatment on the part of her husband drove the defendant to temporary insanity.

The Morning Oregonian, reporting from the September 9 arraignment, described Mrs. Wurtzbarger. "Mrs. Wurtzbarger does not have the appearance of a woman who would commit murder. She is tall and frail. Her eyes are dark and her face, were it not worn by several days of worry would be kindly. She was dressed in a black satin dress, blue hat with a veil and wore a long brown coat when she arrived with the federal officer."[36]

(Note: Her prison record describes her as 5'7" inches and 124 pounds.)

Reporters pressed her about the mystery man, Charles Gallagher, and whether he had anything to do with a motive for the slaying.

From the September 10, 1921, *Morning Oregonian*:

"I wish that I might keep his name out of this," said the woman, as she bit her lips and the tears came into her eyes. "But if I must tell he was a friend before I married Wurtzbarger.

"I was the housekeeper at the state feeble-minded institution last year and Gallagher was employed there. He was an ex-convict and was scorned and shunned by the other employees. I liked him and was kind to him. Several times I went out with him and almost consented

when he asked me to marry him. I would have been better off if I had taken him.

"I have refused to tell where he is until today, for he has been employed in Portland and has been living down his past."

"Did your regard for Gallagher have any influence on you that caused you to kill your husband," she was asked.

"No it did not—I killed my husband because I knew he would kill me. It was a case of self-preservation. I married Mr. Wurtzbarger May 28, and from that time on until I killed him life was only abuse for me. Every day he would threaten to kill me when I asked to be free from him. Every man I had ever known was his enemy. He hated for me to mention my divorced husband who died some time ago. He hated Gallagher and every other man who ever spoke to me. He deserved to be killed."

Mrs. Wurtzbarger was crying and her frail frame shook.

"I have been an invalid for many years," she continued. "I left Arizona six years ago and have been traveling from place to place in an effort to find someplace where I could be relieved of my sufferings from asthma. My strength is almost gone.

"When I went downstairs to get the hammer early Sunday morning it was all I could do to carry it upstairs where my husband was sleeping. I was not angry—I knew I had to kill him, so I used all my strength. I do not know whether I used one hand or both, or how many blows I struck him. I wanted to make a good job it and I did.

"Wurtzbarger was kind to me when we were going together. We met first along last February and were married in May. He professed to love me devoutly and I thought I loved him but after we were married he became a devil and repeatedly struck and beat me. Often times I have carried marks made by blows from his fists for weeks.

"The only avenue of escape from such a brute was murder, and I chose that avenue."[37]

•••••

Marion County prosecutors were not convinced. Why, if she feared her husband was going to kill her, did Mrs. Wurtzbarger not flee from the house when she went down stairs to get the hammer with which she beat her victim to death?"

asked one Marion County official. "She says she went downstairs and secured the hammer while he was asleep. Why did she not then leave the house and go to the nearby home of the superintendent of the Indian school and ask protection?"[38]

The U.S. Marshal who had transported Alma into federal custody did not see the face of a killer when he gazed upon her. "Criminals," he said, "mostly bear marks which characterize the crimes they have committed, but I have never had a case where the absence of this trait is so complete. It seems impossible that such a woman as gentle and retiring as Mrs. Wurtzbarger seems could have been aroused to the deed she confessed."[39]

Charles Gallaher, his role in the drama now public stated, "There is nothing that I would not do for the woman I love. I will remain in Portland, even though I lose my position, and help her if I can."[40]

Alma was formally indicted October 4, 1921.

Gallagher told police and reporters that a week before the murder, Wurtzbarger sent word to him through his stepson Otis and promised to give Alma a divorce if Gallagher would return Alma's letters to him. Gallagher told reporters, "I believe that Wurtzbarger planned to kill his wife, but was afraid to do so with the letters in my possession as evidence. I returned the letters as he requested, and I presume that they are now in the hands of the attorneys at Salem."[41]

"There never was a finer, purer, better woman … I loved her with everything clean and decent and good that was in me. I asked her to marry me, and there was a time she believed she would. But my past was against me. It would have meant that she would have had to take upon herself all the condemnation which the world heaps upon an ex-convict. She chose this other man instead. She found out her mistake later, and she was trying to get away from him when his insane jealousy forced this tragedy. If she could have got away from him we would probably have been married. If I can bring it about we will be yet."[42]

The hammer beating generated big headlines in Salem.

However, another killing had taken place the following day: Aspiring actress Virginia Rappe had died following a liquor-fueled party at the St. Francis Hotel in San Francisco and Virginia's friend had accused comedian Roscoe "Fatty" Arbuckle of raping and killing her. While the Wurtzbarger slaying still demanded front-page coverage, as the days passed the Arbuckle arrest garnered the larger headline and the Wurtzbarger murder retreated to the back pages.

On January 7, 1922, Mrs. Wurtzbarger retracted her "not guilty" plea and pleaded guilty to the charge of voluntary manslaughter. The plea came as a surprise given the earlier claims of self-defense. The U.S. Attorney testified to Andrew Wurtzbarger's mistreatments of his wife and that he had choked and abused her the night of his death. He had told Alma that he planned to kill her as soon as the visiting nephew left. In addition, Wurtzbarger would not allow Alma to see her children from her second marriage.

Mrs. Wurtzbarger's attorneys told the court of threats made against her by Mr. Wurtzbarger, "If you leave me I'll follow you and kill you—and your two children, too. I don't care what becomes of me then."[43]

Federal Judge Bean believed the evidence was strong enough to secure a conviction of second-degree murder. He believed the crime resembled second-degree murder rather than manslaughter in that no struggle had taken place and no altercation arisen immediately before the fatal blow was struck. "Passing sentence is always an unpleasant duty, especially when a woman is the convicted one," said Judge Bean. "But looking at the case from all phases the court cannot but consider her guilty of second-degree murder."[44] He sentenced Alma to ten years confinement in a federal penitentiary.

The penalty for voluntary manslaughter was three to ten years in prison and for second-degree murder it was ten years to life. Thus, the ten-year sentence was the minimum sentence for second-degree murder and the maximum for manslaughter. Alma reportedly took the sentence calmly and declined to make a statement to the court. However, the *Oregon Statesman* reported that she "appeared to be, however, on the verge of a breakdown. Her air in court was one almost of refinement."[45]

Under federal rules, she would be required to serve at least a third of her sentence before she was eligible for parole.

Where she would serve the time was an issue. The Oregon State Penitentiary was an institution for men. However, Alma requested that she serve her time in Salem. Her friends and families supported this request.

On January 25, 1922, Mrs. Wurtzbarger was ordered to serve her prison term in the Colorado State Penitentiary. She had been examined by Dr. Lloyd W. Brooke, a federal physician, who declared that the climate and high altitude would not impair her health. A letter had been sent to Judge Bean, presumably by Alma's attorneys, that imprisonment in Colorado would be fatal to Mrs. Wurtzbarger.

The decision was reversed in early March. "Mrs. Alma Lousie Wurtzbarger will be imprisoned at the Oregon State Penitentiary, effective at once," read the missive to Warden Louis H. Compton.[46] The federal prison board would pay Oregon $40 a month to maintain Mrs. Wurtzbarger at the prison.

In 1924, the March 15 edition of *The Oregonian* ran a small article ran entitled, "Women Prisoners Are Restricted; Females at Penitentiary to Be Put On Equal Basis With the Men."[47] The seven women prisoners would no longer be allowed to wear their own clothes. Purchase requests would be restricted to $2.50, once a month. They would be required to use prison stationery and write on one side only.

Women prisoners took exercise by going on short walks accompanied by a matron, or, in larger numbers, a matron and a guard. They were afforded individual rooms with heavy metal screens instead of bars. They were locked in at 8:30 each night and were permitted to attend weekly shows in the prison auditorium with the male prisoners.

As early as 1923, the warden and woman's matron asked the federal government for her pardon, citing her as a model prisoner with health problems who deserved to be released. The requests were denied until November 3, 1928, when she was finally released. Prison records indicate she moved to Olney, Texas where the trail grows cold.

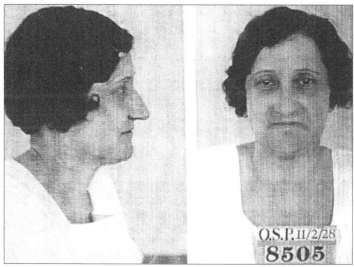

O.S.P. 11/2/28
8505

Photo credit: Oregon State Archives

Wurtzbarger was released from prison in 1928. One can't help notice she looks happier without a man in her life.

Alma—perhaps shamed by the whole sordid episode—did not stay in contact with her family, as her sister wrote the prison asking about Alma's whereabouts.

We can only speculate whether Alma married again or whether seven years in prison had crushed any impulse to ever put her fate in the hands of another man.

6. The I-5 Killer

3700 River Road N.
January 18, 1981

It was about 9:45 p.m. on a Sunday night in Salem when the man the police and newspapers had dubbed "The I-5 Bandit" became the "I-5 Killer."

Salem Fire and Ambulance received the 9-1-1 call for help a little before 10:00 p.m. The call was coming from the Transamerica Title building on North River Road.

The woman was 20-year-old Lisa Garcia and she told the dispatcher that she and her friend Shari Hull, also 20, had been shot. She and Shari were earning some extra money working for Shari's father who owned Pacific Western Building Maintenance. Lit up at night, the windowed storefront was easily visible from the street. They had arrived at the building about 9:10 or 9:15 that night and were done after about 20 minutes. Shari had gone outside and started up the Bronco to leave, but they noticed that one of the windows was still dirty and Lisa went back inside to a backroom to get a spray bottle. When Lisa came around the corner, a man was standing there with Shari, holding a silver pistol.

He aimed the gun at Lisa and ordered the women to go in the back room. There, he demanded they take off their clothes and lie on the floor. Later, Lisa would recall that the man had forced them to perform oral sex on him and he had attempted intercourse; the memory was initially blocked. Shari was crying and begging him not to hurt her. But he didn't care what they wanted—this was all about him.

He shot Shari in the head and then Lisa. Then he shot them both again. When Shari moaned after the second bullet, he put a third one into her. Lisa played dead. Fearing the shooter was still in the building, Lisa waited about five minutes before calling 9-1-1.

The whole ordeal was over in less than 30 minutes. Shari Hull died a few hours later, at about 1:30 a.m.

Hull had moved to Salem in 1970 and had graduated from McNary High School. She was working for her father while looking for a job in the computer field. She was scheduled for a job interview with Northwest Natural Gas Company on that Thursday. Her stepfather described Hull as a fun-loving person who enjoyed four-wheeling, camping, swimming, and travel.

Adding to the trauma, about two weeks following the assault Garcia discovered she had contracted herpes.

Garcia described her attacker to the police dispatcher and paramedics in the ambulance: white, brown hair, about 5'11", about 27 years old, jeans, a hooded dark jacket, tennis shoes. He had a Band-Aid across his nose. Police found no evidence of robbery or fingerprints, as the man had worn gloves.

The description sounded familiar to police.

For the prior six weeks, a man had been robbing businesses up and down the Interstate 5 corridor, wearing tape over his nose as a cheap, but surprisingly effective disguise. The bandit was armed with a pistol and had shot one clerk in the shoulder. He chose places that were lightly staffed, with young women. He had begun with simple robbery but had added sexual assault to his crimes.

On December 1, 1980, the man robbed an ice cream parlor in Bothell, Washington. On December 9, 1980, the man had worn a fake beard, put white tape across his nose and held up a 22-year-old female clerk with a small silver gun at Eddie's Arco Station in Vancouver, Washington, at 5:00 p.m. Two weeks later, on December 13, at 6:00 p.m., wearing the same disguise, the man held up the Baskins-Robbins ice cream parlor on Villard Street in Eugene, Oregon with the same chrome pistol. December 14, the man robbed the Arctic Circle at the drive-in window in Albany, Oregon, clearing $280.

On December 21, the robber targeted Church's Fried Chicken in Lake Forest Park, Washington. That time he sexually assaulted a 25-year-old clerk in the bathroom by making her manually masturbate him. Twenty minutes later, the man robbed two teenage girls at the Baskin-Robbins in Bothell, Washington and netted $500.

Taking a two-week Christmas break, the man next robbed a delicatessen at gunpoint in Olympia, Washington on January 6, 1981. Law enforcement and the media began calling the robber the "Band-Aid Bandit" or "I-5 Bandit." Returning to the scene of an earlier robbery, the man robbed Eddie's Arco Station two days later, but managed to steal less than $100. He had made the female clerk take off her shirt and lift up her bra.

January 11, 1981 at 7:20 p.m., the man robbed the Grocery Cart Market in Eugene and netted $35. Perhaps as a result of his dismal haul, the man had gone out the next night and entered the Central Market in Sutherlin, Oregon, intent on robbery. When the female clerk laughed at his demand for cash, thinking it a joke, the man became angry and reached across the counter and grabbed her blouse, then released her, and then shot her in the shoulder. He emptied the cash register of $300 and left.

A few nights later, the bandit broke sharply from his usual robbery MO. He rang the doorbell of a suburban home in Corvallis, Oregon on January 14, about 5:40 p.m. Two girls—an eight-year-old and a ten-year-old—had been left home alone for an hour. The man at the door asked to use the phone; his car had broken down. They reluctantly let him in. He used the phone and then asked if he could watch TV with them. They declined the offer, growing more nervous with what was becoming apparent: they had let a crazy person into their home.

He ordered them into the bathroom and to remove their clothes. He fondled them and made them fellate him to ejaculation. He told them to put their clothes back on and remain in the bathroom where their horrified mother found them shortly thereafter.

The attack on the two young women in Salem was yet another escalation in the man's violent behavior; with the Hull murder four days later, Salem police realized the man was no simple robber but was a sexually-motivated killer.

Based on Lisa Garcia's description, the police created a sketch of the killer. The description of the killer's hair changed from brown to sandy-colored and his clothing from a dark hooded jacket to a tan jacket, a change that would come back to haunt the prosecution at trial. Marion County Sheriff's Office lead detectives Dave Kominek and Monty Holloway received hundreds of tips concerning the killer's identify. They collected the names of all parolees serving time for sex offenses, murder, and rape.

Once the crime hit the papers, Salem legislators complained that Marion County was a dumping ground for people released from the state hospital and state prisons. Senator L. B. Day-R, Salem, referred to a new county report showing that for every criminal offender Marion County sent to a state institution in Salem, five released criminals stayed in Salem rather than return to their former homes. Representative Peter Courtney-D, Salem, asked the parole board to stop all early releases.

The murder of Shari Hull in Salem did not slow down the robber-turned-killer. The next night, at about 7:30 p.m., he robbed a Vancouver, Washington skating rink when it was mostly empty. On January 26, he returned to Eugene where he robbed the Dari Mart at 1390 Fir Acres at 10:20 p.m. He threatened the 23-year-old female clerk with a chrome revolver while wearing a Band-Aid over his nose. He was described as wearing a brown corduroy coat with its hood pulled low over his face and blue jeans.

A few days later, on January 29, a 20-year-old clerk working alone in a Winchell's Donut Shop in Grants Pass was robbed by a man fitting I-5 Killer's description. The robber fondled both the clerk and a teenage customer before leaving with $70 from the till. About an hour later, the same man held up Richard's Market with a silver revolver in Medford. Similar robberies occurred the same night in Corvallis and Albany, Oregon.

On February 3, the Burger Express in Redding, California was robbed. The fast food place was staffed by an 18-year-old woman at the counter, with an older woman (the owner) in the back. The robber walked them both to the back of the restaurant bathroom and bound the owner with tape, then ordered the 18-year-old to take her clothes off. He fondled the owner's breasts while waiting on the girl. He then forced the girl to fellate him. He attempted anal sex, but failing that, demanded oral sex again. At that point, the owner's husband had arrived. The robber ordered him into the bathroom by gunpoint and then fled with $230. After robbing the Burger Express, the man drove to Mountain Gate, California, ten miles away.

Later that night, Mountain Gate police found residents Donna Eckart, 37, and her 14-year-old stepdaughter dead on a bed, the daughter naked, the mother in her nightgown, pulled up to reveal her breasts, their hands bound. Both were shot. There was evidence that the 14-year-old had been orally sodomized. A .38 caliber gun had been stolen.

The next night, in Yreka, California, the man carjacked a vehicle from a 21-year-old woman and kidnapped her by gunpoint. He quizzed her about her sex life. He demanded that she lay down with her head in his lap and made her unzip his jeans while he fondled her breasts. He ordered her to fellate him and ejaculated in her mouth and hair.

He continued driving until he made a U-turn and pulled off the road. He ordered his kidnap victim into the backseat and directed her to remove her pants, underwear, and shoes. He asked whether she preferred him to ejaculate inside her or in her mouth. When she said inside her, he did the opposite. He next taped her wrists together climbed into the front seat and drove back into Yreka. Before he released her, he ordered the woman to not go to the police. He dropped her off naked and threw her clothes at her where he had first picked her up. She dressed and called police and described her attacker: tape over his nose, silver gun, brown hair, beard and mustache.

Investigating the Hull murder and Garcia assault, detective Dave Kominek hypnotized Garcia to enhance her memory of her attacker. A sketch artist recorded her memory. The man was tall, maybe in his late twenties. He had a Band-Aid across his nose. He wore a hooded jacket and red and white running shoes. She added that she would never forget his face. None of the Salem parolees fit the description, so detectives surmised he didn't live in Salem.

Kominek asked police in the seven Western states for descriptions of similar crimes. Detectives in Shasta County contact Kominek with information concerning their recent crimes and compare the similarities: female victims, sodomy, .32 caliber gun shots to the head; the assailant possibly driving a gold VW Beetle. Other jurisdictions follow suit.

Meanwhile, the robberies and assaults continued up and down the I-5 corridor.

On February 4, the man robbed the Rodeway Inn in Medford. Again a clerk was raped and sodomized. On February 9, at about 8:00 p.m., the man robbed a Corvallis fabric store of $300. He then forced the 30-year-old clerk and her customer into a back room and taped their wrists, ankles, and mouths. He then fondled the clerk and masturbated against her face. A few hours later, in Albany, the man hit the Queen Avenue Laundromat, binding and sodomizing two young women there.

On February 12, robberies and sexual assaults were committed in Vancouver, Olympia, and Bellevue, Washington, by a man matching the description of the I-5 Bandit. In Vancouver he robbed a downtown dress shop, binding the elderly clerk with tape. In Olympia, he forced two teenagers into a freezer, sexually abused them, and then cleaned out the till. In Bellevue, he robbed a Dairy Queen.

In what first appeared as an unrelated event, in the morning hours of February 15, an 18-year-old Beaverton woman was found murdered, shot by a .38 caliber gun. Julie Reitz lived with her mother who found her upon returning from an evening out. There was no evidence of forced entry at the crime scene and police surmised that it was likely Julie knew her killer. Semen was collected at the scene, but the evidence suggested she was not raped. Analysis of the semen indicated the killer had Type B blood. A neighbor told police she saw a gold VW Bug driving up and down Julie's street the night she was killed.

Detectives interviewed Julie's friends. One of them recalled an older fellow Julie had dated. Randy Woodfield. He had worked at the Faucet Tavern as a bartender. He drove a gold VW Beetle. Another one of Julie's friends also mentioned Woodfield, adding that she thought he had a criminal record. Another friend mentioned Woodfield; he had been very interested in Julie and had been seen in Beaverton on Valentine's weekend.

Beaverton detectives checked out Woodfield's criminal record and saw robbery and public indecency convictions. They talked to Woodfield's former co-workers at the Faucet and learned that Woodfield was attracted to young girls and became angry when rejected. They noted Woodfield's physical description and mug shot: brown hair and eyes, handsome — and Type B blood.

Woodfield's parole officer told the detectives that Woodfield had moved to Springfield without first asking permission and gave them the name of his new parole officer. Detectives learned that Woodfield had also been a suspect in the 1980 murders of three Portland area young adults: Darcie Fix, Doug Altig, and Cherie Ayers.

On October 9, 1980, a former classmate of Woodfield's, Cherie Ayers, was raped and murdered. She had been bludgeoned and stabbed repeatedly in the neck. She had recently helped Woodfield plan a class reunion and Woodfield had often been to her home. She had grown up in Newport but had lived in Portland for the last ten years. She had graduated from the University of Oregon X-ray technician course and was working full time at the Metropolitan Clinic in Portland and worked part-time in Milwaukie at the Dwyer Hospital. Ayers lived alone in a single-family residence in SW Portland. Her home had been burglarized. Woodfield had been questioned during the investigation immediately following her death. Detectives found him evasive but the physical evidence did not support an arrest. Woodfield had declined to take a polygraph. Baffled police offered a $5,000 reward.

Six weeks later, on Thanksgiving Day, Darcey Fix, 22, and Doug Altig, 24, were found dead. Darcey's father had gone looking for her when she failed to show for Thanksgiving dinner. Both had been shot in the head, execution-style, in Fix's home at 1754 N. Portland Boulevard sometime the night before. The young couple had been neighbors growing up. They had dated in high school and now, after some time apart, were renewing their relationship. They had spoken of marriage.

Photo credit: Portland Police Department.

As a high school student, Woodfield was a popular star athlete and average student, but there were signs of trouble even then. He was first arrested while a student at Treasure Valley Community College, and then later for robbery in Portland's Duniway Park.

There were no signs of forced entry. An old .32-caliber chrome revolver was missing.

The day after the 1981 Valentine's Day killing, the I-5 Bandit had robbed a Corvallis fast food restaurant and sexually assaulted the waitress.

Law enforcement in the affected 37 jurisdictions in Oregon, Washington, and California met in Roseburg to compare notes on the I-5 Bandit; a suspect in three murders, two shoot-ings, nine rapes and at least a dozen robberies. Ballistic tests connected the California murders with the Salem murder. The surgical tape used to bind the women up and down the I-5 cor-ridor was a match. The composite drawings were similar. The suspect had herpes. He preferred oral sodomy, had attempted anal sodomy and had not attempted regular intercourse.

On February 18, at 3:00 a.m., the I-5 Band-Aid Bandit struck again, robbing a Coburg Road 7-Eleven in Eugene. The suspect displayed a small silver-plated revolver to the 43-year old female clerk, grabbed $30 from the till, and molested her. He then took the clerk to the rear of the store, bound her with tape and fled through a rear door. Photos from the surveil-lance camera were useless. He was described as white, 6' tall, in his early twenties, about 160 pounds, with dark brown eyes. He was wearing a dark knit cap, a black and green plaid jacket, and jeans.

A few nights later, on February 21, at 9:10 p.m., a man wearing adhesive tape across his nose and brandishing a chrome revolver entered the Eugene Taco Time at 1060 River Road but was foiled by an employee—an 18-year-old wom-an—who went out a back door when she saw the man enter. He ordered the other clerk, a 19-year-old female, to squat on the floor but then he panicked and fled without demanding money or harming the woman. This was the 22nd crime at-tributed to the I-5 Bandit since December 13, 1980.

On February 25, 1981, the I-5 Bandit ordered a 19-year-old Corvallis fast food restaurant waitress into the store's restroom and forced her at gunpoint to remove her top and perform oral sex on him. He then ordered her to get on the floor and where he bound her feet and hands with adhesive tape. Once he left, she managed to kick free and call police. She described her attacker as having a piece of tape across his nose, wearing a stocking cap and false beard, and brandishing a silver-colored revolver.

Investigators from the various jurisdictions met again on March 3 in Eugene. Semen collected from the crimes all reflect-ed Type B blood. Police tried staking out the places the bandit had struck previously. There was one suspicious customer, but he nervously made a purchase and left without robbing the store.

Meanwhile, Beaverton police continued to investigate the Julie Reitz murder. They decided to join a previously scheduled meeting between Woodfield and his Lane County parole officer on March 3. Woodfield's Washington County parole officer decided to attend the meeting as well.

Woodfield was a no-show.

Undeterred, the Beaverton detectives and two parole officers decided to pay Woodfield a visit in his Springfield home. After much door pounding, a sleepy Woodfield opened the door. After introductions, the detectives told Woodfield that they were investigating the Julie Reitz case. Woodfield said he didn't know her. Having already spoken with multiple witnesses who had put the two together, police knew he was lying. Perhaps Woodfield would come down to the station for questioning?

At the Springfield police station, Woodfield changed his story when shown a picture of her ("Oh, *that* Julie Reitz," one can imagine him saying.) He had gone out with her once. They were just friends now. He denied being at her house on Valentine's Day. He hadn't seen her in months. He was with friends in Portland on Valentine's Day. He denied having sex with her, and then accidentally admitted to the sex. He declined requests for hair and blood samples and the opportunity to clear himself through a polygraph test.

Woodfield consented to a search of his home. Among other things, police found a receipt for a gun purchase from a Portland G. I. Joe's, a box of athletic adhesive tape, and a gun-cleaning kit for a .38-caliber or .357 caliber gun. When questioned about the gun, Woodfield said he must have acquired the kit before he went to prison in 1975. He was visibly nervous about the adhesive tape. One roll was missing from a box of six.

The tape rang bells for the detectives. Didn't the I-5 Bandit use similar tape? Could this unassuming guy be both Julie Reitz's killer *and* the infamous Band-Aid Bandit?

Springfield police released Woodfield. They didn't have the evidence to hold him—not yet. But now they had a good suspect.

They drove back to Woodfield's rental house but didn't find him home. They stayed and watched the house. When Woodfield's landlady and roommate came home at about 5:30 p.m., detectives asked her questions about her boarder. Susan Matz had nothing but good things to say about Randall. He was gone a lot. He made a lot of long distance calls. Upon request, she handed over her phone bill.

Woodfield had indeed made a lot of long distance phone calls. He was making them from other cities and charging the calls to his home (Matz's) number. Detectives examined the dates and the places from which Woodfield was calling. While they had not committed to memory all of the I-5 Bandit's itinerary, they noted a February 3 call from Shasta, California. Comparing the bill with the I-5 Bandit's string of spree robberies, police were delighted to find they now had a roadmap connecting Woodfield to the towns where the robberies and assaults took place—including calls placed from Beaverton the night Reitz was shot.

The investigation shifted into overdrive. Police took Matz, 29, and her son, into protective custody. The phone bill was shared among law enforcement agencies who begin tracing the numbers to phone booths and comparing it to dates and locations of crime scenes. Springfield police contacted the Salem detectives working on the Hull murder who headed for Springfield to look at the evidence and maybe have a little talk with the suspect—a suspect who resembled the police sketches of their killer. Also called in were the Oregon State Police, Beaverton Police, and Eugene Police.

Kominek checked the phone bill for the night Shari Hull was murdered, January 18. Woodfield had charged a call from Independence to Salem at 9:00 p.m., and then he'd called a Newburg number from Woodburn 90 minutes later. He could have easily passed through Salem on his way from Independence to Woodburn the night of the killing.

Law enforcement was split as to whether to obtain a search

warrant right away, before their suspect could destroy evidence. Salem, Beaverton, and Eugene police wanted to move in right away. Lane County District Attorney Pat Horton wanted to wait. Woodfield was already under surveillance. There was no harm in waiting. If Woodfield was the I-5 Bandit, he had committed crimes in multiple jurisdictions. What police agency had jurisdiction?

That night, the State Police Crime Lab furiously worked to examine the semen and pubic hairs recovered from the first search of Woodfield's room for a match with the crime scenes before their suspect could slip away.

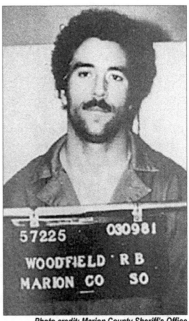

Photo credit: Marion County Sheriff's Office

The Salem DA charged Woodfield with murder, attempted murder, and sexual assault on March 9, 1981.

Marion County detective Monty Holloway got on a plane to show Lisa Garcia, now living in Washington, mug shots, to see if she recognized Woodfield's face from among the others.

The next day, District Attorneys from the various jurisdictions descended on Eugene like crows on a squirrel carcass, but Pat Horton believed Eugene had jurisdiction and argued the Eugene and the Oregon State Police should take over the investigation. This stance infuriated the other jurisdictions. The media had been playing close attention and also threatened to inadvertently tip off Woodfield of the intense interest in him, as if he didn't already realize he was the center of the investigation. *The Eugene Register Guard* ran a story that police expected a break in the case.

On March 5, 1981, Dave Kominek believed he could wait no longer. He and Ron Griesel of the Eugene Police Department knocked on Woodfield's door and questioned him about where he had been, and when. Kominek asked if Woodfield would provide them with a hair sample or take a polygraph, but Woodfield politely declined and his hostility increased with the line of questioning. Griesel then handcuffed and arrested him on a parole violation charge: leaving the state without permission (he was on parole from his robbery of the undercover policewoman in Portland).

Woodfield was interviewed again at the Springfield police headquarters—where was he on certain dates? What kind of shoes did he wear? When was the last time he was in Redding? Did he have herpes? What jobs did he have and when? How did he feel about women? He played basketball on a team? Did he miss games? Did he remember what nights? Did he remember whether he was in Salem on January 18? When was the last time he was in Corvallis? The questioning went on for hours. He admitted to driving to San Francisco to meet a girlfriend at the end of January. Driving back, he stayed at his sister's in Mt. Shasta.

Then he gave the questioning detectives the names of two attorneys he'd like them to call.

A second search of the Springfield house netted police a pubic hair and an unusual .32-caliber long bullet they could use to compare with ones recovered from the Hull murder scene. The bullet was the same type used on Shari Hull, Lisa Garcia, and the two Mountain Gate, California murders. Susan Matz told police that the ashes in the fireplace had been created after she moved out, confirming police fears that Woodfield had burned evidence.

Police also confiscated Woodfield's gold-painted 1974 VW Super Beetle that sported a smashed left fender and a dented front fender and a Green Bay Packers sticker in the rear window.

With a suspect in hand, police found more and more links putting Woodfield near the crime scenes on the day they occurred.

His former PSU teammates expressed shock that this good-looking guy who had everything going for him could be a killer.

•••••

Born to middle-class parents and the youngest of three children, Randall Woodfield's childhood did not suggest the beginnings of the dark journey of a serial killer and sexual deviant. His parents, who grew up during the Great Depression, knew the value of a job. Jack Woodfield got a job at Pacific Northwest Bell after high school and stayed there for more than 30 years. His mother Donna got two years of college under her belt before turning her attention to her family. First came daughters Susan and Nancy, and then Randall Brent, born December 26, 1950, in Salem.

The family moved to Corvallis for a short time and then Jack Woodfield was transferred to Otter Rock on the Oregon coast where the couple became pillars of the community. Randall was an average student who found a success in sports. He played football, basketball, ran track and seemed to be popular and well liked. He made All-State in football. In Newport, he was named Rotary Student of the Month and the most athletic member of his high school class.

Randall preferred younger women, perhaps because they were less likely to size him up accurately. By junior high he expressed himself in an unusual way: he had begun to expose himself. He mostly got away with it and when he was caught, the incidents were downplayed and he was not convicted or held to account. There was no real harm done, right? And no one wanted to lose the star football player.

He graduated in 1969 from Newport High School. His dream was to play professional football. Unfortunately he chose to enroll in Treasure Valley Community College in Ontario, not exactly on the route of NFL talent scouts. He played football for the college as well as basketball and track, breaking the long jump record with a jump of 22', 6.5". He racked up a 2.5 GPA. During his year there he secured a girlfriend, but the relationship didn't last. After she broke up with him, he broke into her family home and ransacked her room, stealing a stuffed animal he had given her. Arrested by Ontario police, a jury found him not guilty; the evidence was weak. Woodfield also stole some cassette tapes, but gave them back when he was caught.

Despite the new environment, Randall could not keep it in his pants and he was caught once again exposing himself.

He transferred to Mt. Hood Community College and after a year transferred to Portland State University in the spring of 1971. He attended through the winter term of 1973. He made average grades and was a long jumper and high hurdler. He became very religious and joined the Portland State University Campus Crusade for Christ and the Fellowship of Christian Athletes. He was so fervent in his newfound religion, he gave his parents qualms. In 1972 and 1973, he spent time in the Lake Tahoe area in connection with the Campus Crusade for Christ.

But having Jesus as his new best friend did not prevent Woodfield from freeing little Randy from the muggy confines of his trousers for a little air. Between 1972 and 1974 he was convicted of indecent exposure four times.

After the 1973 football season his dream came true: he was drafted by the Green Bay Packers in the 17th round and signed with them in February 1974. The dream was short-lived. He was cut from the roster and sent down to the farm team, the Manitowac Chiefs where he played from September to December 1974 and worked for Oshkosh Truck. Rumor had it there had been ten to 20 indecent exposure incidents in Wisconsin. The Packers sent him packing and Woodfield returned to Portland.

Upon returning to Oregon, Woodfield did not bother finishing college, despite having some plans to major in physical education and being close to graduation, credit-wise.

In early 1975, Portland police received reports that a man was robbing women in Duniway Park at knifepoint. In addition to taking their money, he forced the women to fellate him to ejaculation—definitely not your average robber. The police set up a sting operation. On March 3, 1975, Woodfield was arrested.

On April 29, Woodfield entered a guilty plea to a reduced charge of second degree robbery. The oral sodomy charges were dropped.

On June 10, 1975, he was sentenced to ten years in the Oregon State Penitentiary, where guards noted he had a bad attitude and resented female guards. He was released on parole in July 1979, in the Lake Oswego area, to work at Tektronix Inc., but spent most of his time as a convenience store clerk and bartender. He told people he was attending bartending school.

His MO, as far as girlfriends were concerned, was speed and quantity. He was always trolling for women, hitting on most he met. He would become infatuated on the spot. His address book had hundreds of names and he was in phone contact with many at the same time. Unlike other men his age, he got serious very quickly. In the spring of 1980, he moved in with a young woman he had met while bartending at the Cheerful Tortoise near the PSU campus, but this did not stop him from dating others. He met 17-year-old Julie Reitz and told the naïve young woman a tale of women mistreating poor Randall. What interest Julie had in him was quickly snuffed out when she discovered he had lied about his living situation and they agreed to be just friends. Woodfield's live-in girlfriend left him the fall of 1980.

Woodfield did not take rejection well. It was shortly after this breakup, on October 9, 1980, when Woodfield's former classmate Cherie Ayers was raped and murdered.

A month later, Woodfield killed Darcey Fix and Doug Altig. Darcey was killed for the crime of breaking up with Woodfield's friend. Rejection by women appeared to be a sensitive point for Randall.

A few days following the three murders, Woodfield took to the freeway and began his crime spree up and down a 500-mile length of the Interstate-5 corridor. He worked as a bartender in Lake Oswego when not on the road. In the beginning he joined up with some ex-prison associates, one of whom taught him that adhesive tape across a nose was an effective disguise.

Another ex-con friend lived in Medford. Over the Christmas holidays, Woodfield took a vacation from his robbery spree and visited him. They went bar-hopping. He connected with several women there, but while he showed persistence in wooing them, ultimately he came on too strong for the women who brushed him off.

Driving back to Portland, Woodfield stopped in Eugene where he met the woman who was to become his fiancé. She was 22 and home for Christmas. She was attending the University of New Mexico in Albuquerque. They spent hours talking and decided that fate had decreed they be together. They spent the following week together. But like all great love affairs, there were hurdles to overcome. She returned to Albuquerque and to school but promised to keep in touch. Both parties proved to be inveterate letter writers. And no one worked the phone better than Randall.

But being in love did not change Woodfield's need for cash and he returned to the interstate and robbery to support himself. The spree was briefly interrupted when he moved from Lake Grove to Springfield in January 1981, allegedly to find work as a bartender and maybe finish school. However, he may have wanted to put a little distance between himself and his Portland murders. Things were getting hot at work, too. His Portland neighbors later told police that Woodfield's boss suspected him of robbing the bar where he worked. Woodfield probably figured it was time to get out of Dodge. He found a room to rent in Springfield from a woman who had run an ad looking for a roommate to share expenses of her rental home.

Woodfield took a break from robbery and rape to meet his fiancée in San Francisco for the weekend, spending January 30 and February 1 with her, driving both ways. It was on his drive back to Oregon when he robbed the Redding Burger Express, murdered Donna Eckart and her daughter in Mountain Gate and carjacked the Yreka woman.

Once Woodfield was arrested, his Springfield neighbors were happy to talk to the press. Randall was described as athletic; he had been seen jogging in the area, throwing a football with neighborhood children, and took one boy to basketball games a few times. He owned a champagne-colored VW Beetle with a damaged front fender.

On March 9, the Salem District Attorney charged Woodfield with murder, attempted murder, and sexual assault on the two Salem women. He was transferred to the Marion County jail in Salem.

Woodfield was placed in a police lineup and Lisa Garcia identified him as her assailant, as did other victims. He was also secretly indicted March 12 by Linn County on five charges: two counts of first-degree sodomy, two of second-degree kidnapping, and a charge of being a former convict in possession of a firearm.

On March 16, 1981, Randall Brent Woodfield was indicted for the murder of Shari Hull and the attempted murder of Lisa Garcia and on two sodomy charges.

A boy found a gun in the McKenzie River and turned it in to police. It was a .38 caliber and ballistic tests matched it to the one used on Julie Reitz.

Other jurisdictions joined Marion County with indictments.

A Benton County grand jury indicted Woodfield March 31, 1981, on charges of burglary and sodomy against the two preadolescent girls in their Corvallis home and charged with sexual abuse of a 30-year-old woman in a Corvallis fabric shop on February 9, and with sodomy and second-degree kidnapping of a 18-year-old woman Feb. 25 at a Corvallis restaurant. On April 1, 1981, Woodfield was arraigned on seven charges in Benton County. He pleaded not guilty.

Linn County charged Woodfield with sodomy and kidnapping. Woodfield pleaded not guilty.

On March 31, Washington charged Woodfield with robbery and rape in three incidents after a Bellevue Dairy Queen waitress identified Woodfield as her attacker. The Washington charges alleged that Woodfield had robbed a DQ and raped an employee February 12 in Bellevue; that he robbed a health food store in Federal Way December 21, and that he robbed a

Baskin-Robbins in Bothell.

The court appointed legal counsel to Woodfield: Jim Hilborn in Benton County; Charles Burt in Marion County; and Keith Rohrbough in Linn County.

Charlie Burt was a former Oregon State Bar president and was most famous for being John Rideout's defense attorney, the first husband to be indicted for the 1978 rape of his wife. Burt had also successfully defended Jerome Brudos's wife of helping her husband murder three women. DA Burt would give Woodfield a vigorous defense, challenging every aspect of the DA's case.

Chris Van Dyke, son of Dick Van Dyke, was Marion County's new District Attorney. This would be his first murder case since assuming the office the prior year. Thirty-year-old Van Dyke was hampered by Marion County's grim finances. A soaring crime rate of 55% over the prior year and budget reductions left the DA's office with an average of 800 to 1,000 hours of monthly unpaid overtime. Oregon Attorney General Dave Frohnmayer offered to assist the DA's office.

In pre-trial motions, the defense asked the state to suppress and return evidence taken from Woodfield's Springfield house and car when he was arrested as a parole violator March 6. Burt alleged that the search warrant was illegal and that Woodfield's constitutional rights were denied when he was held by Springfield police until he was charged with the Salem slaying March 9 and holding Woodfield on a parole violation was a trumped up charge. Judge Brown ruled that Woodfield had not been denied his rights and ruled the evidence in.

Defense attorney Burt also charged that Garcia's description of her assailant varied. Burt also challenged the lineup, questioning whether the lineup should have been held on the day a picture of Woodfield ran in *The Sunday Oregonian* and was further tainted by a hypnosis session conducted by Detective Kominek. Judge Brown denied the motion, but stated that Garcia could testify on lineup procedures.

Van Dyke agreed to not mention the other I-5 crimes at the trial.

Garcia took the witness stand June 1 in the pre-trial hearing, and described the night in the Transamerica Title Insurance building on January 18. When asked if the man who assaulted her was in the courtroom by Van Dyke, Garcia angrily identified Woodfield.

The trial began Monday, June 8, 1981. Jury selection took two days. The two sides laid out their cases. On the prosecution side, Van Dyke had ballistic tests that showed that the bullets taken from the Salem shooting scene matched those found at a murder scene in Shasta County. Bullets removed from the women were from a .32 caliber gun. Police recovered a Remington Peters .32 Colt Long bullet in a gym bag at Woodfield's home. A friend of Woodfield's, Christi Sue Ree of Milwaukie, testified that she purchased a box of .32 long Colt bullets for a gun he showed her the first week of January. While having lunch together on February 14, Woodfield had told her that he had thrown the gun into the river. She also testified that Woodfield said he sometimes wore a Band-Aid across his nose as a disguise. Another witness, a friend of Woodfield's, testified that Randall had a hooded jacket similar to that described by Garcia.

Blood tests of sperm found in Garcia's mouth showed her assailant had Type A or B blood. Garcia had contracted herpes from her attacker. Woodfield admitted to police when he was arrested that he had herpes.

Pubic hair samples found at the scene were analyzed and found to be microscopically indistinguishable from Woodfield's pubic hair. Phone records showed that Woodfield called a Salem residence from a phone booth in Independence January 18, at 9:01 p.m. Woodfield entered the Transamerica Title building between 9:35 and 9:45. At 10:04, Woodfield was seen by a Marion County deputy sheriff about a mile from the shooting scene, at the intersection of Pine and Broadway streets. Because Garcia had waited five minutes before calling for help, Woodfield would have had time to cover the distance. At 10:30, Woodfield placed a call from Woodburn to Portland, looking for a place to spend the night.

Van Dyke called 29-year-old Douglas Handy to the stand where he testified that he had been with Woodfield when they both committed a robbery together in 1980. Woodfield was wearing a fake beard and a Band-Aid across his nose, and had a chrome revolver. Handy also said Woodfield sometimes wore a hooded jacket and gloves.

Defense attorney Charlie Burt did his best to cast doubt. A person couldn't run from the Transamerica building to where the policeman thought he saw the assailant in such a short amount of time. The bullets were not adequately tested and did not really match. The seminal fluid was not adequately tested to rule out Woodfield. Herpes was common and was not evidence of a connection between Woodfield and Garcia. He tried to quiz Garcia about her sex life but was shut down by the judge. Burt claimed that Garcia was not a reliable witness and the hypnosis, done by a relative amateur, destroyed Garcia's actual memory of the crime.

The defense tried to convince the jury that witnesses had really seen another man the night of the Hull murder: Lawrence Moore who had recently been arrested for shooting up the Oregon Museum Tavern.

When Woodfield took the stand, all eyes were on him. During his 30-minute testimony he described his activities the night of the Hull murder. He said he left his Springfield home between 7 and 7:30 p.m. January 18, and drove to Monmouth. He tried to call a former college football friend at 9:00 p.m. He stopped in an Independence tavern for a few beers—he didn't recall the name—and made another phone call. He then proceeded to Salem via a back road. He stopped to look at cars in a car lot on Broadway and Pine where the deputy had seen him. He explained that his own car had been damaged the prior summer. He watched the police car go by, lights flashing. He then bought beer at a convenience store, called relatives in Salem, then drove to Woodburn to spend the night. When asked, he denied killing Hull and assaulting Garcia. He did admit to being convicted of robbery in 1975 and of indecent exposure in 1972. He admitted that he had purchased a silver-plated gun, but denied having worn a hooded jacket or a Band-Aid on his nose. He threw away the gun because as a parolee, he wasn't supposed to have it.

Dr. George Suckow, clinical director of Forensic Psychiatric Service at Oregon State Hospital, testified that Woodfield suffered from anti-social personality. His symptoms included a lack of stable employment, use of rationalization to explain away his actions, inability to learn from experience, impulsivity, and a criminal history that escalated in severity.

The trial lasted 14 days. Van Dyke estimated the case cost the financially troubled Marion County a quarter of a million dollars.

After deliberating three and a half hours, the jury of four men and eight women convicted Woodfield on every count on June 26, 1981. He was sentenced that October. Judge Brown sentenced him to life in prison plus 90 years—30 years each for the attempted murder of Garcia and two counts of sodomy, the sentences to run consecutively. Judge Brown was only sorry he couldn't impose the death penalty, outlawed by Oregon as unconstitutional at the time of Woodfield's conviction. Brown recommended that the parole board require Woodfield to serve 50 years before he was eligible for parole. Garcia and Hull's mother wept tears of happiness at the verdict.

In August, 1981, Shasta County charged Woodfield with the murder of Donna Eckard and her daughter Janell Jarvis as well as burglary, robbery, and sodomy. Shasta County also charged Woodfield of rape, burglary, robbery, and oral copulation in connection with the robbery of the Redding restaurant and rape of the waitress. It qualified Woodfield for the death penalty.

In November 1981, Benton County prosecuted Woodfield for the Corvallis crimes: sodomy, attempted kidnapping, and being an ex-con in possession of a firearm. Victims described their attacker as wearing a false beard, having a piece of adhesive tape on his nose, wearing a dark stocking cap and carrying a silver handgun. Ex-con Douglas Handy testified about the robberies he committed with Woodfield, and the use of a Band-Aid as a disguise. Former roommate Susan Matz, apparently still under the spell of Woodfield, alibied him, saying he was home with her watching television. The DA gently suggested Ms. Matz was quite confused. Woodfield took the stand

and denied being in Corvallis. The jury convicted Woodfield sodomy and being an ex-convict in possession of a firearm. Thirty-five years were added to his sentence.

In June, 1982, a Linn County jury found Woodfield guilty of two counts of sodomy after an hour of deliberation in connection to the robbery of the Albany Laundromat in February 1981.

Woodfield was convicted of three murders, but was suspected of killing as many as 44 people and committing upwards of 60 sexual assaults. Some victims were able to pick out Woodfield from lineups, but others could not. With his convictions in Marion, Benton, and Linn counties most jurisdictions decided to save their money on prosecutions.

Photo credit: Oregon State Penitentiary

No longer young, Woodfield remains incarcerated in the Oregon State Penitentiary.

In 1984, Woodfield began corresponding with convicted child killer Elizabeth Diane Downs. They discussed marriage in their letters, but when Downs announced the upcoming nuptials to the press, Woodfield denied marriage plans. Woodfield was perhaps anxious to tamp down engagement rumors, since he was already engaged to another woman living in Washington.

In April, 1987, Woodfield lashed back at yet another woman and sued author Ann Rule for her 1984 book about him but the suit was tossed out of court because the statute of limitations had expired.

In May 2012, he was linked by DNA to the deaths of Darcey Fix, Doug Altig, and Julie Reitz. Woodfield would not be prosecuted for a majority of his crimes, but law enforcement stated that it would not hesitate to try Woodfield for other cases if the state ever considered paroling him.

While incarcerated, Woodfield married three times.

In 2011, Lifetime made a movie of Ann Rule's book, *The I-5 Killer*, staring John Corbett as the relentless Salem detective Dave Kominek who brought Woodfield down following Hull's murder.

Woodfield remains incarcerated in Oregon State Penitentiary as inmate #3705001.

It remains unknown if his attitude toward women has improved.

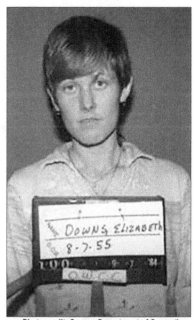

Photo credit: Oregon Department of Corrections

Diane Downs, convicted of murdering her daughter and attempted murder of two of her other children, became pen pals with Woodfield, but their romance was not to be.

7. Over the Wall

The prison break of Harry Tracy and David Merrill in 1902 remains the Oregon Penitentiary's most infamous. They murdered three guards on their "jackrabbit parole." Their trail across two states would run hot and cold and law enforcement's pursuit would be breathlessly reported each day making their names household words until the bloody, climatic finish.

Harry Tracy was born Harry Severns in the Seneca-Pittsville area of Wisconsin in 1875. He had a brother and sister and was reportedly a high-spirited boy. His father worked in the woods; large areas were clear cut and the family was forced to move often to find as-yet uncut timbered areas. Harry was close to his mother, especially after his baby sister died. He reportedly rocked his weeping mother to comfort her and when he began to cry his mother told him crying would not bring her back, he said, "I wasn't crying for my sister, because she's all right … I'm crying for you."[1] He would have been about 15 at the time.

His father Orlando abandoned the family, taking with him the community's funds raised to build a school (he was treasurer). As a teenager, Harry worked in the woods as a cook and for the railroad. Over the years, he worked a variety of odd jobs and pulled petty crimes to make ends meet.

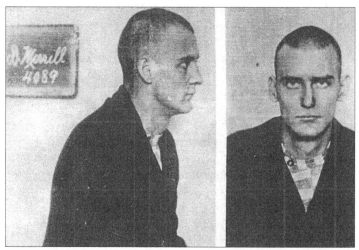

Photo credit: Oregon State Archives

Harry Tracy and David Merrill (above right) a teamed up to commit a series of burglaries in Portland. Merrill was sentenced to 13 years in the Oregon State Penitentiary.

After his death, his life of crime was embellished upon in dime novels, obscuring what really happened. By many accounts he ran with Butch Cassidy's Hole-in-the-Wall Gang, but this is unlikely. While he was familiar with Hole-in-the-Wall and the Powder Springs gangs, there is little evidence he was a member of any gangs, at least for any prolonged time.

Following a Provo burglary conviction in July 1897, Tracy was sentenced to one year in the Utah State Penitentiary in Salt Lake City. On October 8, while digging a ditch and laying pipe outside the prison, Tracy jumped a guard and grabbed his shotgun, perhaps using a "gun" he had whittled from wood and covered in tin foil. He made the guard strip and divided the clothes among himself and three other inmates. The four headed for the outlaw camp Brown's Hole, stealing horses along the way.

Tracy spent the winter there along with fellow escapee David Lant. While there, outlaws Pat Johnson and Jack Bennett came into camp with a posse hard on their heels. Earlier, on March 1, 1898, Pat Johnson had shot his revolver at a young boy named Willie Strang (or "Strong" in some accounts) intending to miss. But he was hung over and wobbly; he hit and killed the boy. The outlaws stole two horses of rancher Valentine Hoy's and took off. The death outraged local ranchers who went out to avenge the boy.

Tracy, Lant, and Johnson headed for Robbers Roost in Utah, a safer hideout. Bennett didn't feel the need, not having been involved in Strang's murder. Lady Luck was not with them and the posse cornered the three. A gunfight ensued and Tracy shot and killed Valentine Hoy. After another chase, they were cornered again. They surrendered.

Meanwhile, a posse encountered Bennett. Not detoured by claims of innocence, they strung him up. The rope was too short and Bennett strangled to death.

(There are math calculations involved in a proper hanging. Too short a drop and the person strangles. Too long a drop and the person is decapitated. Tables were created and used by the military and government executioners to provide appropriate rope lengths for a person's height and weight.)

Tracy and Lant were taken to Colorado and lodged in the Haun's Peak jail to await trial for the murder of Valentine Hoy. When Sheriff Nieman brought Tracy breakfast, Tracy clubbed him over the head, grabbed his keys, locked the sheriff in the cell and he and Lant rabbitted. Nieman took after them and recaptured them a few miles south of Steamboat Springs. The two were jailed again, this time in Aspen.

In the Aspen jail, Tracy again carved a gun out of wood, covered it in tinfoil and he and Lant bluffed their way out. They parted company and Tracy headed to Seattle where would make his living as a small-time robber. It was likely there he met Dave Merrill.

David Merrill was born in 1872 and grew up in Vancouver, Washington as David Robinson. He was frequently arrested and in trouble at a young age and he resented his stepfather. In 1887, Merrill was sentenced to three years in the Oregon State Penitentiary for robbery and he served two years before being released.

Photo credit: Oregon State Archives

As one of the "Black Mackinaw Bandits," Harry Tracy supported himself with robbery and burglary. He was arrested many times, but proved to be an excellent escape artist when it came to jails. He was sentenced to 20 years in the Oregon State Penitentiary.

The pair drifted down to Portland and committed a series of daylight robberies. They held up a trolley car, a drug store, saloons, a butcher shop, and a grocer. Their MO was to enter stores with revolvers during the day and demand money or valuables. They wore black mackinaws and became known as the "Black Mackinaw Bandits."

In February, 1899, Portland police were informed of the identities of the two bandits and that Harry Tracy and David Merrill and could be found at the home of a "Mrs. Merrill," on Market Street near First.

(Since Dave Merrill's mother lived in Vancouver, "Mrs. Merrill" was likely a landlady.)

Knowing the men to be dangerous and dead shots, police staked out the place for a day before taking action. The next day, policemen Warner, Jameson, and Banks each guarded a window and Detective Ford was at the front door. Cordano took the back door. They had been told that the inhabitants had a warning system; when there was a knock on the front door and Mrs. Merrill called, "come in," that was a signal for David Merrill to dash out the back door in case police were at the front door. The plan worked like clockwork; Ford knocked on the front door and when Merrill opened the back door, Cordano was waiting for him.

Looking into the muzzle of Cordano's revolver, Merrill coolly shut the door, locked it and dashed back into the house. Police eventually found him hiding in a bureau drawer in a back bedroom. "Give up or you die right here," said Cordano.[2] Merrill surrendered and was handcuffed.

"Don't take my son that way. He is not a criminal," reportedly cried the alleged Mrs. Merrill. She then pulled detectives aside and asked if she would get a reward if she facilitated a second arrest. In another version of the story, brother Ben Merrill was taken in by Portland Police and after intense "questioning" was persuaded to tell them where they could find Tracy—he would be at the post office that morning. Police hurried there and discovered they had just missed him. They then returned to the Merrill house for a stakeout.

Tracy appeared as expected, easily recognizable by the Black Mackinaw. Policeman Weiner did not identify himself as police and instead engaged Tracy in easy conversation. He suggested they walk to the corner. Tracy agreed, but was growing suspicious. He wasn't overly worried as he was heavily armed. When the two reached the corner of Fourth and Market streets, a Southern Pacific passenger train was passing. "See that train?" said Tracy. "Well, guess I'll take it. So long."[3]

"I guess you won't," retorted Weiner, pulling his revolver. Tracy pulled his own weapon and two bullets whistled passed Weiner's head prompting Weiner to return the favor. Tracy hopped aboard the engine of the train and placed his revolver to the side of the engineer's head and encouraged the engineer to speed things up.

A friend of Weiner's, a railroad man, watched all this, hopped aboard and pulled the emergency air brake. The engineer explained to Tracy that he no longer had control of the

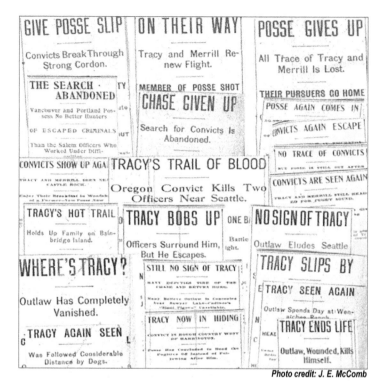

The Tracy-Merrill escape from the Oregon State Penitentiary is among Oregon's most infamous. Newspapers across the country reported daily on the hunt for the two desperadoes.

car. Tracy jumped from the train and ran up Harrison Street.

The neighborhood was roused by the gun shots and citizen Albert Way came running armed with a shotgun. Seeing a crowd was pursuing Tracy and hearing that Tracy had tried to kill a detective, Way aimed and fired. He shot true, striking Tracy in the head and knocking him to the ground. Despite the wound, Tracy was not badly injured and police hauled him to jail.

Police jailed Tracy and Merrill in separate but adjacent cells in the Kelly Butte Jail. When Ned Daugherty, the head jailer, opened Tracy's cell door to take him upstairs to the courthouse for sentencing, Tracy pulled a smuggled gun on Daugherty. Daugherty fell to his knees and said, "It will do you no good to kill me, Harry. I won't open the doors, anyway."[4] After some conversation, Daugherty ran to shelter and shouted to his deputy, "Tom, fire." The deputy did so. Tracy likewise fired as he retreated. Tracy fumbled and dropped his gun rounding a corner and was again apprehended.

At trial, Tracy received a 20-year sentence, Merrill 13. There are two different explanations as to why the sentences were different. One explanation was that years were added to Tracy's sentence when he attempted to break out. Another version was that Merrill got consideration for assisting in Tracy's arrest.

The two were sent to the Oregon State Penitentiary in Salem. Tracy was 24 years old and Merrill, 28. They would share a cell, which would later prompt critics to do some Monday morning quarterbacking. The two spent the next three years working in the prison and biding their time. Inmate 6435 described the two in his booklet, *Sensational Prison Escapes from the Oregon State Penitentiary.*

"Their conduct as prisoners was bad and only a short time after their receipt they began to cause the prison officials constant trouble, and are said to have been ironed with 'Oregon boots' and closely watched," writes the inmate.

Inmate Joseph "Bunko" Kelley, in his book, *Thirteen Years in the Oregon Penitentiary,* thought he knew what prompted the breakout.

While the Pennoyer push were holding on things were quiet and trouble did not begin until Gilbert and Brofield were appointed. Then came floggings, graft, brutality and everything else to make the penitentiary a suburb of the infernal regions. This policy, with the floggings, led up to the Tracy and Merrill outbreak.[5]

Inmate 6435 recalls Tracy's behavior leading up to the break out. He tells of Tracy carefully studying maps of Oregon and familiarizing himself with roads he later took. For several weeks, Tracy, upon entering the moulding room, would search among the boxes and under the rooms dust paper, where the weapons would later be found.

Bunko Kelley believed that Tracy and Merrill had used an escape plan devised years earlier by inmates George J. Jackson and Charles Williams. It was common practice for inmates to accuse other inmates of crimes so as to curry favor with the guards who would be rewarded for discovering plots and mis-behaviors. Kelley believed that Jackson put the idea of escape into Tracy and Merrill at the behest of a guard.

Kelley writes, "The question now is who is the man or officer who put Jackson up to the plot? That man should be tried for his life and hanged for the Tracy and Merrill tragedy came from that plot. The Legislature should find some way of investigating it."[6]

Tracy allegedly promised to pay a sum of money to a for-mer prisoner to smuggle guns into the prison. On the night before the breakout, an individual—in a feat of daring equal to the escape itself—threw a grappling hook over the wall, climbed up the rope hand over hand, and then threw the rope over the inside wall and climbed in. He entered the foundry shop and moulding room and hid two loaded .30-30 Win-chester rifles and ammunition. He left the same way he got in.

At night, only one guard would be on duty inside the yard.

The morning of the escape, Tracy, Merrill, and 163 other inmates shuffled into the foundry shop as usual at 7:00 a.m. with Tracy and Merrill near the head of the line. They were guarded by Frank Ferrell, John Stapleton, and Frank Girard. As soon as they were in, Tracy and Merrill headed for their floor in the molding room, removing their coats and hats as usual. Tracy went to the wall where his patterns were piled up, and removing the paper, found the two rifles. He motioned for Merrill to come over and showed him the weapons. They waited until all the convicts were in the building. Guard Fer-rell was rolling a cigarette near the door. Ferrell turned and saw them.

"You've had your day; now it is mine," said Tracy and

fired into Ferrell.

Ferrell fell, uttering, "Oh my God," and died moments later.[7]

Tracy is said to have walked toward Ferrell to note the effect of his shot and then ordered the prisoners into the opposite part of the moulding room. Next, he went to a window that faced the yard and began firing at the guard towers.

Kelley wrote that Merrill wasn't trying to hit a guard, just induce them to leave the wall. He and Merrill began to make their way out of the building, encountering Guard Frank Girard. Girard, unarmed as were all the shop guards, fled for his life.

Inmate Frank Ingram stepped out to stop Tracy from firing on Girard. Tracy responded by shooting Ingram in the leg above the knee, shattering it so badly it had to be amputated. He was later pardoned for his effort to stop the breakout.

(Buncko Kelley refutes this version of events and says that Ingram was trying to back up against some barrels when he fell over and Tracy thought he was reaching for the gun and he shot him. Kelley reports that Ingram lay for two hours before officers removed him.)

Tracy and Merrill continued to fire at Girard and guard John Stapleton, but the two ducked into the prison and out of sight. The convicts fired at the southwest and northwest guard posts, without hitting a guard. Guard Thurston Jones saw the pair from his tower post and started shooting. Tracy shot at Jones from a distance of 150 yards, dropping him and Jones tumbled from the wall. Next they shot at the guards on the north wall, Tiffany and Ross, Ross's hat suffering a bullet hole.

The two grabbed the ladder in the carpenter shop and headed for the northeast wall, racing across the yard. Ladder in place, Tracy led the way up, returning fire as he did so. Guard Tiffany continued to fire at them from the east tower. The two desperadoes jumped to the ground on the other side. Guards Tiffany and Ross leapt after them and followed them around a corner, coming face to face with the two escapees.

Tracy and Merrill ordered the two guards to give up their weapons and ammunition. The guards threw down their guns

Photo credit: State Library of Oregon

Seen here in 1911, the Oregon State Penitentiary is the oldest in the state, opening in 1851.

and ammo. The cons marched the two guards ahead of them, captive. Guard Oscar Bair on Post No. 4 fired on the fugitives. Tracy and Merrill returned fire, shooting Tiffany in the chest. He died with his wife's name on his lips. Ross dropped to the ground from the concussion of the gun and kept still. Tracy and Merrill left him, believing him dead.

None of the other 163 prisoners in the foundry building tried to escape. According to Bunko Kelley, the guards could have easily apprehended the prisoners when the convicts were scaling the wall, "but there was no organization. They all seemed to lose their heads."[8]

The day after the escape, officials suspected that recently released Harry Wright, who was friends with both men, had been the one who smuggled in the guns. Warden Janes said he was positive the three had concocted the plan prior to Wright's release, designating a place for hiding the weapons before-hand.

Ex-con Charles Monte would later brag that it was he who smuggled the guns in and as a result, drew a life sentence. In-mate 6435 scoffs at the idea of Monte as a nimble saboteur.

He said, "It is supposed they induced some ex-convict with whom they had been familiar, to return and bring the firearms with which they made their escape. A year or two later it developed that a former convict, Charles Monte by name, who served time with Tracy and Merrill, and was quite intimate with them, had made the boast that he was the party who had scaled the walls and arrested, tried and convicted, and on July 15, 1905, was sentenced to life imprisonment. His boasting nature and desire to show off as a 'bad man from Bit-ter Creek,' fell to zero when a life jolt was handed him, and at the time much doubt was expressed as to his ability and nerve to pull off such a stunt. To know the man, nothing but a boast-ful, whining mongrel, was to immediately become convinced that he was utterly incapable of such a deed of daring. How-ever he was kept in confinement over nine years before he was released, a sadder but not much wiser man."

Governor Oswald West would pardon Monte in 1914, given that Monte had a solid alibi for the night in question: he was robbing the Aurora post office the night before the escape. Monte hadn't wanted to bring up the alibi at trial, fearing a federal rap.

Tracy and Merrill disappeared into thick brush along Mill Creek. They were next spotted at noon by farmer John Bau-mann two miles southeast of Salem. They were still wearing their convict clothes and carrying rifles and small sacks that presumably contained ammunition.

"It is an awful affair, and I will never rest until I run the fiends down," swore state prison superintendent J.D. Lee.

Several posses were hastily organized and were soon in pursuit. The Washington State prison sent a posse. Company F and then Company D of the Oregon Militia joined the chase.

Blood hounds were called in from Walla Walla, Washington, and were on the job the next day. *The Morning Oregonian* predicted, "If the trail is not too cold by that time, it will be a question of little more than a day before the murderers are either brought back to answer for their crime or are stretched out cold in the spot where they make their last stand."[9]

After it was all over, a cynical Inmate 6435 reported the bloodhounds "did no greater service than to encourage the morale of the posses with strenuous baying."

A $500 reward for the capture of each man was announced by the prison's superintendent, and it was soon increased to $1,000 for Tracy, as reports had him as the one who had killed the guards. There was no money in the state budget for this, but prominent citizens stated that they would personally pay the reward.

The Morning Oregonian noted, "If the men are located there is little doubt that the state will be spared the expense of any trial, and the cowardly murder of three respected citizens will speedily be avenged."[10]

The next morning at about 4:00 a.m., the outlaws surprised woodchopper August King while cooking his breakfast. The men demanded breakfast and King was happy to give them some, not knowing the identity of his guests. At noon, King's employer stopped by and upon hearing about the encounter, notified the authorities. The posse and the bloodhounds ("Don" and "Hunter") did not arrive until dusk and their subsequent search was fruitless. Sheriff Durbin was consoled that he had trapped them in the nearby timber. He posted a few of his men on the roads and told the rest of the posse to return at daybreak.

But trapped they were not. At 9:30 that evening, the two secured a meal at the home of Alonzo Briggs of Gervais, who did their bidding facing the business end of a gun. Fed, they went out and "buggy-jacked" a buggy, taking the two men's guns and a coat along with the transportation. The empty buggy returned ten minutes later, but the short trip would baffle the bloodhounds.

Much to their embarrassment, the men who had lost their

buggy to the two desperados were members of one of the posses.

The fugitives returned to Salem and held up suburban resident J. W. Roberts at his south Liberty Street home. They took his hat, coat, vest, and trousers and left Roberts some of their convict clothes. They announced to Roberts who they were, that they were prepared for a fight to the finish, and that they would never be taken alive. They asked Roberts about boats they could take to Portland, but next stole two Clydesdale horses from Felix LaBranch's barn on Center and 12th Streets. The bloodhounds were brought in but lost the scent near the School for the Blind.

The Governor directed a squad of 25 state guardsmen be sent to Gervais to relieve the guards who had been on duty all night. Because of their Portland roots police theorized they could be headed north. It would also be easier to pass unnoticed and secure passage upon a vessel or train to take them out of the area. Portland police were ready with repeating rifles and ammunition.

The next morning at 4:00 a.m., August King was once again surprised by the pair. The men had spent the night not far from their pursuers. They were hungry and wanted breakfast. King reported, "They were very polite, and offered to pay any price I wanted for some food. All I had was a loaf of bread, which they received. They did not sit down, as they did yesterday morning, but held their guns all the time, and even poked the barrel of a rifle into the bunk to see if I had any one concealed there.

When they opened the door Tracy said, "Pardner, I suppose you know now who we are.' I said that I did, and advised them to leave, as the posse was after them. They told me I would receive word from them one month from today, after having inquired as to my name. They cautioned me not to raise an alarm or notify the officers, and then departed."[11]

At about 2:45 p.m., a young boy saw the pair in a Gervais wheat field and notified authorities. The fugitives saw the posse about the same time the posse saw them. Tracy and Merrill took cover. Shots were exchanged. The fugitives positioned themselves such that they could pick off their pursuers in an ambush. Sheriff Durbin recognized their strategy and ordered the posse members to fall back to a nearby orchard.

Durbin placed men on the roads surrounding the stand of timber in which the fugitives were believed to be hiding and halted all travel on the four roads in the area. Nevertheless, the men slipped through the perimeter in the middle of the night and Day Four of the manhunt found the escapees breakfasting in Monitor, five miles away.

With 250 militia men, sheriffs, constables, city marshals, brothers of the fallen, assorted citizens, and private detectives tracking them, the fugitives dropped in on Mrs. Barney Aker of Monitor. They told her they were escaped convicts and they were hungry. They locked Mrs. Aker and her friend in a room to ensure they would not notify authorities and when Mrs. Aker went to the cooling house to get milk, Tracy accompanied her, rifle on his arm. Mrs. Aker later reported that the fugitives were nervous and jumped when a mill whistle blew while they were eating. They told her they did not want to harm anyone, but those who were after them would have to look out.

There had been rumors of sightings near Barlow, but the men seen turned out to be hobos, joking that they could terrorize the country by claiming to be Tracy and Merrill.

The trail turned cold. By Saturday, five days after the escape, the militia was called off. The men had not been seen since Thursday. The state increased the reward to $3,000 or $1500 for either man.

Meanwhile, the two desperadoes continued north. A pattern emerged. Tracy and Merrill would stop at a farmhouse, demand a meal, rest, and then tie up their hosts before leaving, but not very well. They would take with them provisions and maybe horses. The hosts would free themselves, notify police who would bring bloodhounds to track the criminals. The bloodhounds would find a scent, causing hopes to soar, and then the dogs would lose the scent provoking frustration.

On Monday, the pair poked their heads up in Vancouver,

Washington and robbed bachelor Henry Tiede of clothes and provisions, after announcing who they were. They also took time to read about their exploits in *The Morning Oregonian*, clipping pictures of themselves for keepsakes. They tied up Tiede and left. Tiede worked himself free and notified authorities.

In one version of the story, Tracy read about the prison break and manhunt over a farmhouse kitchen table near Castle Rock. In its description of the two desperadoes, the paper told of their arrest in Portland and that Merrill had fingered Tracy for a lighter sentence. Tracy said nothing to Merrill and the two soon departed.

The bloodhounds were called back and the hunt heated up once again. In the excitement, a posse member shot another posse member. The need to amputate the leg was feared. It put a damper on the spirits of the trackers.

The July 2, *The Morning Oregonian* carried a short letter to the editor from prison superintendent J.D. Lee that refuted rumors that Tracy and Merrill had been repeatedly flogged, thus triggering the escape.

As an answer to all of them, allow me to say that neither Tracy nor Merrill was ever struck by a lash of any kind, whip or rod, not even by a Brockway spanker. Other stories, quite as startling, but equally unfounded, are in circulation. The man who should attempt to review and refute them would find himself confronted by a Sisyphean task. I shall not attempt it. At the proper time a calm and complete vindication of our management can be presented to the public.

On July 2, a lone Tracy stepped into the Capital City Oyster Company in South Bay near Olympia, Washington at 5:00 am demanding breakfast and brandishing his Winchester. Upon finishing a hearty breakfast of bacon and eggs, he directed Captain Clark and three others to ferry him to Seattle via their launch anchored nearby and left two others tied. They set off at 11:00 a.m. Tracy was not in any hurry to reach friends in the Seattle area before the veil of night.

After threatening to shoot guards as they chugged past the federal prison on McNeil Island on general principle (and Capt. Clark talking him out of it), Clark asked after Merrill. Where was he?

Tracy told the sailors he had discovered that Merrill was responsible for his arrest while reading a newspaper near Castle Rock. Merrill was also careless, and "left a trail like a log" according to *The Morning Oregonian* report of the conversation. A quarrel ensued and they agreed to resolve it with a dual, each pacing out ten steps before turning and firing. Tracy's stories of what happened vary. In one, Tracy looked over his shoulder and saw Merrill start to fire on the count of nine. Tracy fired and Merrill went down. In another, Tracy spun around on the count of eight and shot Merrill twice in the back.

Police were skeptical of the story, thinking Tracy was spinning a yarn to help Merrill escape. A body was discovered July 15 near Chehalis by Mary Waggoner and her son while picking blackberries. The body was partially decomposed, the face unrecognizable, but bullet wounds were found in the head, back, and left side. Three .30-30 shells were found nearby. Mrs. Waggoner and Sheriff Deggeller brought the "unrecognizable body" to the prison guaranteeing it was Merrill. She asked for the $1,500 reward.

She was rebuffed by prison superintendent Lee. Lee thought $300 was adequate recompense, since she had not "captured" the corpse. The warden went on record saying he thought Waggoner should get it.

According to Bunko Kelly, the warden did not like Lee and was "trying to run Lee out of the job. Such was the gossip." Kelley also states that Lee was Governor Geer's brother-in-law "and that is one thing that should not be allowed in any state institution."

Merrill's body was viewed by Oregon inmates. Bunko Kelley did not believe the body was Merrill's. The dead man had gray hair and Merrill did not. Also, said Kelley, "Merrill was a smooth-skinned man, and he had a burned ankle from the time he wore the Oregon boot two years before. There was a big scar on his ankle from the burn and the band of the boot wore a dent into the skin to the bone."[12]

The body brought back to the prison had no such scar.

Clark dropped Tracy off at Meadow Point, two miles north of Ballard. "I'll send you a lot of money to make up for kidnapping you and the launch, Captain Clark," said Tracy as he jumped from the boat, "for I will have a lot of dough pretty soon now. And I won't forget you other fellows. You have acted pretty decent by me. Well, so long."[13]

Tracy took with him one of the men on the boat, Frank Scott. Scott walked Tracy into Ballard. "While I was mortally afraid of Tracy," said Scott, "yet he made a fellow feel at home."[14]

Tracy spent the night in a waterfront shack in Ballard. At sunup, Tracy headed off down railroad tracks. A University of Washington employee spotted him and called the sheriff who quickly threw together a posse and took out after Tracy. The posse included Deputy Sheriff Raymond, Deputy Sheriff Jack Williams, Deputy Sheriff Nelson, Deputy Sheriff Brewer and news men Karl Anderson and Louie B. Sefrit. They caught up with Tracy near deserted cabins at Wayne Station near Bothell at about 3:30 p.m.

Rain fell in torrents as the men marched toward a cabin. Without warning Tracy popped up from behind a stump, flung his .30-30 into position and fired. A bullet grazed Anderson's face and sent him tumbling. Tracy fired twice more and Raymond reeled backwards, fatally wounded. Sefrit fired, drawing gunfire from Tracy. Sefrit, who no doubt hoped to live to write future news stories, went down as if shot and didn't move. After a few minutes, Tracy was satisfied he was dead and moved toward the shacks.

Seeing some movement behind the brush, Tracy fired, putting three bullets into Deputy Jack Williams. Officers Nelson and Brewer exchanged fire with Tracy. Tracy ran for the woods. The posse in tatters, it limped back to town with its wounded and dead. Seattle Sheriff Ed Cudihee, who had not been in town when the call came in, swore he would hunt Tracy down.

Photo courtesy of the Oregon Historical Society

Surrounded by the law, wounded, Tracy shot himself rather than be captured alive. Posse members found him the next morning, gun still in hand.

Miles down the road, Tracy stopped a farmer named Johnson in his buggy, claimed to be a deputy sheriff tracking Tracy and directed him to drive to Fremont, a Seattle suburb. Tracy stopped and dined at the home of a Mrs. R. H. Vanhorn. A boy delivered groceries to the home at about 9:00 p.m. and Mrs. Vanhorn told the startled boy that Tracy was sitting at her kitchen table. The boy ran to his horse to tell the authorities.

Sheriff Cudihee, Patrolman Breese, Neil Rawley, a game warden, and J.I. Knight, a local insurance man, armed themselves and headed for the Vanhorn place. Unaware of the danger, Tracy exited the house between two other men. Breese stood up and called out "Drop that gun, Tracy." In response, two shots rang out in quick succession. Breese went down. Rawley went down. Tracy took off running into the darkness. Cudihee fired two shots, but was unsure if either had struck home.

For the next month, there were Tracy sightings where he would rob those he encountered, but law enforcement was always a step behind. Armed men staked out roads leading in and out of Seattle.

Seattle was said to be suffering from "Tracyitis." Citizens claimed to have seen Merrill everywhere. Citizens fired shots, believing a man to be Tracy, only to discover they had fired at deputies. Someone reported a Tracy sighting back in Salem. A play was performed in Seattle about the outlaw. In light of criticism regarding the failure to capture the outlaws, Governor Geer's (Oregon) private secretary defended the government's reputation in failing to catch the outlaws. He wrote that the escapees had many advantages. They had thrown the dogs off their trail by using red pepper, taking cable cars, and wading through water. Citizens were too terrorized to report an encounter right away. Untrained men anxious for the reward and reporters got in the way.

On August 5, Tracy pinned a note to a well where horses were watered a mile north of Odessa, Washington. It read: *To Whom It May Concern: Tell Mr. Cudihee to take a tumble and let me alone, or I will fix him plenty. I will be on my way to Wyoming. If your horses was any good would swap with you. Thanks for a cool drink. Harry Tracy.*

This oversized clue as to his whereabouts seemed to support some theories that Tracy was out for the notoriety and that he was not trying to escape as much as provoke a fight to the death.

The trail was hot again.

A man from the Eddy ranch notified Sheriff Gardner that Tracy had spent the two days and nights there, 11 miles southeast of Creston, Washington not far from Spokane. Once again Tracy had announced who he was upon entering the cottage on the ranch.

Five men took to the trail: Deputy Sheriff C. A. Straub; Dr. E.C. Lanter; attorney Maurice Smith; railway section foreman Joe Morrison; and Frank Lillengren. They hastened to the Eddy ranch and spotted Tracy. Seeing the men, Tracy ran. He dashed behind a boulder and fired on the men, who returned the favor. They saw Tracy stumble and crawl into the nearby wheat field, the breeze disguising his movements.

Tracy had been shot in the leg and it was broken in two places. The posse decided to wait him out. At about 10:30 p.m. they heard a single shot. Not sure what had happened and fearing a trap, the men continued to wait until daylight before wading into the field.

There they found Tracy behind a boulder covered in blood, an artery in his leg severed. He lay dead from a self-inflicted gunshot wound to his head. His revolver was still in his hand, his .30-30 Winchester rifle by his side. He had tried to staunch the blood flow with his handkerchief, but to little effect. He still had plenty of ammo left.

They took the body to town on a wagon and relic-hunters stripped the body for souvenirs.

Three of the five members of the final posse escorted Tracy's body back to Salem and he was buried next to David Merrill in the prison cemetery. The graves have since been covered over by new buildings.

8. Ladies Night

2395 Front Street
May 7, 1981

Ladies Night always drew a big crowd at The Oregon Museum Tavern—half-price drinks for the women, live music, a friendly crowd. Thursday, May 7, 1981, was no exception. Between 200 and 250 people were there to meet friends, have fun—and maybe fall in love and live happily ever after.

The Museum, as it was generally called, was particularly popular with the ex-McNary High School crowd. A McNary grad was sure to run into an old classmate if they dropped by the tavern, especially on Ladies Night. After a young woman had disappeared in February after stepping out of the tavern for some air and had been found murdered, the crowds dropped off. But by May, business at the tavern had largely rebounded, people forgetting their fears that, maybe, a killer was in their midst.

It was close to 10:30 p.m. The dance floor was packed. Jenny and the Jeans was halfway through its second and final set—it was warming up the crowd for the featured band, Sequel—when patrons heard the sound of fire crackers. At least they thought they were firecrackers. But then people starting running or hitting the floor and screaming. And then there was the blood. Everywhere.

Police did not lack for witnesses.

The shooter had walked through the front door of the tavern. He had shoulder-length thinning blond hair and a scruffy beard; he was balding at the crown of his head. He stood spread eagle, pointed the gun at arms' length and shot into a cluster of people standing near the cigarette machine near the front door. At least three people fell, wounded. He then stepped outside, reloaded, stepped deeper into the tavern and fired in an orderly pattern fanning left to right, again holding the gun at arms' length.

Bullets rocketed into the lounge, game room, and dancing area. Witnesses reported that there were two distinct rounds of shooting. In their attempt to escape, panic ensued; patrons knocked over tables and chairs, breaking glasses and pitchers. Victims fell near the stage, near the bathrooms, 60 feet away from the shooter.

When the gunman paused to reload a second time, people saw an opportunity and four men tackled him to the ground and disarmed him. One struck him in the head with a pool cue. Another broke a beer bottle over his head. They held him until police arrived.

Within minutes police and ambulances arrived. Medics worked quickly, moving from body to body, checking for vital signs and the severity of the wounds. They left the dead to work on the living.

Ambulances came from Marion County Fire District 1, Stayton, Monmouth, and Woodburn. The last victim was taken to the hospital at 11:05, about 40 minutes after the shooting. Salem Hospital called in about 80 additional workers to assist with the wounded. A triage station was set up in the entranceway of the emergency room. It was the most complex disaster the hospital had handled. The hospital had held a drill a few weeks before, enabling them to do their best for the injured. Relatives and friends of the injured poured into the hospital to get news and give support.

Four nice kids died that night; three at the scene, one, Allen Wilcox, at the hospital.

Victim Eric Hamblin, 24, was a regular at the tavern. A 1975 graduate of Silverton Union High School, he was a member of the golf team. He had learned auto painting at Taggesell Pontiac where he was well liked, and then followed his boss when he left for C.E. Miller Auto Body Rebuilders. He opened up his own specialty car painting shop in West Salem, restoring classic cars.

Lori Jean Cunningham, 22, was a regular at the Museum on Ladies Night. Cunningham grew up in the Hillsboro area, moved to Cloverdale in her last years of high school. She had moved to Salem shortly after graduation and was attending Merritt Davis College of Business to become a legal secretary. That Thursday she was there with her best friend Darlene. That they were good friends spoke well of them; they had both dated the same man and decided they must have a lot in common. They were planning on shooting some pool. Cunningham had gone to the bar to get some quarters for the coin-operated pool table when she was shot.

John Cooper, 27, was a McNary graduate, class of 1971. He was a partner in his family's business, Precision Tool Grinding Company. He raised birds in his West Salem rental, was becoming interested in photography, and drove a black 1980 Corvette that he loved. According to one friend, Cooper had recently joined the Jehovah's Witnesses. Cooper was hanging out that Thursday, with a plan to meet his older brother later. John's mother had buried her husband just six months earlier. Allen Wilcox, 24, was a McNary grad, class of 1974. He had worked five years at Brattain International Inc. as a parts person and apprentice mechanic. At the time of the shooting he was working counter sales at Salem Auto Parts. He and his roommate had been avoiding the Museum since the disappearance of Terry Monroe from its premises, but that Thursday he felt like going out. An estimated 500 people attended the funeral.

Nineteen others were shot and injured; some would never fully recover. One victim, 36-year-old Dennis Scharf, was paralyzed.

The shooter was quickly identified as a tavern regular: Scio resident Lawrence Moore, 25. Police took him into custody and tried to control the scene.

The FBI defines a mass murderer as someone who kills four or more victims in one location in one incident. The incident may stretch over a period of minutes or hours, but the killings are all part of the same emotional experience. Mass murderers who go to a public or semi-public place and open fire are making a statement, a statement that is so important to them they are willing to sacrifice their own lives to communicate their point.

Photo credit: Oregon State Penitentiary

Lawrence Moore, aka Inmate #5794821, has been serving a life prison sentence at the Oregon State Penitentiary since December 1981 for the aggravated murder of four people.

The gun used was a Belgian-made Browning 9 mm semi-automatic handgun. The gun holds a magazine, each holding 13 cartridges. It is considered a short-range handgun. Bullets fired from a Browning are capable of doubling in size on impact. With a semi-automatic, the trigger must be pulled each time the gun is fired.

The slayings represented Salem's worst multiple homicide in its history. In addition to Salem's deep shock, the shooting made national news. It was front page news in *The Chicago Tribune* and was covered by the *New York Times. Good Morning America* and *The Today Show* covered the shooting.

Moore was charged with four counts of homicide and jailed in a 5'x10' isolation cell, seldom spoke, and refused reading materials. The question of his mental competence arose almost immediately. A psychiatric exam was scheduled.

Callahan filed notice with the court that Moore was not responsible for his conduct because of his mental condition. According to newspaper accounts at the time, Oregon law stated that a person was not responsible for criminal conduct if at the time of such conduct as a result of mental disease or defect, he lacks substantial capacity either to appreciate the criminality of his conduct or to conform his conduct to the requirements of the law.

The use of insanity as a defense is known as the M'Naghten Rule of 1843. Daniel M'Naghten tried to kill British Prime Minister Sir Robert Peel. Peel is remembered for organizing London's police force and London cops are referred to as bobbies in his honor. M'Naghten failed to kill Peel, but did manage to shoot Peel's private secretary. M'Naghten was found not guilty, as his mental condition deprived him of the ability to know the wrongfulness of his action or conform his conduct with the requirements of the law.

"Guilty but insane" has never been popular with the general public who view such a verdict as getting away with murder. It's rarely clear cut. For example, Charles Whitman, the man who shot people from the clock tower at the University of Texas in Austin in 1966 is often thought of as a classic, cold-blooded, premeditated murder. But during the autopsy, doctors found a tumor in his temporal lobe. Had that caused him to start shooting?

If the jury agreed that Moore was guilty, but insane, Moore would be turned over to the Psychiatric Security Review Board to determine if he was a danger to himself or others and should be committed to the state mental hospital. The board would also decide if and when Moore should be released.

To obtain a guilty verdict, the jury would need to find that Moore was not under the influence of an extreme emotional disturbance.

Three psychiatrists examined Moore. All three found that his mental condition made him not responsible for his actions the night of the shooting. *The Statesman Journal* reported that generally, if all the doctors agree, then the defendant usually avoids a jury trial and instead is tried by a judge.

·····

Lawrence William Moore was born in Longview, Washington, but grew up in the rural areas east of Salem and in the Santiam Valley. Moore was eight when his parents divorced in Kelso, Washington in 1964, after 12 years of marriage. His mother claimed mental and physical cruelty in the divorce proceedings and his father did not contest the divorce. His father remarried eight months later.

His mother, Mona Mae Moore was 31 when the Cowlitz County Superior Court declared her mentally incompetent and committed her to the state hospital in Steilacoom, Washington in 1964. She was diagnosed with chronic schizophrenic reaction. Her symptoms included hearing voices that gave her orders. Sometimes the voice sounded like children being hurt and other times she heard the voice of her father. She was institutionalized at least five times over the next three years. Lawrence and his brother and sister went to live their father in Mill City, Oregon; Mona took care of her youngest daughter when she was able.

Mona moved to Mill City to be closer to her children and tried to be a good mother. However, she was often disheveled and incoherent, and spent time staring at walls or walking aimlessly about the town. A psychiatrist opined that Mona needed psychotherapy and the anti-psychotic drug Mellaril to function. She moved to Salem in 1970, but was unable to live on her own. The Marion County Circuit Court committed her to the state hospital in October 1973, but released her two months later when doctors found cancer. Mona and released her into the care of a friend. She died in 1976.

Larry attended elementary school and junior high in Mill City-Gates School District. He graduated from Stayton High School, the class of 1973. He made good grades and was on the honor roll his senior year. He won a special award for welding in his senior year. He ran cross-country, although he was not vividly remembered.

Classmates reported that no one knew him well. He was shy and quiet. While fairly good looking, he did not have a girlfriend. School officials recalled that Moore was a good dresser and not a discipline problem. He attended Chemeketa Community College in 1974 and 1977, studying computer programming but did not graduate.

He worked as an ironworker at Stevens Equipment Inc. in Salem, and then later worked in a lumber mill in Lyons. He was quiet and kept to himself and was remembered as a good worker. The mill closed in June 1980 and Moore was laid off. Moore was hired in December by the mill's new owner but he quit at the end of January. He walked off in the middle of a shift, complaining of being overworked.

He moved back in with his parents and occasionally went to The Museum on Ladies Night, but patrons reported that he didn't mix with women and never danced. He didn't drink much and didn't smoke. The Museum's bartender recalled that Moore was predictable. He would order a Miller's, and then walk over to the archway, next to the cigarette machine and lean against the wall. He wouldn't speak to others. He'd stay awhile, and then turn and leave. Moore became reclusive.

Moore's attorney successfully argued that Moore couldn't get a fair trial in Salem, given the amount of publicity the shooting had garnered (days of front page coverage). The trial was moved to Eugene and delayed several months.

When the Oregon Supreme Court ruled in June 1981 that the voter-approved state law requiring a 25-year minimum sentence for murder was unconstitutional, District Attorney Chris Van Dyke revised the charges against Moore to four counts of aggravated murder. Conviction of aggravated murder carried a minimum 15-year sentence before the possibility of parole is granted. The DA also charged Moore with 20 attempted murders.

Jury selection began October 6, 1981. A jury of six men and six women were chosen after two days of questioning the 29 prospective jurors.

Lawrence Moore signed a stipulation admitting that he had fired the fatal shots. Because of this, the trial would be shorter and focus on Moore's mental state that night. Moore admitted that he entered the tavern at about 10:30, May 7, opened fire and killed four people.

In his opening statements, Moore's attorney laid out Moore's insanity defense. The customers at the Oregon Museum were conspiring to poison Moore. They were part of a larger conspiracy of millionaires and Jews to acquire all the money in the world, including Moore's.

According to Moore's attorney, Moore knew he was going to die on May 7 and he decided to kill as many of the conspirators as possible. Callahan went on to explain that after Moore turned 21, he frequented a Salem lounge, The Loft, where he was poisoned for three or four years, although he did not realize it until the spring of 1980. Moore believed that poison was in his drinking water, and in the dust on the road, spread by motorists. The night of the shooting, a policeman asked Moore why he had opened fire. Was it a robbery gone wrong? Moore told him that the bartender was putting poison in his drink.

Callahan went on to explain that Moore bought a gun and told his father about the poisonings. His father, no doubt desperate to help his son, made a deal with his son: If he went to The Loft with his son and talked to the bartender, Moore would see a psychiatrist. Moore agreed, and did see a psychiatrist, but soon determined that the doctor was also part of the conspiracy against him.

Deputy District Attorney Dale Penn, in his opening remarks argued that Moore was guilty under the law because he was not under extreme emotional disturbance and that immediately following the shootings, officers noted that Moore showed no signs of being emotionally distraught.

Further evidence that Moore wasn't crazy was testimony that Moore had shot one man in the arm and after making eye contact, pointed his weapon elsewhere. In another case, Moore pointed his gun at a man but when he recognized the man from high school, fired in a different direction. Moore was choosing his targets. Lori Cunningham's friend testified that she had seen Moore at the tavern on nights other than the shooting, and she would catch him starring at them.

Moore took the stand October 9, the fourth day of the trial. He testified that the shooting was self-defense. The people conspiring against him were millionaires, Jews, prostitutes, and bartenders. They wanted his money. Most of The Museum customers were syndicate members. Female bank tellers would act as prostitutes for the organization.

Moore described several instances where different people in different bars had put poison in his drink, and overhearing others plotting to kill him.

When at a Las Vegas hotel, a clerk kept him in the lobby for 20 or 25 minutes and by the time he got to his room, it had been dusted with toxic dust. A bottle of pop he bought at a bus stop contained a chunk of poison. A bartender at The Museum opened a bottle of beer for him and dumped poison in. He quit his job in January because people were dusting down his work area. When he was driving, people would dust down his car by pouring toxic dust from the back of a pickup truck. Someone had broken into his apartment and poisoned all the food. He moved home until he discovered his parents were also poisoning him.

His stepmother testified that after Moore confessed to his father that he was being poisoned, his behavior changed dramatically. He no longer ate meals with the family. He lost weight. He wouldn't sleep on his bed, but slept on the floor. Before he went to sleep he would open the doors or turn on the fan to air out the house. Moore talked and smiled to himself a lot, especially when he was outside, alone.

Three psychiatrists testified and agreed that Moore was suffering from paranoid schizophrenia and supported the defense's position that Moore could not be held responsible for his actions.

Aaron Alexis, the Washington Navy Yard shooter, James Holmes, the Aurora Colorado movie theatre shooter, Jared Loughner, the man who shot Congresswoman Gabby Giffords, and Seung-Hui Cho, the gunman at Virginia Tech were all believed to be suffering from paranoid schizophrenia.

The average age of onset of paranoid schizophrenia in males is 18 years and affects about one percent of the population. It accounts for about one-quarter of mental health costs. The key symptoms are delusions and hallucinations. A common delusion is that the individual believes he is being singled out for harm, such as a co-worker is poisoning their lunch or that the government wants to harm them. Delusions can result in violence if the person affected believes they must defend themselves. Auditory hallucinations are common, where the person hears voices no one else hears. The voices may command the person to do things or be critical. Symptoms of schizophrenia include anger, emotional distance, anxiety, violence, argumentativeness, loss of motivation, difficulty paying attention, neglect of personal hygiene, difficulty in speaking and organizing thoughts, suicidal thoughts, and self-importance or a condescending manner.

Moore traveled out of state to try and escape his persecutors and find a safe place, but concluded that there was no safe place. On the night of the shooting, Moore was originally motivated to go to the tavern for the music, however, it became clear to him on his way that the conspirators were still after him. He was frustrated that the police did not believe him. He paced in front of the tavern for several minutes, before deciding that something had to be done to expose the conspiracy.

Psychiatrist Dr. Maltby agreed that while Moore understood that pulling the trigger and killing people were wrong, he lacked the capacity to appreciate the criminality of his conduct or to conform his conduct to the requirements of the law. Maltby had seen Moore the prior August and had diagnosed Moore then as a paranoid schizophrenic and prescribed medication. He returned a few days later reporting that he was sleeping better and getting along better with people. He did not keep his third appointment and Dr. Maltby did not see him again until trial preparation.

Dr. George Suckow was the clinical director of the Forensic Psychiatric Service at Oregon State Hospital. Both Hogue and Suckow had initially been retained by the DA's office, but both ended up supporting the defense. Among Moore's symptoms of paranoid schizophrenia, said Suckow, were his tendency to withdraw from others, his delusional thoughts about a plot and his flat affect where he displayed little or no emotion.

Portland psychologist Peter DeCourcy testified that Moore had neither the capacity to appreciate the criminality of his acts nor conform them to the law. When DeCourcy examined Moore at the request of Deputy District Attorney Penn, he found that Moore, suffered from paranoid schizophrenia and was delusional and divorced from reality.

DeCourcy later complained that Penn had told him that Moore would not be tried if the psychology professionals agreed Moore was mentally ill. When asked about this promise by reporters, Penn declined to comment.

Moore's sister and father compared Moore's symptoms with those of his mother's and suggested Moore be hospitalized. His father testified about a time he went to his son's apartment only to be greeted by his son, deer rifle in hand.

Penn argued that Moore would not have requested legal counsel if he was truly unaware of the consequences of his actions. He also pointed out that not all schizophrenics were criminals. In cross examination, Penn got Dr. Hogue to concede that paranoid schizophrenics were often intelligent and manipulative, although Dr. Hogue countered that he strongly doubted that Moore had misled him. Penn suggested that DeCourcy had asked Moore leading questions and made suggestive comments. Penn also pounced on the fact that in his written notes DeCourcy had incorrectly noted Moore's beard but not his moustache. Prison guards did not think Moore was insane.

In his closing arguments, Deputy District Attorney Penn argued that the jury might find Moore mentally ill, but that he might still be responsible for his actions. The murders were not related to his mental problems. Moore opened fire that night because women had rejected him, argued Penn. Jurors must find that the crime was the result of the mental disease or defect and they must find that Moore did not have substantial capacity to conform his conduct to the requirements of law. Moore's actions the night of the shooting proved he was in control of his actions.

In his closing arguments, Callahan reviewed Moore's past actions and delusions and asked jurors if there could be any doubt about Moore's mental health.

The question of guilt went to the jury at 2 p.m. Thursday. It took the jury about nine and a half hours to arrive at a guilty verdict.

Lawrence Moore was convicted of four counts of aggravated murder. The aggravated murder statute was designed for particularly brutal acts. Aggravated murder carries a minimum 30-year penalty if the murder was a killing for profit, if the defendant had an earlier murder conviction, or if the victim was killed by a bombing. Aggravated murder carried a 20-year minimum sentence if the victim was a police officer, a Corrections or parole officer, a judge, juror, witness in a criminal proceeding or court employee. The 20-year minimum also applies to cases in where there is more than one victim, as in the Moore case.

Moore was sentenced December 15, 1981, to serve four, 20-year sentences concurrently—80 years—in prison without possibility of parole. The District Attorney's office agreed to drop the 20 attempted murder charges, in view of the sentencing.

Larry Moore is incarcerated at Oregon State Penitentiary in Salem, as inmate #5794821, serving a life sentence.

By the time of the sentencing, The Museum's business had bounced back and had returned to being one of the most popular rock clubs in town.

9. The Bug House

2600 Center St.
November 18, 1942

Until the vomiting began, it had been just another quiet day at the asylum. But within minutes of forking up dinner, scores of patients at the Oregon State Hospital were vomiting blood and crawling about the ward dining rooms on hands and knees, so weakened they were unable to stand. The hospital staff of six doctors and ten nurses worked frantically through the night trying to save victims.

Hospital superintendent Dr. J. C. Evans said, "They had nausea, vomiting blood and showed evidence of an acute toxic condition. Respiratory paralysis and violent cramps in the legs preceded death. Those who were not strong passed out immediately and died."[1]

The toxin struck swiftly. Within 15 minutes of eating, victims were complaining of violent cramps. Within an hour, the first death was recorded. By ten o'clock, five hours after the meal, ten had died. By midnight, the toll reached 32. By 4 a.m., the total had reached 40. The dead were all from four wards of the hospital.

"As soon as I had swallowed the first spoonfuls of my eggs my face became numb,"[2] reported a 29-year-old patient. "My teeth began to ache. Pretty soon my legs became paralyzed. They have been paralyzed most of the time since, my face is still numb." The man recounted this, his lips still blue, one day

Photo credit: State Library of Oregon

Oregon State Hospital around the turn of the century.

following a mass sickness befalling the hospital. Still, he was one of the lucky ones. By the end of the week, 47 people would be dead and over 400 sickened from the Wednesday night dinner.

R. C. Tillett, in charge of a ward where eight men lost their lives, said men began complaining immediately upon forking up the eggs. Minutes earlier, Tillett had made a patient return a portion of eggs from his plate, thinking the patient had scooped up more than his due, likely saving the patient's life. A nurse in a women's ward, Mrs. Alie Wassell, took a bite of the eggs, realized something was wrong and ordered the patients to stop eating. There were no deaths on Mrs. Wassell's ward, although she was at death's door for many hours after her bite.

The hospital's morgue, accustomed to no more than two or three bodies, was soon overflowing. The hospital's nondenominational chapel was pressed into service, the floor of the 30'x50' floor covered with bodies. When no more space was available there, bodies were placed in hallways. Salem undertakers began injecting the bodies with embalming fluid as soon as the next day. District Attorney Hayden did not want to move the bodies until a cause of death could be determined, so for hours the mental hospital looked like a scene from a 1970s horror movie.

•••••

The Oregon State Hospital opened in 1883 with the best intentions. At the time, the hospital was on the outskirts of Salem in its bucolic countryside. Citizens could take the electric trolley car out Asylum Avenue (later renamed Center Street) to gawk, picnic on the grounds, or visit the hospital cemetery. Oregon first took on responsibility for people with mental disorders in 1843, 16 years before statehood. The provisional government adopted laws and appropriated $500 "for purposes of defraying expenses of keeping lunatic or insane persons in Oregon," according to a 1945 article in the *Oregon Historical Quarterly*.

By 1861, Dr. J. C. Hawthorne opened a private institution in Portland to care for people with mental illnesses. (The street where the facility was located was called Asylum Street but was renamed Hawthorne when the neighbors complained.) The state contracted with Hawthorne initially to care for 12 patients. By 1874, the doctor housed 194 patients—and received 52 percent of the total state budget to do so. The numbers of patients grew steadily until the state opened its own institution in 1883, when 370 people were transferred from Portland to the J building in Salem.

As decades passed, the numbers of patients grew exponentially. A hospital superintendent complained in 1928 that counties were committing the elderly, alcoholics, the physi-

Showing the alleged cause of insanity as stated in commitments of patients admitted from December 1, 1894, to November 30, 1896, inclusive.	Males.	Females.	Total.
Brain softening		1	1
Business trouble	4		4
Childbirth		4	4
Christian science		1	1
Concussion of brain	1		1
Congenital		1	1
Cerebral embolism	5		5
Domestic trouble	4	6	10
Disappointment in love	1	2	3
Dissipation	2		2
Dementia		2	2
Epilepsy	22	8	30
Exposure and solitude	1		1
Exposure and sickness	3		3
Fright		1	1
Financial trouble	7		7
Grief	2	5	7
General debility		1	1
Heredity	10	15	25
Hydrocephalus	2		2
Idiocy	5	3	8
Intemperance	28	3	31
Ill health	3	4	7
Injury to head	16	1	17
Injury	4	1	5
Injury and religion	1		1
Intemperance and epilepsy	1		1
La grippe	1		1
Loss of sleep	2		2
Lead poisoning	1		1
Morphine habit	18	5	23
Masturbation	24		24
Meningitis		2	2
Menopause		6	6
Morphine and cocaine	4	1	5
Mental strain		2	2
Melancholia	2	1	3
Nervous prostration	3		3
Old age	8	2	10
Overstudy	2		2
Overwork	2	4	6
Opium habit	4	3	7
Paralysis	6	1	7
Paranoia		1	1
Pneumonia		2	2
Puerperal trouble		4	4
Partial paralysis	2		2
Religion	9	6	15
Removal of ovaries		1	1
Spinal meningitis	3		3
Spiritualism	2	2	4
Syphilis	5		5
Solitude	2		2
Scarlatina		1	1
Starvation		1	1
Suppressed eruption	1		1
Sunstroke	5		5
Typhoid fever	1	1	2
Trouble	2	1	3
Tobacco	1		1
Unknown	199	76	275
Uterine disease		11	11
Worry	3	5	8
Totals	432	200	632

Photo credit: State Library of Oregon

Oregon citizens were committed to the state hospital for a variety of conditions. *(7th Biennial Report of the Oregon State Insane Asylum.)*

cally disabled and others who didn't belong, just so they wouldn't have to care for them. Patients sometimes lived four, five or more decades behind the J Building's barred windows, enduring the treatments of the day.

In the 1930s, that meant forced sterilizations, wet-sheet restraints and insulin-induced comas. In the late 1940s and early '50s, surgical lobotomies were performed. At the same time, a crude form of electroshock therapy was used on as many as 50 patients a day. Sexual abuse of patients was reported in the 1990s, but likely had been an ongoing problem. Never properly funded, the dilapidated hospital became more so; its run-down institutional condition inspired Michael Douglas and Milos Forman to film *One Flew Over the Cuckoo's Nest* there in 1974.

At the time of the poisoning in 1942, about 3,000 people were committed to OSH.

•••••

Those patients (news accounts just as often referred to them as "inmates") who were served the toxic meal were the 487 inmates who worked in various jobs on the hospital grounds, kitchen, garden or elsewhere. These patients were served the scrambled eggs for dinner for added nourishment because they constituted the working forces of the institution, aside from the paid staff.

"Our best patients have died," observed Dr. J. C. Evans, the hospital's superintendent.[3]

Governor Sprague made a tour of the hospital the next day and said that the mass poisoning was the worst catastrophe ever to occur at an Oregon state institution.

The bodies were not yet cold before patients and police alike suspected foul play.

Marion County District Attorney Miller B. Hayden headed up the investigation personally and made rapid progress. Captain Walter Lansing of the Oregon State Police began questioning the staff and patients. He said, "It is not fair to say it definitely was homicide but the fact that the police are hanging around shows we're still investigating that possibility."[4]

Dr. Frank Menne, pathologist from the University of Oregon medical school in Portland, tested samples of the food and stomach contents of the victims. Dr. P. B. Dunbar, assistant chief of the federal Food and Drug Administration, sent chemists and inspectors to Oregon from his Washington D.C. department. San Francisco's American Medical Association sent J.D. Walsh and M. L. Belgangie to Salem to conduct their own inquiry. Also investigating was L. E. Barrick, the county coroner, but by noon the next day said an inquest was unlikely unless evidence of negligence or a criminal act was responsible. Governor Sprague announced that the state Board of Control might begin an investigation of its own.

Representatives for the Agricultural Department in Washington, D.C., announced it was halting the distribution of frozen eggs pending results of the investigation.

Hospital superintendent Evans began his own investigation. "Some patients who have furlough privileges could have slipped some poison into the food. On the other hand, since many such eggs are shipped to the army, there is the possibility that some saboteur poisoned a can." He added somewhat circumspectly, "The theory of bacterial poisoning, caused by spoilage or chemical reactions within the eggs also cannot be discounted."[5]

The egg yolks—part of a shipment received by the state from the federal government's surplus commodities corporation—were stored in the kitchen basement cold storage room and kept at a temperature of zero to ten degrees below zero. Some of the same shipment had been used by the hospital and other institutions without ill effect. In fact, some of the yolks from that shipment had been used just that day at lunch, as part of the rice pudding. The yolks had been packed in 30-pound tins.

Initially, investigators suspected ptomaine, but as death occurred so rapidly, a theory evolved that potassium cyanide had been dropped in the eggs. By mid-Thursday, chemists and bacteriologists said that theory was wrong and reverted back to the food poisoning belief. By six p.m. Thursday, Dr. Joseph Beeman, of the crime detection laboratory at University of Oregon medical school, announced that sodium fluoride was the probable cause. He found a considerable quantity of fluoride in the organs of those who died and the cooked eggs. Fluoride, used to strengthen teeth in tiny quantities is also used in roach powder poison. A fatal dose is five grains—about the size of an aspirin.

Governor Charles Sprague suspected foul play. "I lean heavily toward the theory that a criminally insane patient at the hospital was responsible for the placing of sodium fluoride, more deadly than a poison-fanged snake, in the dinner dish," he said. "As soon as I received the report that deaths at the state hospital were caused by a chemical poison I directed the state police to take charge of the investigation and to leave no stone unturned in an effort to fix responsibility for this mass murder," said Governor Sprague.[6] "The poison was evidently added in the preparation of the food."

Now that the cause was known, police had to determine whether the eggs had been contaminated intentionally or by accident. Food for the wards was prepared in a central kitchen. All persons who had access to the kitchen—about 30 employees and 50 patient-workers—were questioned by the police and the DA. Additional investigation narrowed that down to 30 people in the kitchen Wednesday night: four paid employees and 26 patient "trustees"—those patients deemed responsible enough to assume duties around the hospital.

Many of the patients questioned suffered from dementia praecox or alcoholism. "To understand our difficulty," said Captain Lansing, "it must be understood that a great deal of our discussion must be with the patients of this institution, and their information is not reliable." He told of getting several "beautiful stories" from patients only to have them refuted.[7]

Cook Mary O'Hare reported that five tins of the yolk had been brought up from the cellar Tuesday night. Contents of two of the tins were used for that Wednesday's lunch rice pudding. The other three tins had been used for the dinner. While O'Hare rolled out biscuits, A. B. McKillop mixed up the eggs. The yolks had still been frozen when she began the dinner preparation.

McKillop, on the kitchen staff since July, told police that he had been in charge of cooking the scrambled eggs. He said he put the egg batter in big bowls Wednesday night, and then went to the basement for milk powder. He was away from the eggs for about five minutes while the eggs were stirred by a mechanical mixer.

Tests found no fluoride in the uncooked batter. Dr. Menne fed bits of egg yolks taken at random from cans in the hospital to rats and the rats survived. Rats that were fed the cooked eggs were not so lucky and died within minutes, proving that the batter had been adulterated at the hospital.

By Saturday, three days after the event, investigators were leaning toward a theory that a hospital patient or employee, with homicidal intent or through error, had placed the cockroach killer in the scrambled eggs. The poison was similar in color and texture to the milk powder. "When we determine who brought the powder into the kitchen we will have got to the bottom of the case," said Captain Lansing.[8]

Large amounts of roach power were kept in the hospital basement in the kitchen's locked fruit compartment. This room was directly across the corridor from where the powdered milk was stored, in another locked room. Only regular kitchen employees had keys. McKillop reported seeing no one in the fruit cellar when he went to fetch the milk powder.

By Saturday night, Captain Lansing had his confession. Assistant Cook A. B. McKillop broke down under questioning and reversed his previous statement. He confessed that he had broken a hospital rule and gave keys to the storeroom to one of the hospital trustees to fetch the milk powder, being too busy to do so himself. He had tossed in the powder brought to him into the egg mixture without a second thought. Both McKillop and Cook Mary O'Hare had deduced what had happened shortly after the vomiting commenced in earnest.

"He broke a hospital rule in sending a patent to get the milk," said Dr. Evans, "but he was busy…" (Some might say he was "scrambling.") "… and I understand that this has happened before with other members of the staff and other patients. We cannot deny that we may have had to be niggardly in providing sufficient help."[9]

Captain Lansing contacted the press once he had his confessions to the bitter annoyance of District Attorney Hayden who did not think the information should have been given to the public. "Giving the news to the press completely wrecks my case," he complained. "Why, the press even knew about the confessions before I did."[10]

Lansing and Evans evenly explained that they felt the need to notify the press so relatives of patients could be assured that more poisonings would not be occurring.

State police were reluctant to arrest the two cooks, but did so when ordered by Hayden. Lansing thought they should be able to remain at the hospital, but Hayden insisted they be jailed. McKillop was arrested and charged with manslaughter. He entered a plea of not guilty. A $10,000 bail was set.

O'Hare was arrested and charged with being an accessory-after-the-fact. No coroner's inquest was necessary, but Hayden's inquiry gained new life and he questioned the two cooks. He discovered nothing new. He tried to interview the trustee who had mistaken cockroach powder for milk powder, but the man — "a nervous individual, although not insane" — suffered a complete breakdown and had to be placed under a doctor's care.[11]

Hayden held a one-hour press conference at 3:00 a.m., during which time he again protested that the public should not have been informed that the poisonings had been solved. Coroner Barrick and Treasurer Scott supported Lansing and Evans decision to release the information.

District Attorney Hayden lost out again when a grand jury failed to indict them. The trustee was never charged.

George Nosen, the poor sadsack trustee at the center of the cockroach powder storm had a tragic history. Born in 1915, he was brought to the hospital by his Medford parents in August 1942 for treatment of epilepsy. Nosen had been injured in 1938 when a 200-pound sack of feed fell on him. The accident resulted in chronic seizures and personality changes. His psychiatrist Dr. Peter Batten stated that Nosen was, "dramatically different after that accident."[12] Nosen was 27 at the time of the accident.

Following the poisoning, he was considered by many of his fellow patients to be a mass murderer. He became a pariah at the hospital where he spent the rest of his life. He was eventually diagnosed with paranoid schizophrenia. He became a thin, chain-smoking man, often starting fights. Dr. Dean Brooks, former superintendent of the hospital remembered Nosen as, "extremely sensitive about the poisoning incident."[13]

Three brief attempts at life outside the institution in 1971 failed and he died at the state hospital in 1983, 41 years later at the age of 68, after suffering a heart attack during a fight with another patient who was 75 years old. A witness said Nosen was struck in the head and stomach and collapsed. Dr. Batten who was the Marion County Medical Examiner as well as Nosen's psychiatrist, said Nosen had a long history of scrapes with other patients and repeated the diagnosis of paranoid schizophrenia. The death was initially ruled as resulting from natural causes, but six years later, Batten changed the cause of death to homicide. No charges were ever filed against Nosen's batterer, who had subsequently died.

The incident is cited for the beginning of reforms in mental health hospitals. In the late 1950s, journalists and government commissions exposed the dirty, overcrowded and dehumanizing conditions within many state psychiatric hospitals. President Kennedy called for a system that would emphasize community-based care. New drugs such as Thorazine, effective in controlling violent behavior, hallucinations and delusions, made the vision possible. Congress passed laws that stopped federal Medicaid payments to state-run "institutions of mental disease" in an effort to push states into building community-based mental health centers that would be eligible for federal subsidies.

An investigation covering the years 1989 through 1994 found widespread sexual abuse of patients including children and teenagers, reports of which were routinely ignored. So many emotionally disturbed children were on suicide watch at one time that the corridor was lined with their mattresses at night so staff could keep an eye on them.

In 2003, Dr. Charles Faulk, a senior psychiatrist, withheld anti-psychotic medication causing a man to become depressed, lose 40 pounds, cry, and hallucinate. When pressed by staff to medicate the man, Faulk gave him six electroshock treatments instead.

In 2008, the U.S. Department of Justice found the hospital had violated patients' Constitutional and statutory rights.

While state institutions are no longer the preferred method of treating the mentally ill, the Oregon legislature and county governments have failed to build community-based settings on the needed scale. Numerous studies estimate that about one-third of the homeless have had some kind of mental illness diagnosis. Failure to adequately treat the mentally ill in this state ensures we will see additional tragedies in the future, for both the individual personally suffering from an illness and a society that attempts to cope with the consequences of indifference.

10. Obsession

November 25, 1975
Public Service Building

The top law enforcement officer of the state lay bleeding on the ground in front of Salem's Public Service Building just steps from the Capitol Building, two bullets lodged in his weakening body. A man stood over him, the gun now tossed onto the grass. State workers on their way into work overheard the injured man—in shock and bleeding badly—ask, "Wimpy, why did you do this?"[1]

The murder of Holly Holcomb was never a whodunit; it was always a question of why, and how a perceived miscarriage of justice nearly 20 years earlier festered and grew into a cancer that found resolution with a death.

What could have happened to provoke a man with a keen sense of right and wrong to kill another man with a similar life philosophy?

•••••

Holly Vernon Holcomb Jr. seemed destined for a career in law enforcement. Born January 7, 1917, in Quitmon, Mississippi, Holcomb moved to Vernonia, Oregon, with his family when he was six years old. He grew up there and attended Vernonia schools. He attended Oregon State University from 1935 to 1939 where he played football and pledged a fraternity. He took a job with law enforcement when he was two terms shy of graduation. He married Bonnie Jean Strahan in 1938, who, coincidentally, had also been born in Mississippi and had moved to Oregon at a young age. Holcomb eventually logged 37 years among the ranks of the Oregon State Police.

When Holcomb joined, the Oregon State Police was a relatively new agency; it was established in 1931 with 95 officers. Most of the officers were transferred from various other law enforcement agencies.

Photo credit: Oregon State Police

Holly Holcomb was Oregon's third state police superintendent.

The majority came from the old State Traffic Department, with the rest coming from state agencies responsible for fish and game laws, forestry, prohibition, criminal, and arson laws.

When Holcomb joined in 1939, the state police had only had two previous superintendents: Charles Pray (1931-1946), a former state parole officer and a former Department of Justice agent, and Harold G. Maison (1946-1966).

Holcomb's state police career began in Medford and Klamath Falls. In 1941, he was transferred to West Slope, near Portland. In 1942, he moved to St. Helens, where he remained until he joined the Air Force in February 1943. Holcomb was a pilot, and he spent 13 months flying C46 cargo planes with the

6th Combat Cargo Squadron in the South Pacific. He earned the Philippine Liberation Ribbon, Air Medal, Asiatic Pacific Theatre Ribbon, American Theater Ribbon, and World War II Victory Medal.

Once back in America, he returned to the state police in 1946 and shot up through the ranks. Holcomb was promoted to sergeant and put in charge of the St. Helens office. In 1949, he transferred to the larger Roseburg office. In 1955, he was promoted to lieutenant and assigned to the arson squad, then to captain in charge of the Milwaukie office. In 1962, he was appointed deputy superintendent. In 1966, Governor Mark Hatfield promoted him to the top spot, the Superintendent of the Oregon State Police, when Harold Maison retired.

By all accounts—except one—Holcomb was well-liked and respected.

·····

In many ways, Robert Harlan "Wimpy" Wampler was a lot like Holly Holcomb—born a year earlier, Wampler also joined the military and then joined the state police. Wampler was always a law-and-order sort of guy. Born in 1916 in Portland, Oregon, Wampler attended Portland schools and spent five years in the Marine Corps. He joined the state police in 1940 when he was 24 and was promoted to investigative sergeant in 1951. Unlike Holcomb, Wampler's career did not enjoy a rapid, upward trajectory. He resigned in 1953 to work for the National Automobile Theft Bureau but rejoined the department in 1956. When he returned, it was not as a sergeant, but as a patrolman with the rank of private first class, which he accepted, albeit unhappily.

Holding a rigid view of right and wrong laden with a heavy dose of obsessive tendencies created problems for Wampler, problems that would later prove to be his downfall—and the downfall of Holcomb. The paths of the popular and gregarious Holcomb and the slightly odd, never-quite-fitting-in Wampler would cross in 1958, and would have life-altering consequences for both of them.

1958 Misconduct Charge

In 1958, Rep. Richard "Dick" Groener (D-Milwaukie) had a beef with the police. The Milwaukie legislator had six driving convictions since 1936 and 13 traffic accidents since 1940. Groener's most recent violations had been in March and September 1958 for speeding. Groener charged that Oregon State Police Superintendent Harold G. Maison pressured patrolmen into making arrests under a quota system with the inference the arrests were unwarranted. Groener stated that officers who had complained to Maison had been penalized for their efforts and that the Oregon motoring public was being unjustly cited (especially him).

Groener knew state trooper Robert Wampler and might have developed his theory with a little help from him, as a ticket quota did not fit within Wampler's sense of fair play. Groener took Wampler with him on a visit to Governor Holmes to discuss the quota system. Groener thought this meeting likely resulted in Wampler's later troubles.

A couple of months later, in June, state police superintendent Maison, Lt. Holly Holcomb, and Capt. Vayne Gurdane called Wampler into the office in Milwaukie and accused him of insubordination. Wampler was warned that talking to others was prejudicial to good order and if he had grievances, he should bring them to his supervisors.

Wampler described this meeting, saying he had been grilled by Holcomb and Gurdane as possibly having cooperated with Groener on his charges. Wampler told his superiors earlier that he didn't have anything to do with Groener's charges and had tried to talk Groener out of making them, although he didn't disagree with them.

On October 1, 1958, Maison told Pvt. Robert Wampler that Holly Holcomb had charged Wampler with insubordination and conduct unbecoming the department. The charges stated that Wampler had asked another officer to sign a statement criticizing state police policies and that in August he complained about department operations to the wife of an officer.

Holcomb told Wampler that he would face a police disciplinary board for a hearing on the charges.

Groener called foul, charging that a disciplinary board staffed with hand-picked Maison officers would result in Wampler being railroaded.

There had only been five state police disciplinary trials in ten years.

The disciplinary board consisted of state police assistant superintendent Lee Bown and two state police captains, Capt. John Eric Tucker of Milwaukie and head of the Arson Division, and Capt. Paul Morgan, the Medford District Commander.

The board had the option of acquitting Wampler, dismissing him, suspending him or reducing his rank. The law required a ten-day notice of the proceedings to the accused.

Rep. Groener asked that the state police be placed under civil service—that the hearing under the three policemen would be a mockery. He further charged that Maison was intolerant of criticism and was forcing officers to issue a minimum number of citations on each shift. Maison was out to get Wampler for accompanying Groener to a meeting with Governor Holmes, charged Groener.

Publicly, Governor Holmes stated that Superintendent Maison had his full support. At a Clackamas County Labor Council meeting held at Thora B. Gardner Junior High School, Governor Holmes and Rep. Groener exchanged heated words on the topic during the coffee segment of the evening. While all agreed profanity was employed, accounts varied as to whether it was Groener or Holmes doing the swearing. Reportedly, Groener reminded the governor that in 1957 Holmes planned to fire Maison, which Governor Holmes denied saying.

While an internal hearing of an employee of a state agency might not seem newsworthy today, the hearing was front page news in both the Salem and Portland papers.

Wampler asked that the charges be dismissed and that only perjured testimony could support them. It was usual practice for accused state policemen to be represented by a department officer, but Wampler questioned the witnesses himself, leaving only the summation to his representative.

Despite Groener's concerns, the disciplinary hearing continued as scheduled and was held in the Public Service Building in Salem, which housed the headquarters of the Oregon State Police. The hearing would take most of two days. Superintendent Maison testified that Wampler had implied that he had the support of the department and was critical of all commissioned officers in the department.

Photo credit: State Library of Oregon

Fixated on what he viewed as the corruption within the Oregon State Police, Wampler ran for governor in 1962 and again in 1970. (1962 Oregon Voters Pamphlet photo.)

Capt. Gurdane testified that Wampler had come into his office in a highly nervous state and told him of the things he didn't like about the department. He didn't like the uniforms, particularly the Sam Browne belts. He also complained about unsubstantiated arrests, appointments made by the superintendent, as well as the superintendent's operation of the department.

Wampler reportedly clashed with board member Bown when Wampler attempted to show that other officers criticized the department, too. Wampler made little headway on this, but one of his witnesses, Pvt. Herb Frasier, Lake Grove, testified that Officer Wallace Ummel had said that one sergeant was stupid and that another did not do any work.

Officer Wallace Ummel testified that Wampler had said that Maison was a "dictator" and unfit for his office at the West Slope state police office on June 23, 1958. Wampler had statements from a number of state police officers outlining grievances and asked Ummel if he would make a similar statement. Ummel told him if he had any grievances he would take them to his superior officer and that he had nothing but admiration for Superintendent Maison and the department.

Holly Holcomb, Wampler's boss, testified that Wampler had come to him with complaints and said he could bring 30 officers to Salem to substantiate them. Holcomb had urged Wampler to air his complaints with Superintendent Maison in Salem and volunteered to even accompany him, but Wampler declined. Holcomb then ordered him to do so. When Wampler heard that charges were being filed against him, he declined to discuss his grievance anymore.

Recalled the next day for the defense, Officer Ummel testified that once he agreed to appear at the hearing for the defense, he received several unsettling anonymous phone calls at home, strongly recommending he not do so.

Wampler cross-examined all the state witnesses except Maison. Wampler had a list of 16 defense witnesses, mostly fellow officers. Wampler did not testify in his own defense because he didn't believe there was any proof of the allegations against him.

Shortly after the police board adjourned, they made their decision which was conveyed to Wampler in his Milwaukie home. The board found that Wampler had spoken critically of the superintendent and solicited other officers to join with him in his efforts to bring about changes in the management of the department and its policies, resulting in unrest and dissension among the membership.

The board fired Wampler.

Wampler appealed the firing to the Clackamas County Circuit Court claiming the hearing should have been in his home county of Clackamas. The circuit court and then the state Supreme Court upheld Wampler's firing in ruling that the police board properly held its hearing in Marion County.

The trial was over, but the humiliation would eat away at Wampler, every day.

That same day Wampler was fired, State Representative Richard Groener was found guilty of speeding and fined $25. "Certain officers in Marion County like to arrest me,"[2] complained Groener. When asked whether he had it in for Groener, the citing patrolman needed help in recalling the politician. Groener told the press he planned to appeal.

Following his termination, Wampler got a job as a Clackamas County deputy sheriff. He was a president of the Clackamas County Peace Officers Union, a member of the Lower Columbia River Peace Officers Association, the Milwaukie Elks, American Legion Post 180, the Tri-City Chamber of Commerce, and the Oregon City Hilltop Boosters.

In 1962, Robert Wampler, then 46, threw his hat in the ring for governor, running as an independent candidate. In the *Oregon Voters' Pamphlet*, Wampler stated, "I would insist upon the immediate resignation of the present superintendent of state police and demand a policy of sound enforcement of criminal law." In the three-way race, Wampler finished a distant third.

(Incumbent Mark Hatfield won 197,556 votes; Robert Thornton won 151,494; Robert Wampler won 14,293 votes.)

Wampler repeated his run for governor in 1970, this time as a Republican. Again, he finished in third place.

(Incumbent Mark Hatfield won 180,413 votes; Andrew Gigler had 24,741; Wampler had 22,246.)

Wampler resigned from his job as a Clackamas County deputy to job to run for the top job, that of Clackamas County Sheriff. He ran three times—in 1964, 1968, and 1972—but failed to unseat Sheriff Joe Shobe.

Wampler worked periodically for Clackamas County as a temporary deputy, filling in for vacationing deputies. His main source of income was from his dry cleaners, Wampler's Quality Dry Cleaners and Laundry in Oregon City.

Friends and neighbors were well aware that Wampler had been fired by the state police, with Wampler often referencing what he believed to be a travesty of justice.

Wampler dropped in on his old friend Dick Groener in 1974. Groener recalled that Wampler was still very bitter about his discharge from the Oregon State Police. Groener told him to forget about being fired and to let it go, but Wampler had kept saying he had to exonerate himself. He had even asked Groener to go see the governor and try to get Holcomb fired.

He had seemed obsessed.

Murder

Early on the morning of November 25, 1975, Robert Wampler, 59, drove to Salem. He didn't tell his wife Ella Mae of his plans, whom he left sleeping when he left the house. When she awoke to find him gone, she assumed he had gone to the dry cleaners.

Wampler parked outside the Public Service Building, across the street from the State Capitol Building, the very site of his 1958 humiliation.

Then he waited. And brooded about the past.

It was about 7:50 a.m. when Wampler saw Holly Holcomb, 58. Holcomb was walking toward the Public Service Building, where the state police still had their offices. He was accompanied by his deputy superintendent Major Bryon Hazelton.

Wampler, described by the press as a tall man with grey, thinning hair, approached the pair and asked to speak to Holcomb, who agreed. Holcomb was smiling and made a little shrug, which Hazelton interpreted to mean everything was okay, so he proceeded into the building alone. A few minutes later, multiple witnesses heard two shots fired.

Hazelton heard the two shots and raced back outside. The .38 caliber pistol had been tossed on the grass. Wampler made no attempt to flee. State police rushed from the building and surrounded the shooter. Hazelton took Wampler into custody while others called for an ambulance.

Holcomb, 58, was rushed to Salem Memorial Hospital with two bullet wounds but could not be saved. He was pro-

Photo credit: J. E. McComb

Oregon's Public Service Building as it appears today. The pavers used to be diagonal parking. The shooting occurred in the area near the low hedge.

nounced dead at 9:50 a.m.

The community was jolted by the shooting. That a prominent member of the community—the top state trooper, no less—could be gunned down in the middle of the city, outside state police headquarters and steps from the state capitol where laws were made was incomprehensible.

Wampler appeared before Judge Norblad who ordered that Wampler be held without bail; he scheduled a preliminary hearing for Friday at 11:00 a.m.

No time was wasted in getting Wampler in front of psychiatrists and the first examination took place the evening of the murder. Judge Norblad delayed the entering of a plea by Wampler until December 15—enough time for psychiatrists to do their work.

Governor Straub expressed shock and sadness at the killing and ordered the state's flags to be flown at half-staff. Former Governor Tom McCall said that with the death of Holcomb, Oregonians had lost a leader of sound judgement.

Those who knew Bob Wampler were also stunned. Sylvia Jackson, a Wampler employee at the dry cleaners had known Wamper for five years and reported he had always been kind and generous—the best boss she had ever worked for.

The funeral was scheduled for that Friday, November 28, at First Baptist Church. Local news accounts estimated the crowd at Holcomb's half-hour service to be in the neighborhood of 1,200. He was buried at Restlawn Memory Gardens as Air Force jets flew overhead in memory of his WWII service.

Trial

Psychiatrists for both the defense and prosecution found that Wampler understood the charges against him and was able to assist in his own defense.

On December 15, 1975, to the charge of murder, Wampler pleaded innocent by reason of mental disease or defect.

The attorneys for the defense were Walter Aho and Robert Stoll of Milwaukie. Gary Gortmaker, Marion County District Attorney, acted on behalf of the state.

The trial was to have begun in January but was postponed until March 1 due to a variety of pre-trial issues of discovery and evidence.

On the first day of the trial, the attorneys for the defense moved for a mistrial, claiming the press and police had created a circus atmosphere outside the courtroom. Jurors had passed within view of television lights and police checking courtroom observers with metal detectors, but Judge Barber denied the motion. Barber also denied the request for a change in venue. The defense asked for a mistrial based on news reporting, and was also denied that motion.

Jury selection took some time, as the defense questioned prospective jurors at length and instructed jurors about the law regarding pleas of not guilty for reason of mental disease or defect. Attorney Robert Stoll told prospective jurors that Wampler was innocent by reason of lack of responsibility; he didn't have the conscious intent to shoot Holcomb; he was suffering acute emotional disturbances or mental defect or disease.

Stoll also began describing Wampler, a career policeman who had made many arrests and who respected law and order; his life's goal was to be a police officer. Denied this, Wampler suffered catastrophic emotional effects. There was no question that Wampler had killed Holcomb; the issue was about Wampler's state of mind at the time of the shooting.

Prosecutor Gortmaker and defense attorney Stoll clashed repeatedly throughout the trial and accused each other of misconduct. To the jury, Gortmaker suggested that no one was perfectly normal; it would be up to the jury to decide what degree of abnormality frees a person from responsibility from his actions.

The second day, the trial began in earnest, with witnesses called to the stand. Byron Hazelton recounted what had happened the morning of the murder. When Hazelton ran out of the building and encountered Wampler on the building's porch, he grabbed Wampler by the coat lapels and asked him why he had shot Holcomb. Wampler did not respond. Hazelton then turned the suspect over to other police while he ran to Holcomb 20 yards away. Hazelton testified that Holcomb did not carry a firearm when dressed in civilian clothes.

Other witnesses who saw the two men together got the impression the two men were arguing. One witness thought she saw anger on both men's faces.

A state worker passing by the two men heard Wampler say, "Why didn't you believe me, you son of a bitch?" He saw Wampler throw the gun to the ground.

Holcomb then told the witness, "Call an ambulance. The son of a bitch shot me."[3]

When Lt. Hollis Watson took Wampler into custody, Watson testified that Wampler seemed at ease and in full possession of his faculties. Watson read Wampler his rights. The only statement Wampler volunteered was that Mr. Holcomb had framed him 17 years ago and got him fired from the state police.

Gortmaker said the .38 caliber revolver had been shot twice, and had misfired twice. Gortmaker stated that the defense had the burden of proof to show that Wampler had acted under mental disease or defect.

A lifelong friend of Wampler's, Virginia Ward, testified that Wampler believed his dismissal from the state police was unjust and he became increasingly despondent about it, raising the issue in conversations, saying he needed to clear his name. Mrs. Ward thought Wampler needed psychiatric help, but didn't think Wampler would appreciate the suggestion so didn't voice it. She noted that his motivation to run for governor was to clean up the state police department and put some honest people in the government.

Wampler and his first wife divorced in 1966 in great part because of his despondency over his firing. She described Wampler as extremely conscious of honesty and truthfulness. When he and other policemen became concerned about pressure to write more tickets, he became their spokesman. After the hearing, she had discussed her husband with another officer—about how he might need psychological help, but he never got it.

Former state policeman Paul McAllister, then working as a Deputy District Attorney for Umatilla County, testified that he was pressured to resign following Wampler's dismissal for insubordination by Holly Holcomb due to his association with Wampler. McAllister was at Wampler's home when the message that Wampler had been fired was delivered and was seen. He testified that Wampler had been fired for discussing internal grievances with others of equal or lesser rank, a violation of department regulations. Because McAllister was seen at Wampler's house, Holcomb called him into his office several times in the following two months to question him about his association with Wampler and considered resigning. He testified that he began to receive phone calls at home after hours from Sgt. John D'Angelo and Holcomb asking him when he was going to quit. When he didn't quit, McAllister testified that he received a letter saying his oral resignation had been accepted.

Frank Beers, a retired state police lieutenant testified about internal problems within the department at the time of Wampler's firing. Beers stated that the police force was run like the military; Maison had no system of promotion. If a trooper was charged with a department violation, they usually resigned rather than face the hearing board because the hearing was rigged with the superintendent's underlings, adding that Wampler was an excellent policeman.

Groener testified that he had met Wampler when Wampler was a patrolman in the Oregon City area. Groener complained that the state police emphasized the number of arrests, rather than the quality of the arrests, as demonstrated by arrests of each trooper being posted on a bulletin board in a competition. Police Superintendent Maison denied the charge, but Groener claimed that Governor Holmes had directed Groener to investigate. Wampler accompanied Groener to a meeting with Governor Holmes. Wampler complained to the governor that he would be fired if he was involved in such an investigation, but that Holmes assured him he would not be fired.

After Wampler was fired, he didn't speak to Groener for ten or 12 years, but when Governor Straub was voted in, Wampler went to Groener's house and asked Groener to join him in asking the governor to ask Holcomb for his resignation. Groener suggested Wampler forget about it, but Wampler insisted that he had to clear his name.

A West Linn attorney testified that he thought Wampler had a mental disorder because of his obsession over his firing and that might excuse Holcomb's murder.

A former state trooper took the stand and testified that the rule prohibiting policemen from complaining about procedures to those of equal or lesser rank was largely ignored and that Holcomb had violated the rule as well.

Ella Mae Wampler testified that her husband had gone to Salem to deliver some liniment to friends, liniment that was found in the car after the shooting. The night before the shooting she had not noticed any unusual behavior on the part of her husband. The firing was not discussed. The morning of the shooting her husband had awakened at 5:30 a.m. and said he couldn't go back to sleep. Wampler had been more irritable than usual, and she reported that he regularly wrote down license plate numbers of cars parked in front of their house and descriptions of planes if they were circling low near the house. Portland psychologist Andrew Berger assessed Wampler and found him to be morbidly obsessive and that he exhibited schizophrenic disorganizations and paranoia and difficulty controlling his impulses.

At one point, Wampler told Berger that a room in the courthouse might be bugged and that the state police and the Wampler family had appeared on the scaffolding of a building across from the jail and were going to assassinate him with the help of the state police. The tests administered to Wampler indicated that Wampler was trying to suppress any thought that he might be mentally ill and would not admit to any problem. Berger stated the firing caused Wampler to blame all the bad things that had ever happened to him on this one event. Wampler had a morbid preoccupation with his firing and was constructing conspiracies against him.

Portland psychiatrist Dr. Henry Dixon testified that Wampler was a paranoid schizophrenic and believed he was persecuted. Dixon thought Wampler should be hospitalized. Due to his psychological impairment, Wampler had saw himself as an always-correct and law-abiding person; he had no insight that he had a mental disorder.

Wampler's attorneys did not want Wampler to testify in his own defense. However, DA Gortmaker got a videotape of a psychiatric examination entered in as evidence and it was played for the jury. In it, Wampler described how his firing from the state police was a gross injustice and he wanted to clear his name. He hadn't planned to drive to Salem, but upon leaving his house he saw the liniment he had promised a friend in Salem and decided to take it to him. He arrived in Salem at about 7:30 a.m., too early to drop off the liniment, so he thought he would see Holcomb in an attempt to clear his name.

Wampler told psychiatrists that the last thing he recalled was Holcomb denying that Wampler had been framed and being called a lying son of a bitch. His next memory was when he heard someone ask "Wimpy, why did you do it?" He turned and saw Holcomb on the ground.[4]

Two prosecution witnesses testified that Wampler was not suffering from a mental disease. Dr. James Hogue, testified that Wampler had dropped his head and seemed sad when told three hours after the shooting that Holcomb had died. Dr. Peter Treleaven, clinical director of the Oregon State Hospital testified that Wampler saw himself as an honest, upright, correct person who was unjustly fired.

The prosecution and defense gave their summations. DA Gortmaker told the jury that Wampler was not mentally ill and did not suffer an extreme emotional disturbance when he shot Holcomb, and therefore could have controlled his actions. The defense argued that Wampler suffered from paranoid schizophrenia and was not therefore responsible for the shooting.

Judge Barber instructed the jury telling them that the state must prove beyond a reasonable doubt that the defendant was not suffering from an extreme emotional disturbance. To be innocent by reason of mental disease or defect, the defendant must prove that he lacked substantial capacity to appreciate the criminality of his conduct or to conform his conduct to the requirements of the law. Barber told the jury they could consider the lesser offenses of manslaughter in the first or second degree. The jury retreated to deliberate.

After four hours of deliberation, the jury returned with a guilty verdict, unanimously agreeing that Wampler intentionally and without mental defect shot Holcomb to death. In response to the verdict, *The Oregonian* reported that, "Wampler rocked slightly on his feet, then looked down and squeezed his eyes closed. When he raised his head, he showed no emotion and told his attorneys he preferred to be sentenced immediately."[5]

Judge Barber sentenced Wampler to spend the rest of his

Photo credit: J. E. McComb

The Oregon State Police Fallen Trooper Memorial was created in 2016 to honor all the state troopers who died on the job. It is located just feet from where Holly Holcomb was shot outside the Public Service Building that had housed the state police administration.

life in prison, a mandatory sentence.

Postscript

Robert Wampler served eight years in the Oregon State Penitentiary and was paroled when he was 68 years old. The Holcomb family objected to the early release, but Wampler wasn't viewed as a risky parolee. He spent his remaining days quietly, tending the dry cleaning business and dying at age 81. He is buried in Willamette National Cemetery.

The Holly V. Holcomb Award was established in 1988. The award is given to officers who distinguish themselves by reacting to a situation in a heroic or positive and professional manner to reduce the risk of loss of life or injury to another person during the course of their duties.

In 1980, a Marion County court convicted District Attorney Gary Gortmaker of eight criminal counts of first-degree theft and misappropriation of handguns seized in criminal cases. He was charged with pocketing investigation expense funds. Gortmaker was sentenced to four years in prison, fined $500 and ordered to pay $15,000 restitution. He served five months. He was suspended from the Oregon State Bar. Gortmaker had not sought a fifth term. Chris Van Dyke was elected to replace him. Gortmaker attempted to have his law license reinstated in 1989 but was denied.

Dick Groener served in both chambers of Oregon's legislature beginning in 1955 and ending in 1982. In 1981, he was found to be driving a lobbyist's 1978 Cadillac. Groener explained there had been an oversight in transferring the title and that Groener had really paid for it. Soon after, Groener introduced legislation to create a news media ethics commission to hear complaints about news stories. It did not pass.

In 1982, Dick Groener was found to have violated Oregon ethics laws, having used his office to obtain financial gain for himself. He had used his position to pressure the Workers Compensation Division to refer injured workers to a firm in which Groener was employed. Groener died in 1996 from complications due to Alzheimer's.

11. Despair

It was not yet noon on an early spring day when Officer Sam Burkhart first called out to Mrs. Lucy Jellison. He had already gone through the house and found no one. Seeing the tent pitched behind the house, he proceeded to investigate. He called her name again and then, hearing nothing in response, drew back the tent flap.

Huddled on two beds made from boxes filled with straw were the bodies of Mrs. Jellison and her four children: Epsey, aged 15; Harland, 13; Maud, 11; and baby Raymond, aged 3.

An empty bottle of cyanide lay near the beds.

•••••

It would be fair to say that Lucy A. Ford was unlucky in love. Born in Ohio in 1870, she married Elmer Storey. They had a son, Russell, but the marriage didn't last and they divorced. She moved to Kansas, married a man named Charles Jellison and had three children: daughters Epsey and Maud and son Harland. That marriage too fell apart and they divorced. Lucy moved to Oregon and, with hope (or economic need) triumphing over experience, wed again, to John Swanson. That too, ended July 1911 when John brought suit of divorce, but not before Lucy had another son, Raymond.

Her life had been a hard one. Not much is known of her early life, before Salem where she spent her last four years. Maud had been born in a boxcar when Lucy was picking hops.

Her youngest, Raymond, was born in house bare of comforts at the end of 12th Street. Lucy and her children had been living off scraps of bread. Lucy was often too ill to work, the disease not identified in newspapers. Working so much did not leave her much time to raise her children. She told her friend, "O, you don't know how much it grieves me to see them running wild like this."[1]

A friend later described Lucy as well-educated. She was a few weeks shy of graduating from the Monmouth Normal School and might have found work as a teacher. She had recently taken a civil service exam and was third on the list for appointments to the post office.

The first clue that anything was amiss when Salem Chief of Police Hamilton received a letter the morning of March 2, dated and postmarked the same day at 6:30 a.m.

I know the law requires investigation. Do as little as possible. The plain fact is I cannot earn enough alone to keep my family. Some one induced my boy to leave, and I am now too ill to work. I cannot see them starve. There is a little money, $21, in my purse. Make it bury us all together.

I am sorry to make so much disturbance, but I am too confused to think.

Mrs. L.F.J.

Upon receiving the note, Chief Hamilton and Officer Burkhart hurried to the address. They went through the house and found no one. They proceeded to the backyard where a tent had been erected. Later they would learn that Lucy had sublet the house and moved to the tent in the yard, not being able to pay the rent on the house.

After police had checked each body for signs of life and finding none, they discovered another note stuck under a lamp.

Let Mrs. Pratt have my trunk. Tent and everything else left here is for Mrs. Carrie St. Clair. I am sorry to make this bother. Forgive me. Mrs. Pratt lives at the corner of 12th and Rural Avenue. I hated to lie to get the stuff.

Until February 17, Lucy had worked at the Royale Cafeteria, earning $10 a week. She quit, telling co-workers that she was moving to Colorado to her sister's. Her fellow waitresses, realizing Lucy's destitute condition, had sent food home with her and believed her circumstances would soon be improving with her move. Her oldest boy Russell was working with W. S. Fitts at his fish market, earning about $6 a week there. Even with their resources pooled, the little family could afford but one or two meals a day. Russell had left home one or two weeks earlier (accounts vary) and was living with his stepfather John Swanson in Lebanon, apparently taking his $6 a week salary with him. *The Daily Capital Journal* reported mother and son had quarreled.

Lucy wrote to a friend: *This last blow has been one too many. It is not possible for me alone to earn enough to keep my family.*[2]

It was believed that second husband Mr. Jellison had visited her recently, but there is no record what they discussed or evidence that he ever assisted her financially.

With hunger gnawing at the vitals of her children and indescribable sorrow and despair eating out her heart, she resolved to end it all by plunging her children, as well as herself, into the great unknown.

The Daily Capital Journal opined that "Mrs. Jellison was probably temporarily insane as she was not apparently in need of any of the necessities of life, as there were provisions in the house at the time the deed was committed and the children were fairly well-dressed and did not show that they were in need of anything, although she must have had a pretty hard way of getting along with so large a family."

•••••

A mother killing her own children (maternal filicide) has a long history. Killing one's own children did not used to be crime, but that changed in the 16th and 17th centuries when France and England made filicide punishable by death and women were presumed guilty unless found innocent. With the Infanticide Acts of 1922 and 1938 in England, the law recognized that birthing and caring for an infant can detrimentally affect a mother's mental health and maternal infanticide was treated more gently, as manslaughter.

Recognized motivations of parents that murder:

1. Altruistic filicide: The parent kills the child because the parent perceives it is in the best interest of the child.
2. Acutely psychotic filicide: The parent in psychosis kills the child with no rational motive.
3. Unwanted child filicide: The parent kills the child because the child is a hindrance.
4. Accidental filicide: The parent unintentionally kills the child as a result of abuse, including Munchausen syndrome by proxy.
5. Spouse revenge filicide: The parent kills the child as a means of exacting revenge upon the spouse such as for infidelity or abandonment.

The most common (49%) motive is altruism. The strongest risk factor is a history of suicidality and depression or psychosis. Women most at-risk of filicide are socially isolated, indigent, full-time care providers, and victims of domestic violence. Often, the mothers had experienced inadequate mothering themselves, due to absence, alcoholism, mental health issues and abuse. One study found that between 16-29% of mothers successfully commit suicide following a filicidal act.

Lucy's letters indicate that she had considered sending her children to live elsewhere when her bad fortune curdled to something worse, but confessed she could not bear to be parted with them. Later, when her friend suggested placing the children elsewhere until Lucy got on her feet, Lucy tear-

VICTIM OF SOCIAL ISOLATION LOSING IN HARD FIGHT YIELDS TO DESPAIR

TWO LAST LETTERS WRITTEN BY MRS. LUCY F. JELLISON WHO COMMITTED SUICIDE

Heart Rending Story of Her Life Struggle Told by Her One True Friend---Children Born in a Boxcar, Who Learned to Lie and Steal and Snatch Things Just Because They Never Had Enough to Eat---Awful Indictment of Social Conditions---Need of Higher Socialization of the Community Life Along Broader Lines.

The Capital Journal editorial of Saturday, entitled "The Crime of Isolation," has been widely read and commented upon in connection with the tragic death of Mrs. Lucy F. Jellison, who killed her four children with cyanide of potassium and then took the poison herself. The editorial statements are remarkably sustained by the following letters written by Mrs. Jellison just before her death. Letter

no use talking. I must be with the biddies more. And even if I could be now, I fear it is too late to rectify some things. They have been left alone too much already. I have never left them for an hour willingly nor for aught but work.

There has been no lecture, no entertainment in any form, not even church nor a neighborly visit. I have gone

can you tell WHY it has not been answered? I fear I am a bit of a fatalist, else may be an infidel. I hardly believe that, though. There has always been a very real God to me, although not just what most of the ministers tell us. My dear, even yet I pray with all my soul, "Father, if it be possible let this cup pass from me," but I cannot finish it in the same spirit as our Leader did. Were I only concerned I could. But if I had no biddies I could make my way easily. "Go for my wandering boy tonight. Go search for him where you will. But being him to me with all his blight. And tell him I love him still"---It is an untold agony to me that he feels so hard to me. It is true that I've punished him, but it was to try to keep him from forming habits that were detrimental to him as an individual and to the state, too. And it seems I've made a grievous mistake. I do not understand. These next three never were good like he used to be. They can do, but will not. I can take any one alone and work with them and they will do fairly well, but together there is nothing.

What can I do? It is not right to rear them so. I wish you knew all my life. There is so much you could make use of but I've no time for more. Just this. I've lost my grip and grit and all is dark. Forgive me, dear, and forget as soon as possible. Should I

Photo credit: Daily Capitol Journal, March 11, 1912

Following her death and the death of her family, the community rallied in her memory and asked themselves what could have been to save her.

fully told her, "No—no. My children are undesirable … There is not one of them but will steal, not one but will lie. We have lived so hard—so hard—they have learned to snatch like little animals. They have longed for simple comforts, and O so often my poor babies have been hungry—hungry—not only one time, but for days and days! Forgive me, dear, for saying this to you, but you must know that no one would take my children into a home and keep them."[3]

Lucy may have had additional concerns. Her friend says that "worse than all else, at this time, came the knowledge of further wrongs to her children." The friend asks newspaper readers, "You mother of little girls, answer in your own mother-hearts why it was that during the last three weeks of her service at the cafeteria she always took (15-year-old) Epsey with her—ostensibly to help her with her work but does not your mother instinct tell you more than that?"[4]

Because of the way Lucy had adjusted her life insurance, police believed she had planned to take her life and those of her children for some time. She had life insurance on herself and her eldest son Russell. She had paid his up for three years, but hers was due to expire on the day after she died.

A gentleman friend of hers, A. B. Leech, employee of Portland Railway, Light & Power Company, had visited Lucy the night before the murder-suicide, leaving at 8:45 p.m. She had asked him to buy her some cyanide of potassium "to kill some old dogs." Unwittingly, he had provided her the means of her death and that of her family.

While descriptions of the family at the funeral home stressed how peaceful the family looked, death by potassium cyanide is anything but. When you watch an old movie featuring Charlie Chan or Miss Marple and they lean over and smell the breath of the deceased and declare a faint, fruity smell of almonds lingering about the lips of the corpse—that's cyanide.

Within a few minutes of ingestion the individual collapses, frequently with a loud scream. In lesser amounts, death can stretch out to between 15 and 45 minutes. The last minutes of a cyanide death are marked by convulsions, gasping for air, a bloody froth of vomit and saliva and then—death. Cells die rapidly due to oxygen starvation. As muscle cells and nerve cells fail, body-rattling convulsions frequently result. Following death, the skin is mottled with blue. If swallowed, cyanide salts burn going down.

The coroner's inquest was held that evening. Another letter of Lucy's had surfaced and was read. It was addressed to Leech.

Remember all the time you still have a work to do. I want you to do me one more favor. Find the lad (Russell) and try to soften his heart toward me enough so that he will heed my last wishes for his benefit. I want him to go to school. It was a grief to me always that I had to keep him out. He will need a good friend. I could wish he would go to the Oregon Agricultural College. Mr. Ressler there used to be the kind of man I would wish for his friend.

I pray you do not grieve for us. You must live to watch over your own. I've done what little I could to help you over some ruts. I wish I need not have given you this blow. I cannot help it. When I've been cross with you lately it was to keep from breaking down. Forgive me and be good and don't worry. It is only another pebble crushed beneath the iron heel.

My lad has gone quite a way down. I pray something may happen to stop him and send him up. Then indeed my life and death will not have been in vain. Remember, I told you I should remind you of your promise to help me if I asked. I ask you to be kind to Russell and not fret over any of us. I have appreciated our friendship, even if I did scold. I wish you the best of success, and thank you for all you have done for me.

Be strong and forgive me the shock. Had I been able to think of any way to get away without shocking anyone I would have done so. I could not raise the money to get any place. I am not able to work and I cannot sit here and go through what we did once and know all the time of that gnawing misery for Russell. Poor boy. If only I had bidden him Godspeed. I am ill with a horror at this time. You would not make it easy for me, but of course you are right. I fear I cannot hold out but I must try. I cannot leave them to face alone what I have tried so hard to do and failed—failed. And I was stronger than any of them. No I cannot leave them here. But woe is me, to have to send them home. At least they are innocent.

Time is passing and I must go to work. But O God, have mercy. I have prayed for some other way, but find none. My brain reels. Good-bye.

•••••

Yet another note had been found in the tent: *For all time,* written four times, once for each victim. Beneath these words: *The rest are at peace. God help me.*

The jury found that Mrs. Jellison had always acted in a rational manner and at no time up to when she was last seen alive on Friday night had there been any indication of insanity. The verdict was "death due to poison—cyanide potash—

administered by the mother, first to the children, and then to herself with suicidal effect."

The community was at once caught up in the tragedy. The services were held in the undertaking parlors of Lehman and Clough. *The Daily Capital Journal's* March 4 (rather longish) headline read as follows:

Simple Pathetic Services
Sermon by Pastor Avison
Husband and Son Present
Hundreds Attended the Services
at the Undertaking Parlors This Afternoon
That Marked the End of the Most
Pitiful and Pathetic Tragedy in Salem's History—
Everything Goes to Show that
Human Sympathy and a Little Friendship and Kindness,
A Little Aid and Encouragement
Might Have Prevented the Tragedy.

The bodies attracted quite a bit attention at the funeral home with a stream of morbidly curious. Salem citizens draped the children with spring flowers during their brief visit.

There were no flowers for the mother.

Former spouse John Swanson and son Russell Storey were summoned and they purchased a cemetery lot for the family. The names, birth dates, and single death date of March 2, 1912, were engraved on five wooden slabs at the head of three new graves in the Odd Fellows Cemetery (now the Pioneer Cemetery on Commercial and Hoyt Streets).

Sadly, their graves are now unmarked; nothing but a spread of grass remains at lot 625. Perhaps the simple wooden slabs were never replaced with something more permanent. Vandals have broken many (if not most) of the old headstones; there is no way of knowing if the little Jellison family's markers would have survived bored teenage angst, even if there had been the money for tombstones.

From the March 4, 1912, *Capital Journal:*

Photo credit: J. E. McComb

Lucy Jellison and four of her children—Epsey, Harland, Maud, and Raymond—are buried in Salem's Pioneer Cemetery in Lot 625, their simple grave markings now long gone.

As the simple but pathetic services were held over the dead, but few eyes were dry and occasionally in the audience a sob could be heard from some woman overcome by sorrow, the pitifulness of it all. In a grave coffined alone, tonight at the cemetery the mother sleeps. By her grave's side arises another fresh mound, the couch of Harland and Epsey, brother and sister, and in the third the remains of Maud and Raymond, the last baby boy of the dead woman and the husband who stood by the grave today with head bowed down with grief.

But anyway, they sleep tonight. Wrapped in the dreamless drapery of eternal peace, the mother sleeps beside her children in their graves in the little cemetery on the hill tonight, careless alike of storm or sun, praise or condemnation. Beyond the reach of man, and in the benificient [sic] care of God who made them, and who alone can judge them.

Beneath the load of human sorrow other hearts in this world may break, but the hearts that have become as dust will never break again.

From other eyes in this world the light of joy and happiness may fly and die; but the eyes that have been curtained by the everlasting dark will never know again the touch of tears."

From other lips in this world may come the agonizing cry for bread, and the cry, as her's [sic], goes unheeded, but from the lips that death has kissed into eternal silence there will never come another word of pain or joy.

They will sleep tonight, their bodies in the beautiful cemetery, Salem's city of the dead, and the world can never again bring to the weary mother the agony and suffering she feared for her children, but with her little brood, no longer clad in the biliments [sic] of poverty, but robed in draperies of spotless white, hand clasped in hand, together they will tread with joyous feet the flowers decked fields of Paradise.

12. Snitches Get Stitches

January 17, 1989
2575 Center Street

On January 17, 1989, President-elect George H.W. Bush was preparing for his inauguration in Washington, D.C. In Florida, Ted Bundy, denied his final stay of execution, was confessing to additional crimes, including the murder of an Oregon State University student.

And in Oregon, Department of Corrections Director Michael Francke, 42, was missing.

•••••

Michael Francke had been hired by Governor Goldschmidt 20 months earlier, in May 1987. Goldschmidt was promoting an ambitious legislative package of bills to add 900 prison beds to Oregon's overcrowded prison system and build an $8.3 million, 195-cell isolation building within the state's penitentiary. Francke, a progressive-thinking Corrections director from New Mexico, seemed perfect for the job.

But Michael Francke's tenure had not been smooth. He had overspent his agency budget and was under intense legislative scrutiny and criticism for making spending decisions without legislative approval. He and Governor Goldschmidt were often in conflict due to their different philosophies. He had centralized operational and administrative control of the

Hired away from New Mexico in May 1987 to head up Oregon's Department of Corrections during a period of prison expansion, Michael Francke inherited a largely non-centralized prison system where prison superintendents ran their respective prisons independently, entrenched in outdated policies and procedures.

prisons, reducing individual prison superintendents' power and control, and there were reports he was looking to make additional changes in upper management. He had reportedly sent his resume to a New Mexico firm earlier that month.

Making matters worse, Francke's wife had left him the week before and had taken their young son with her. His finances were not in good shape either—he had to borrow money at times to cover his spending habits and obligations to his first wife, child support, and tuition.

At work, he seemed more worried than usual. He asked his second-in-command to step up efforts to intercept drugs going into the prison. He checked out a shotgun from the penitentiary's arsenal and sometimes carried it in the trunk of his

Photo credit: J. E. McComb

The Dome Building where the Corrections Administration was housed and where Michael Francke had his office. The north porch, where Francke's body was found, is on the left behind the trees.

car or stashed it under his bed. He was sleeping with a .45 caliber pistol under his pillow.

On the night of January 17, 1989, Francke was working late. He was scheduled to testify before the Senate Judiciary Committee the next day and needed to prepare for the usual legislative grilling.

As the director of the Department of Corrections, Francke worked in the "Dome Building," across from the Oregon State Hospital on Center Street. The Dome Building housed the Corrections Department's administration office along with the offices for the state's Board of Parole. On the afternoon of January 17, Francke attended a meeting with his assistant directors and members of his executive team that ended between 5:30 and 5:45 p.m. He then met with colleague Elyse Clawson and two others in his office until 6:30 or 6:40 p.m.

But shortly after 7:00 p.m. and two hours after the sun had set, no one could find Francke.

Elyse Clawson and her assistant Mary Blake noticed the dome light on in Francke's car. It was parked in its usual space, not far from the front door. They walked out to the state-owned Pontiac Bonneville and found one of the doors open. Other than that, nothing appeared to be amiss. They closed and locked the car.

Colleagues checked his office where they expected to find him working on the next day's presentation, but he wasn't there. They called him on his pager but there was no answer. Francke had mentioned that he had a dinner date that night and his worried colleagues called area restaurants looking for him.

Richard Peterson, Francke's top aide, returned from home and conducted a room-to-room search of the building. He was joined by Dave Caulley, the agency's financial officer, but they found nothing. The two encountered Larry Hill, a maintenance worker who was doing a security check of the building and who was also keeping an eye out for Francke. When Hill circled back an hour later, at about 10:30, the only car left in the lot was Francke's.

Finally, Stephen Rubino, an Oregon State Hospital employee, was making a routine check of the hospital grounds and came across Francke's body at 12:40 a.m. He found Francke lying face up in front of the door of the somewhat secluded north porch of the Dome Building. Rubino did not immediately recognize the pale face. The door into the building was locked, but a door window near the brass door knob had been broken as if Francke was trying to get into the building by turning the knob from the inside. A bloody handprint was to the left of the doorknob. Francke's glasses were lying near his feet. His car keys were a few feet away. His office keys were still in his pocket.

He had been stabbed in the heart and lung and also had slash marks on his right hand, arm, and leg, perhaps caused in part from fending off a knife attack. State Medical Examiner Dr. Larry Lewman stated that Francke had bled profusely.

Blood droplets on the concrete sidewalk and stairs leading to the porch marked Francke's route and began about 95

Photo credit: J. E. McComb

A wounded Michael Francke made his way up the steps to the Dome Building and down the north portico where he tried to enter the building through this door where he collapsed.

feet from his parked car. Investigators found no blood spatter that would definitively indicate where he might have been assaulted. Rubino called the hospital communications center via radio and police quickly descended upon the crime scene.

Police theorized that Francke had been attacked at his car as he was leaving for dinner.

Francke had then made his way across 25 yards of parking lot and wet grass to the Dome Building's side porch. He had likely approached the north side doors because people were still working at that end of the building and might be able to hear him.

The main doors had been locked since 5:25 p.m. and the area vacant. Francke had broken the window with such force that glass shards were scattered several yards into the room, a large administrative office. At the time, the door lock was broken such that it couldn't be opened from the inside or the outside without a key.

According to police reports for the prior year, the parking lot outside the Dome Building had seen one minor assault and four thefts. Employees thought the number was likely far higher, as many thefts were not reported.

·····

Unlike most Salem homicide victims, Michael Francke was smart and well-educated. He was born in Kansas City, Missouri and grew up in Prairie City. He earned his law degree from the University of Virginia School of Law. He spent four years in the Navy as a Judge Advocate General, stationed in Los Angeles.

He then went to work as an attorney general for New Mexico. He became general counsel to the Corrections Department, then director of the investigations division and the Medicaid fraud control unit and the deputy attorney general in charge of the criminal division.

Next he was appointed as a District Court Judge in 1980 and served as the administrator of the Santa Fe County Juvenile Detention Facility. In 1983, he was named the head of the New Mexico Corrections Department. In May 1987, Oregon's governor hired him for the same post, here.

Francke was buried in Sante Fe National Cemetery with military honors. Oregon held a memorial and the legislature also memorialized him. Francke left behind wife, Bingta, daughter Marlo, 20, and sons Joel, 16; and Trey, 1.

The murder shocked the community. His friends noted that Francke put his job first, with 18-hour days the norm rather than the exception.

But new bosses with new ways of doing things can cause friction with established employees and associates. One such associate was Scott McAlister.

McAlister worked at the Department of Justice for 17

years as the lawyer for Corrections. Legal issues, lawsuits, questions involving prisoner rights, all would be directed to McAlister. As a result, he was intimate with the department and worked extensively with Francke. McAlister resigned 11 days before the murder to work in Utah. In his resignation letter to Attorney General Dave Frohnmayer, McAlister said he could no longer work for Corrections because of the management there, citing philosophical differences.

Photo credit: Marion County Sheriff's Office

After an unexplained delay, police released this sketch of a man seen in the Dome Building the day Michael Francke was killed. He was never identified but some thought he resembled Tim "Rooster" Natividad.

Francke's death was a setback for Oregon. Francke was open to new ideas in an area moribund with 19th century ideas of punishment and rife with corruption and supported education and mental health programs within the prison.

The Investigation

A team of 20 detectives was assigned to the case. Investigators interviewed about 1400 people, including 800 state hospital workers, in the weeks immediately following the murder.

The police team, in turn, was broken into groups to investigate different angles of the investigation: Francke's personal and professional associates; state hospital patients out on leave; other crimes reported in the area; New Mexico connections; more recent Oregon connections; and witnesses to that night's events, including a man seen running away from the scene.

Family, friends, co-workers, and the community immediately speculated that his murder was connected to his job. It seemed impossible that the Corrections chief could be murdered as a random victim of crime, when he had spent his career enmeshed with the criminal element.

Marion County District Attorney Dale Penn told the press that his office was primarily working two motives: a possible robbery of Francke in the parking lot and revenge in connection with his job either here or in New Mexico. Penn admitted Francke received death threats, some recently.

Michael Francke's younger brother Kevin offered another theory. About a month before the murder, Michael had told Kevin that he was preparing to reveal an "organized criminal element" in Oregon prisons. Allegedly, no paperwork or computer files on his investigation were ever found, but there were rumors that over 20 bags of shredded paper were removed from the Dome Building around the time of the murder.

A reward fund was established and increases in the fund were regularly publicized in the newspapers. By May, it was up to $22,000.

And so began what became the state's most expensive homicide investigation in Oregon history. Investigators would interview over 3000 people in four states and spend more than $900,000 before someone was convicted of the crime.

1986 Investigation

The theory of possible prison corruption wasn't hard to believe. At the urging of then-state senator L.B. Day (R-Salem), the state police investigated allegations of employee misconduct at the prison in 1986. The ten-month investigation uncovered a vast drug smuggling network that brought in large quantities of drugs and thousands of dollars.

In addition to the widespread drug smuggling, state police found guards were gambling on duty by placing bets via the phone. Job applications of friends and relatives were falsified with more prison experience with the approval of higher ups so they could be hired. There was widespread theft and financial irregularities at the farm annex. Inmates possessed ammunition and makeshift firearms.

Photo credit: State Library of Oregon

State Senator L. B. Day was an attorney and Teamster administrator who held numerous state and federal offices in his life time and served in the Oregon State Senate representing part of Salem from 1977 until his death. He initiated an investigation into prison corruption in 1986. (1982 Voters Pamphlet photo.)

At the conclusion of the 1986 investigation, the prison superintendent resigned to work in Arizona; the prison security manager was reassigned; two married Corrections officers were fired for making unauthorized copies of keys and for taking inmates home with them and giving them alcohol; one C.O. was fired for regularly smuggling in marijuana; one officer was fired for theft and supplying marijuana to an inmate; one officer was cited for three counts of second degree theft and was later forced to resign. Some believed that the investigation had been halted before higher ranking Corrections officers could be included. The 1986 report suggested that the problems were longstanding.

On October 12, 1986, a prison guard claimed that after

he told the Salem City Club about widespread use of drugs in the prison he was harassed by inmates and guards until he resigned. Curtis Coffin told the reporter that he had been charged with drug smuggling and jailed for two weeks in retaliation for his comments. District Attorney Dale Penn scoffed at the idea that inmates and guards had framed Coffin and denied he had been set up, but agreed that the prosecution rested on a single inmate who had refused to testify. The charges were later dropped for lack of evidence. Corrections Director Fred Pearce countered the assertion that there was widespread drug use in the prison and reported that during the last random drug test only ten percent of the inmates tested positive for drugs.

Corrections Officer Dave Larson was one of the guards who had told Senator Day about prison corruption. Larson was threatened after he came forward, and when Day died of a heart attack the day before a scheduled press conference to voice concerns about the 1986 investigation, Larson believed his protection died as well, along with the investigation that he felt was less than thorough.

Larson also expressed concern about the interconnections between the police who were investigating the Francke murder and Corrections officers who were the subject of the investigation, some of whom were related. Larson had met with Francke and reported that Francke was most upset about the same event that had upset Day: In August 1986, an inmate being questioned about crimes was allowed to have sex with his wife at the Oregon State Police office in Salem. FBI agents, Corrections officers, and two state police detectives watched through a two-way mirror. The two peeping state police officers were involved in the 1986 prison investigation. One was investigating the Francke murder. Larson thought there could be a connection between prison corruption and Francke's death; that someone might be willing to kill to protect their pension.

On January 25, a week after the murder, police released a description of a suspect who was seen running from the crime scene at about 7 p.m. the night of the murder: a man with dark, collar-length hair, wearing dark pants and a light-colored coat—possibly a trench coat—that extended below his waist. The witness wasn't sure about the race, but didn't think he was black. The description spurred a surge of phone calls—roughly 200—with possible leads.

The suspect had run down the driveway and across 23rd Street, disappearing into a parking lot on the north side of Salem Hospital's Physical Medical and Rehabilitation Center, about 175 yards away. Five hospital patients who were out on leave to attend a nearby Narcotics Anonymous meeting between 6 and 8 p.m. the night of the murder had reported seeing the suspect. Others had also reported seeing the man, but DA Penn declined to identify them at the time. Police worked up sketches based on witness accounts.

From the beginning, the police and District Attorney liked the theory that Francke had interrupted a car prowl and the burglar had stabbed Francke to escape. Often the simplest explanations are the most sound. Francke's family was skeptical. Nothing was missing from the car, to their knowledge. Patrick Francke told the press that police had found Michael's wallet, credit cards, and car keys. He found it suspicious that the attack had taken place on a Tuesday night—the only night of the week where someone could be sure to find Michael Francke at work in the Dome Building. He felt certain the killer knew Francke's schedule either first- or second-hand.

Kevin Francke's wife Katie later told the press that she had spoken to Michael four days before the murder. She reported that he told her that he had uncovered something about drugs and a criminal organization. In the same interview, Katie reported that she saw Michael's ghost the day after his death and he said the name of a Corrections official involved in his death.

The family hired a psychic who accurately described the Dome Building and said three men were on the scene when Michael was attacked; one wearing a trench coat. The psychic said that the murder was planned, but not for that night; something had happened that moved up the killing. It was planned at a cabin near a lake and that the plotters were high up in Oregon government; one of the plotter's names started with a hard "K" sound, she said.

Ghosts. Psychics. Conspiracies. The relationship between the family and police grew strained. The police stopped communicating with the Francke family in the spring of 1989. The autopsy the family had been given was full of redactions. Police failed to interview family members. The events as described by the DA didn't hold together for them. The psychic had a different version of the murder. The whole thing spelled cover-up to the family.

The theory that Corrections employees had arranged for Francke's murder when Francke uncovered illegal activities in the prison was a theory that would not go away.

As the investigation hit the two-week mark, another homicide would take place that would later play a part in the Michael Francke murder saga. On January 31, Elizabeth Godlove, 25, shot and killed her boyfriend, Timothy David Natividad, 24, in a domestic dispute. The two lived together at an Iberis Street apartment with their four-year-old son. Police found Natividad lying on the floor near the apartment's entrance, wounded by a single gunshot to the chest. He died en route to the hospital. The apartment manager and his friend found a .44 caliber revolver in a bush about 50 yards from Godlove's apartment. With Natividad's extensive record of domestic abuse and Charlie Burt as her lawyer, a jury acquitted Godlove after four hours of deliberation.

A week after the Francke murder, police asked the public for help in finding another man, seen in the Dome Building the day of the murder at about 6:30 p.m. Police described him as about 5'10"; dark, well-groomed hair; a black neatly groomed mustache; an olive or dark complexion, early thirties, slim, and wearing a black or navy pinstripe suit. Prosecutors later came to believe the man was the Xerox repairman. A Corrections employee familiar with the repairman insisted he wasn't.

A sketch of the man was not released to the public until

late June—a delay that may have hampered the man's identification.

Once a month had passed, the flood of tip calls ebbed. The hundreds of interviews had served to rule people out, more than identify likely suspects. The team of full-time investigators was reduced to about 15.

In February, the state police and FBI rounded up the usual suspects and polygraphed a number of dubious characters who had been in Salem at the time of the murder.

The state police polygrapher charged that the FBI did not have the authority to give lie-detector tests to Oregon suspects. The state trooper ruled that suspect Crouse had passed the test; the FBI disagreed. The trooper then complained to the state Board on Police Standards and Training whether polygraphers needed to be licensed in Oregon.

Among the suspects was an ex-con by the name of Johnny Crouse, 32. His parole officer tipped police that Crouse knew something about the Francke killing. Crouse reportedly had a quick temper, a history of assaults with knives, and a history of breaking into and stealing from cars.

The first time investigators questioned Crouse in February, he told them that he was a possible witness. While walking home from a visit to his parole officer on January 17, he saw a group of five men near the Dome Building and a commotion. He said he saw them "drop some guy"[1] and four of the men piled into a car and drove off while a fifth man he believed to be Mexican ran away on foot.

During a second interview in April, Crouse repeated his initial story, but when DOJ Investigator Randy Martinak expressed skepticism, Crouse revised his story and said a man named "Juan" had approached him "to take care of Francke for $300,000."[2] Juan gave Crouse a $1500 down payment and Crouse waited for Francke to emerge from the Dome Building. Crouse confronted Francke at his car and slugged and stabbed him.

Later that same day, Crouse's story changed again. Crouse said Francke had grabbed him and a struggle ensued and Crouse stabbed him when it looked like he was going to lose the fight.

The next day, Crouse refined his story and told investigators how he had stabbed Francke, including a downward thrust into his heart. Crouse was allowed to call his brother and have the call recorded, and ask if his brother remembered Crouse telling him about the murder.

Detectives took Crouse to the murder scene where he again described the night of the murder. When Det. Martinak grabbed Crouse by the shoulder, Crouse reacted violently and said he didn't like to be touched like that. Crouse said he had walked past the car and upon seeing theft-worthy objects in the car, proceeded to break in with a wire. Francke caught him while in the car, grabbed him, and said, "Come with me."[3]

Crouse accurately described Francke and said that his fear turned to fury as he struggled to escape and swung at the man with his arms. When that failed, he slashed at him with his knife until, still failing to escape, he aimed for the man's heart. Crouse then ran away. He did not know who he had stabbed until the next day. When he found out he had stabbed the head of Corrections and would face the death penalty, he told his apartment manager that he was going to "split" because "something heavy was going down." Soon after, he told his brother that "he had done something wrong"[4] and would be on the run. He never returned to his job and missed his next scheduled meeting with his parole officer on January 19. In a recorded phone call, Crouse confessed to his brother and later to his mother, stating it was "a freak accident."

A few days later, Crouse recanted his confession. A few days after that, he recanted his recantation and described how he hit Francke with a round house punch with his right hand connecting with Francke's face on the left side, which matched injuries found on the body. He was given a polygraph test and judged to be telling the truth when he confessed. In June, Crouse told Patrick Francke that he had not killed his brother, but supported Patrick's theory there was a conspiracy among some DOC officials to kill Michael. He gave a final interview that November where he repeated his claims of innocence and was granted immunity for hindering prosecution.

Penitentiary inmate Konrad Garcia told a counselor that Timothy Natividad matched the picture of the man in the pinstripped suit and had killed Francke. Prior to the killing, Natividad had told him that if Garcia killed Francke, he could get him released early and that Scott McAlister had arranged the murder. The counselor passed the information along to the task force, but nothing came of it.

Photo credit: Marion County Sheriff's Office.

Frank Gable was a small time meth dealer when he was arrested for the murder of Michael Francke. The prosecution relied on testimony from his circle of associates, who later recanted.

To placate the conspiracy theorists, some Corrections officials and former assistant attorney general Scott McAlister took polygraphs. All passed and denied involvement.

In May 1989, police pulled over ex-con Frank Gable and his wife Janyne. Gable was wanted for stealing his foster father's car. Gable was also wanted for questioning about the Francke murder. Police found a .22 caliber gun, which, as an ex-con, he was not supposed to have. The police report noted Janye's arm was in a cast and she was sporting two black eyes.

They ran him downtown and questioned him. An inmate at the prison had notified authorities that Gable might know something about the murder. Gable told the trooper he didn't know anything about the Francke murder. The first he heard of it was when he drove his wife Janyne to work at 6:30 am the morning of January 18. It was then he saw police barricades near the Dome Building.

Police arrested Gable and found him a cell, albeit occupied. This turned out to be more awkward than usual, because his cellmate was an old meth associate, one who thought Gable had ratted him out to the police: Mark Gesner.

Gesner had been arrested for meth. Gesner reported that the police had told him that if he had any useful information regarding Frank Gable and the Michael Francke murder they might be willing to drop the charges. Gesner would be the first of many to claim Gable had confessed to him.

Investigators pulled Johnny Crouse back in for additional questioning. During that five-hour interrogation, Crouse told police that he knew who had killed Francke, a name he had disclosed to his attorney, but would not tell police. The killing had been a hit ordered by two Corrections officials. He said he knew where the killer's clothes had been buried, but when officials took him there they found nothing. Those familiar with Mr. Crouse opined that Crouse was lying.

In July 1989, District Attorney Penn assembled a grand jury for the Francke case. It would meet off and on for a year. Coincidentally, the foreman was a Department of Justice employee and longtime friend of Scott McAlister, the DOJ Corrections attorney who had resigned shortly before the murder. By the time the grand jury had completed its work it would hear from 153 witnesses over eight months.

Also that July, Keizer police paid three weeks' rent for the Gables at a Keizer apartment complex. Gable had reportedly told the manager that he was working with Keizer police to catch gun smugglers.

On July 17, a business person called police and reported that Gable was beating his wife on a street corner. Police picked him up, but Gable was released 40 minutes later when his wife declined to press charges. The apartment manager reported that Gable would often use her phone and make lots of calls asking people "if they needed anything." She also reported Gable was visited by unsavory people arriving on foot. She asked Keizer police to move him.

Also that July, Kevin Francke threatened legal action unless the police turned over an unexpurgated version of his brother's autopsy.

On August 31, police released three sketches of people seen around the Dome Building at the time of the murder and asked the public's help in identifying them for questioning.

On September 15, Dome Building employees called police and reported a break-in. The burglars had found and used keys to open the offices of the Corrections Department assistant director and an employee who worked with agency computers. Stolen items included a radio and empty soda cans. Computer discs may have been tampered with. A witness reported seeing two men loading a pickup at about 1:00 a.m. and said that the burglars had parked under a light and seemed to be taking their time. One of the men carried a box that appeared to be heavy. Police would not say if the burglary was connected to the Francke murder.

There was tremendous pressure to solve the case. And everyone wanted to try, including the legislature and the governor. Some legislators were pushing for a special investigative committee to be formed. In a memo dated August 22, the governor's legal counsel laid out the pros and cons to Governor Goldschmidt in response to his suggestion of appointing special investigators or an investigative team. She noted that an "investigation initiated by the legislature would obviously be less desirable than one we might set up."[5]

There are at least three possible interpretations as to why Governor Goldschmidt wanted to keep control of the investigation and out of the legislature's hands. First, there's the political inclination to not cede executive power to a legislative body on general principle. Secondly, a parallel legislative investigation might go down any number of rabbit holes, not follow strict rules of evidence, and muddy the waters for possible prosecutions. The third possibility was that Goldschmidt didn't want the truth to come out for any number of reasons including skeletons in his own closet.

A month later, Governor Goldschimdt appointed a retired

Oregon Court of Appeals judge—John C. Warden—to investigate allegations that Corrections employees were involved in illegal activities, whether there were reasonable grounds to believe that the death of Michael Francke was connected to such activities; and whether existing means of investigation and enforcement were adequate to respond to such activities. Warden would be assisted by six retired FBI agents.

Police still had a number of suspects, but by September were looking hard at one: Frank E. Gable, 30. At the time, Gable was sitting in the Coos County jail on domestic violence charges and for parole violation with a $100,000 bail.

•••••

Gable was born in Lemmon, South Dakota. His father died of throat cancer when Frank was four. His mother was alcoholic and physically abusive and sent Frank to live with a family friend, Les Gederos, when he was eight. Gable's sister testified that Gederos sexually abused Frank and his brother. Frank dropped out of school in the seventh grade. He spent 45 days in the Pine Hill School for boys on a 1975 theft charge. When Gederos moved to North Bend, Oregon in 1976, Frank moved with him.

In March 1979, when Gable was 20, he was convicted of second-degree robbery and first-degree forgery in Coquille and sentenced to two and a half years at the Oregon State Correctional Institution, but was paroled in December. Three months later, he was convicted of assault. He served a 30-day jail term.

In February 1981, Gable was convicted of first-degree burglary and sentenced to a ten-year sentence and served two. While incarcerated he was written up 22 times for disciplinary issues. Twice he was sent to the minimum security farm annex. He was paroled back to Coos County in June 1983.

In 1984, Gable was convicted of second-degree robbery at the Bay Way Market in Coos Bay and sentenced to ten years. In the after-sentence report, the chief deputy of the Coos County District Attorney's Office described the crime. Gable had grabbed a clerk from behind, put his hand over her mouth, and forced her to the ground. He demanded she give him money and food stamps. The Chief Deputy of the Coos County District Attorney's Office wrote to the parole board recommending that they not release Gable early, warning the board that it was only a matter of time before Gable really hurt someone or himself.

While in prison, Gable was diagnosed with a severe personality disorder and was labeled dangerous. He tried to pull himself together. He earned his GED and an associate of arts degree from Chemeketa Community College. He started reading the Bible. He enrolled in the prison's drug rehabilitation program housed in Salem Hospital across from the Dome Building. While in the prison's rehab program, Gable met his future wife.

Janyne Vierra worked as a nurse in the state hospital medical clinic from November 1984 until April 1989.

Gable was paroled on the Bay Way robbery charge on August 9, 1988. Vierra and Gable married two weeks after his release. Frank moved in with Janyne at the Chandelle Park apartments, about a half mile east of the Dome Building and got a job. For a few months, Gable's life stabilized. Then Gable began using drugs again—including injecting methamphetamine—and he quit his job in November and focused on the drugs. Gable had a habit of keeping a duffle bag with spare clothes because the drug caused his to sweat so much. According to his wife and friends, Gable often carried knives, a baseball bat, and a handgun.

The marriage was not a positive move for Janyne. She became more involved with drugs, particularly meth. On meth, Gable became abusive. Janyne would come home to find a variety of nefarious types using her room as a shooting gallery. She lost her job due to attendance issues in April 1989, when Frank beat her and broke her arm.

The Gables were served with an eviction notice the day after the murder for having a noisy party the night before, and later, for nonpayment of rent. They were evicted two months later, March 6. Within months of the murder, they had lost their apartment, their car, and Janyne's job. Frank was selling anything of value.

Janyne was looking for a way out. On April 28, 1989, Gable was served with a restraining order, ordering him to have no contact with his wife after she accused him of domestic abuse. In her request for the restraining order, Janyne stated that Gable had fractured her wrist and elbow during an argument. Janyne moved some things to her mother's house and sent her daughter to live with a sister in Tacoma.

In May, 1989 police questioned Gable, but he provided no useful information. The car theft charges were dropped and it was at this time that Gable approached Keizer police about becoming an informant and he worked for them briefly.

Gable moved back to Coos Bay and got a job at the Marshfield Bargain House as a general laborer. Once there, asked Janyne to join him. She resisted, but "then he said he was coming to get me and that if I wasn't waiting for him, he was going to burn my mom's house down."[6]

It was a persuasive argument. She went.

Later that same month, Frank and Janyne had a spectacular fight. Gable threw Janyne into a dresser, knocking one of Gable's collector plates to the ground and breaking it. Gable became enraged, took the sharp edge of the now-broken plate and cut Janyne's leg nearly to the bone. She would need 27 stitches. He said it was an accident. Janyne reported that not only was it not an accident, Gable had reopened the stitches when she returned home. That was it. She reported the assault to police and later filed for divorce. Gable was arrested September 5, 1989 on domestic abuse charges.

Police interviewed Gable and gave him the first of his many lie detector tests on September 13, 1989. Police told him the polygraph was to eliminate him from the pool of suspects. Gable, without benefit of legal counsel, agreed. Gable knew he was in trouble. It was later reported that Gable had failed the lie detector test. He matched one of three composite drawings made of men in the area of the murder scene.

Two days later, Gable was picked up and interviewed again about the Francke case from about 5:30 p.m. to 11:00 p.m. and given a second lie detector test, which he reportedly failed. He was then taken into custody on a charge of assaulting his wife and blood and hair samples were taken.

Gable was given a ten-year sentence, then placed on probation, then ordered to serve a year in prison as a condition of the probation. He was jailed in the Coos County Jail in Coquille.

Gable acquaintance Mike Keerins told police that September that Frank had confessed to him when they were cellmates in May. Keerins said that Gable had told him that he was prowling state-owned cars thinking they might contain guns that had been issued to state officials for protection. Keerins reportedly passed several polygraph tests.

Legislative Interest

In November, the legislative Joint Interim Judiciary Committee met and began taking testimony on the various investigations and audits that the Francke killing had set in motion.

During the last few months of 1989, a prison guard filed a complaint with the state Ethics Commission, stating he had been ordered to take a crew of ten prison inmates to McMinnville to salvage and clean bricks for state Senator Cub Houck's (R-Salem) construction company, for later re-sale. Oregon law prohibits a public official from financially profiting by virtue of his office. Prison superintendent Hoyt Cupp was fuzzy on the details. Houck claimed the prison labor wasn't free— Houck was paying the prison the same wages as any other workers. Unfortunately, there wasn't any paperwork to support this claim. Houck's lawyer, John Dilorenzo, blamed poor Corrections record keeping. The Ethics Commission accepted Houck's explanation and dismissed the complaint.

Less than a month later, another inmate filed a similar complaint against Houck, this time for a prison farm annex inmate crew working at a Salem Hospital project. (Inmate participation was cut short when one inmate escaped.) Because Houck had not mentioned this job when asked about other inmate jobs, the commission revived its inquiry. The Ethics Commission subpoenaed Houck's records for the two projects. Houck refused to turn over the records, citing a new state law (sponsored by Houck) that prohibited the Ethics Commission from launching an investigation without probable cause—cause that couldn't be established without the records.

(The law took effect October 3, 1989—the day after the complaint had been lodged.)

Photo credit: State Library of Oregon

State Senator Carlos "Cub" Houck was an owner of Houck-Carrow Construction and represented part of Salem in the Oregon Legislature in the 1980s and became embroiled in controversy when he used prison inmates on some construction jobs without paying the Department of Corrections. (1986 Voters Pamphlet photo.)

Further investigation revealed that Houck had never paid for the inmate labor, with Houck explaining that he had never received a bill. Houck complained about the Ethics Commission director's investigation into his business dealings; the director would resign later that year.

Judge Duane Ertsgaard tossed the subpoena and issued a restraining order against the Ethics Commission.

Fun fact: Judge Ertsgaard's wife had worked in the Secretary of the Senate's office while Houck was a state senator and saw him nearly every day.

In the end, despite what it considered substantial evidence, the Ethics Commission agreed to drop the matter and in return, Houck agreed that there was the appearance of a violation.

A legislative committee met to examine possible prison corruption. State Senator Jim Hill (D-Salem) had been a driving force; people had come to him and complained about wrongdoing in the prison. An inmate told Hill that she had been ordered to falsify and pad inventories, remove metal state identification tags from prison furniture, and sign for bills for which she had no authority. The furniture had been

Photo credit: State Library of Oregon

State Senator Jim Hill represented part of the Salem area from 1987 – 1993 and chaired the Senate Judiciary Committee when Michael Francke was murdered. He was skeptical of the car-burglary-gone-wrong theory and began a legislative inquiry into prison corruption. (1990 Voters Pamphlet photo.)

taken by Corrections staff, she claimed. The warehouse fire had been set to disguise the theft. She had also told Michael Francke about the theft and he had said he was going to fire the people involved.

According to Gable's federal appeal filed in 2014, the A-Shed fire was one of the topics on which Francke planned to brief the legislature the day after his murder.

A problem the legislative committee immediately ran into was that of immunity—the committee's ability to offer immunity to witnesses could impair the District Attorney's ability to prosecute the murder case. The concern slowed legislative action.

On December 15, Judge Warden released the findings of his investigation. The team found widespread corruption and significant illegal drug use and distribution within the various prisons, with prison staff carrying in drugs. Favored inmates were allowed freedom to move about without searches and facilitate drug distribution.

One inmate—a "con boss"—made cell assignments, exacted payments from other inmates, controlled prison jobs and payroll and gave orders to inmates and Corrections staff. The con boss was protected by a senior officer and used his own computer to maintain prison records. He had his own office with radio, TV, VCR, and tape deck and sometimes slept there. The lieutenant who was supervising the con boss said he had no idea what information was on the computer. When the Warden team confiscated the computer to discover what information was contained on it, six of the files had been modified within a half-hour of the "unannounced" visit.

Warden's investigators found guards used excessive physical punishment (e.g. beatings) in violation of the prison's own administrative rules and punished inmates who filed lawsuits. Guards planted evidence in cells. Corrections officers provided marijuana and sold alcohol to inmates. Administratively, there was nepotism, cronyism, and favoritism in employment, work assignments, and discipline. Promotion and favored treatment was given to staff who intentionally lost at private poker games. Guards would be punished if they reported misconduct. Guards weren't disciplined for law violations. Contracts were awarded to relatives without competitive bids.

Something investigators didn't find was a link to Francke's murder. Judge Warden concluded "that there are reasonable grounds to believe that some officials of the Department of Corrections are involved in significant illegal activities or other wrongdoing, that there are not reasonable grounds to believe that Michael Francke's death was connected to those activities, and that the existing means of investigation and enforcement are not adequate to respond to such activities."[7]

Warden also noted that while Corrections employees had been helpful, "The single element which has been absent in the responses of some officials in the institutions is candor. Therefore, it is unlikely that a complete, clear picture has, or can be, developed from the brief investigation of Corrections that we have been able to maintain." He added that while he found no conspiracy, "What does appear to exist is an atmosphere, wherein those who seek personal gain of property, power, or authority, can pursue those ends with little difficulty."[8] Warden forwarded the names of 15 Corrections officers his team thought were involved in illegal activities.

That month also saw questions raised about a 1988 prison warehouse fire of suspicious origin. State police re-investigated the A-Shed fire when accusations were made that the warehouse was burned down to prevent the detection of stolen property or to obtain an insurance settlement.

The Department of Corrections reported the value as $670,400 for the building and $500,000 in stored materials. A lower sum was negotiated with the insurer. One DOC employee stated that the material listed in the building's inventory was not actually in the shed the prior 18 months. A later investigation found that some of the items claimed as lost in the fire had been sold before the fire, the inventory list falsified.

The Secretary of State conducted four audits concerning financial records and accounting procedures. The limited scope disappointed lawmakers, but the Audits Division didn't have the staff needed to investigate criminal activity. The audits revealed possible theft from inmate accounts and a variety of other financial problems and lack of accounting practices.

In November, two prison administrators, a recreational therapist, and an administrative assistant were suspended and later fired for marijuana offenses.

In late December 1989, the former Oregon DOJ attorney Scott McAlister resigned from his Utah job, citing what he believed were unfounded complaints about his management style and allegations of sexual harassment. During his year in Utah, McAlister had been accused by the ACLU of having conflicts of interest, of violating inmates' rights, covering up investigations of wrongdoing by prison guards and mishandling prisoner complaints. McAlister had also criticized a Utah judge's decision to allow American Indians to build a religious sweat lodge at the Utah State Prison.

In January 1990, the Legislative Emergency Board funded the prison ombudsman position and other proposals to curb drugs and improve hiring as recommended in the Warden report.

About this time, small-time meth peddler Shorty Harden had come to the attention of Francke investigators. Harden had a warrant out for his arrest on a variety of charges: possession of a controlled substance, being an ex-convict in possession of a firearm, probation violation, possession of methamphetamine, and delivery of a controlled substance. He was questioned for nine hours. Harden's residence was searched and his knife collection confiscated.

Harden was among a cadre of criminals that dealt in guns and meth, among them Frank Gable, Mike Keerins, Robert Cornett, Mark Gesner, and Earl Childers. The men had known each other for years, with Gable a relatively newcomer.

Gable associate Janice Lesh, 23, stated that Frank Gable had become upset in the summer of 1989 when he couldn't find a briefcase and laptop computer he had stored in her ex-husband's Ford Pinto, but had relaxed when she told him it had been destroyed. Kevin Francke reported that one of his brother's three briefcases was missing.

In addition to police questioning Gable's associates, Gable's wife told police that on the night of the murder her husband had been out all night and had only returned the next morning, shortly before taking her to work. Driving by the cordoned-off crime scene the next morning, Janyne said Frank freaked out and would not go back on the grounds.

Gable could see where this was all headed and did not like it. From his perspective, his criminal associates were merely giving the police stories about him in order to get criminal charges dropped against themselves.

Interest in the case was enormous and pre-trial press coverage extensive and included a number of people coming forward with their theories and possibly relevant recollections concerning the case. At the end of March and beginning of April, 1990, DA Penn subpoenaed Phil Stanford and Phil Manzano of *The Oregonian*, Steven Jackson from *The Statesman Journal*, and reporters for KGW, KOIN, and KATU, requesting that they turn over published and unpublished information regarding their interviews with Gable. The newspapers cited the Oregon Shield Law that protected reporters from having to turn over their sources or unpublished materials. No materials were turned over.

The police believed they had their man, and the pressure was on to develop enough evidence to indict Gable before he was released from the Coos County jail. The District Attorney reconvened the grand jury and heard from various Gable associates as well as the person who had installed Francke's car alarm. Apparently the installer's brother, sister, and brother-in-law all knew Frank Gable and were together in a Salem house that was raided for drugs three days after Francke's death. One of those arrested claimed a cop had pulled her aside and asked for information about the Francke case and mentioned a $1000 reward. The installer denied giving Gable the tools to disarm the alarm and said he had not met Gable until after the murder.

Gable was arrested for the murder of Michael Francke on April 8, 1990, just days before he was scheduled to be released from jail on his earlier charges. He was transported from the Coos County jail to the Lane County jail in Springfield. Detectives interviewed him for hours. Gable continued to deny that he had killed Francke.

The next day the grand jury charged Frank Gable with murder. The indictment offered seven different alternative theories of aggravated murder and murder. DA Penn explained that it wasn't unusual to list multiple theories of a single crime since the theory was based on what the criminal was thinking at the time, and he could be thinking several things. The aggravated murder charged carried a possible death penalty; the regular murder charge had a possible penalty of life in prison.

(Gable's attorneys would later, in July, challenge the grand jury indictment, citing the relationship between the jury foreman and Scott McAlister, and that the foreman could be motivated to steer away from investigating McAlister.)

The District Attorney's Office declared eight people to be material witnesses in the Francke case. Prosecutors ask judges to declare people material witnesses if there is concern the person won't show up to testify. Material witnesses can be jailed or ordered to report in to authorities regularly.

- Michael O. Keerins, 33, was already in custody on a probation violation. Keerins told police that Gable had confessed to him while both were in jail.
- Cappie C. "Shorty" Harden, 34, was being held on drug charges. Harden claimed to have witnessed Gable stab Francke.
- Randall J. Studer, 31, was being held on charges of first-degree sodomy and two counts of first-degree sexual abuse. Studer was Gable's brother-in-law and told police Gable had confessed to him.
- Mark M. Gesner, 24, was serving a 21-month sentence on federal gun charges. Gesner shared a jail cell with Francke and would testify that Gable gave him a bag to dispose of the day following the murder and had confessed to him.
- Earl F. Childers, 41, had been recently released from Marion County jail on his own recognizance. He claimed to have seen Gable near the crime scene and that Gable had confessed to him about the murder.
- Daniel P. Walsh, 23, had been released on his own recognizance from Marion County. Walsh claimed that Gable had confessed to the killing to him.
- Jodie Mae Swearingen, 17, was being held in the youth corrections facility Hillcrest School (for Girls). Swearingen

said she was with Harden the night of the murder and had witnessed the stabbing.

• John "Kevin" Walker, 26, was being held in Benton County on charges of menacing (he had pointed a gun at a motorist) and being an ex-convict in possession of a firearm. Walked claimed that Gable had confessed to him.

That June Gable was charged with unlawfully possessing a weapon and faced a 15-year-to-life sentence as an armed career criminal. In a surprise twist, Gable and his attorney in that case, Karen Steele, fell in love. She would informally assist in his murder defense and emotionally support Frank throughout his trial.

In a pre-trial affidavit submitted to the court by prosecutors to support their request for no bail, the DA's office offered a statement from inmate Richard Kientiz, who claimed that Gable had offered him money to kill Shorty Harden. In exchange, Gable would kill an inmate who had stolen from Kientiz.

Some of those involved had implicated Timothy Natividad for the murder. Gable's attorneys sought and received permission to have Natividad's knives examined and compared with Francke's stab wound. The court granted permission, but analysis failed to link Natividad's knives to the crime.

Defense counsel asked police investigators for the autopsy report and Natividad case file. Defense attorney Bob Abel said witnesses reported that they had seen wounds on Natividad shortly after the Francke murder. Police reports indicated that a woman thought Natividad had killed Francke because her husband, an inmate, was having problems in the prison and Natividad had asked her husband if he wanted to get even. She said that Natividad had wanted to find someone to kill somebody. The DA denied defense counsel's request for the file, stating that there was no clear link to the crime.

In September 1990, Elizabeth Godlove told police that her then-boyfriend, Timothy Natividad told her a week after Francke's death that he had killed a man. She believed it had been Francke. Natividad owned a pin-striped suit, like the man seen at the murder scene. Natividad had been increasing his use of meth and had become more erratic and threatening.

(Fun fact: Elizabeth Godlove and Kevin Francke married in 1994.)

In a tangential matter, former DOJ Corrections attorney Scott McAlister was arrested in Utah in May 1990 for possessing child pornography. "Young Arabian Nights" and "Pre-Teen Sex" both had Multnomah County court exhibit stickers from a 1977 obscenity case. McAlister had allegedly given his secretary, whom he was dating, a box of pornographic films as a seduction tool. Instead, she took the films to the FBI. According to Multnomah County records, McAlister had taken possession of the exhibits when the case was appealed. Federal law prohibits knowingly receiving, distributing, or transporting child pornography.

The feds declined to press charges and passed the case to the Salt Lake County attorney's office. McAlister pleaded guilty to misdemeanor pornography distribution and was sentenced to a week in jail. McAlister's ex-girlfriend and employee filed a civil suit against him and the State of Utah when he allegedly demoted her when she refused to participate in group sex with him. The state settled with her for $95,000.

Jodie Swearingen, who had told the grand jury that she was with Shorty Harden at the Dome Building and saw the murder take place, had gone into hiding.

(Fun Fact: In the 1995 movie made of the Francke murder, *Without Evidence*, penned by Phil Stanford and Gill Dennis, Swearingen is played by Angelina Jolie and Godlove by *Breaking Bad's* Anna Gunn.)

She called defense investigators and told them she had lied to the grand jury. She had done so at the behest of Harden and then police had coerced her into supporting Harden's story. Her story had varied. In one version she told police she watched from Shorty's car and saw the two men struggle with each other 15-20 feet from the car.

In another version, she was standing near the front of the Dome Building. In a letter Swearingen wrote in 1989, she said that she wouldn't testify against Gable for fear of her life. She didn't want to snitch because those involved in the drug trade would get angry and kill her. She also told the defense that police had put her with Shorty Harden two or three times so they could get their story straight.

Police admitted that the two had been in contact but denied coercing Swearingen or coordinating testimony. Swearingen claimed police interviewed her for hours. Each time she failed to corroborate Harden's testimony police would say they didn't believe her and continue questioning her to bully and intimidate her. Police traced a phone call and arrested Swearingen in Denver.

Swearingen also said she knew who the killer was, but she wasn't saying, except to say it was not Frank Gable. Swearingen's attorney tried to keep her from being jailed as a material witness—where she was held in protective custody and routinely handcuffed and subjected to strip searches—but failed. Her attorney charged that prosecutors were using the material witness law to coerce favorable testimony from witnesses, holding them until they agreed to say what prosecutors wanted them to say. The prosecutors vehemently denied the charges. One report has Swearingen being interviewed 44 times by state police and given 23 polygraphs, sometimes three in one day.

The trial had been tentatively scheduled for January 1991, but the defense asked for a delay to sort through the more than 29,000 pages of evidence much of which they had received just the prior September. The trial was initially pushed back to March 4, and then delayed again until the beginning of May.

Trial

On February 12, 1991, Marion County sent out 3,000 jury summonses from which to draw a jury for the Francke case. Jurors were sworn in April 26.

Two weeks after the summonses were sent out, *Unsolved*

Mysteries aired a TV segment on the Francke murder and reen-acted the theory that Francke had been abducted by three men and then returned to his office and killed.

The prosecution was annoyed. This was not their theory of the crime and could be poisoning the jury.

Gable's murder trial began May 1, 1991. For the defense: John Storkel and Bob Abel. For the prosecution: Sarah Moore and Tom Bostick. The two sides gave their opening state-ments, a high-level summary of the case.

(Fun fact: The two prosecutors would later marry.)

The prosecution's theory of the case was simple. Michael Francke walked out to his car around 7:00 p.m. and surprised Frank Gable rifling through the contents of Francke's car looking for "snitch papers." Gable lunged out at Francke and stabbed Francke three times and fled west across 23rd Street, into the old hospital grounds. Gable then drove north on Med-ical Center Drive and turned right on D Street. Meanwhile, Francke made his way to the north side of the Dome Building porch where he broke a window attempting to get in, or get attention, but died shortly thereafter.

The prosecution argued that the physical evidence sup-ported this theory, as did witness testimony and Gable's own statements made during questioning and statements made to others.

The defense argued that despite the state spending near-ly $1 million during the investigation, the prosecution had no murder weapon, no physical evidence tying Gable to the scene, a weak motive, and had relied upon the testimony of ca-reer criminals pressured by police to finger Gable, motivated by revenge and looking to reduce their own criminal charges. Investigators had failed to secure the crime scene and evidence had been compromised.

Police did not investigate the body until daylight and did not take the body's temperature to establish time of death, leaving open the possibility that others had killed Francke at another time. The State Medical Examiner had performed only a routine autopsy and did not measure the wounds making it impossible to identify the murder weapon. In all of his police interviews, Gable had maintained his innocence. Investigators had determined that Francke's body had been on the porch at least two hours before his discovery, so he could have been stabbed later than 7:00 p.m. negating the eyewitness testimony.

The prosecution called upon a number of experts to describe the crime scene.

(Fun fact: On day two of the trial, Ted Kulongoski, then-insurance commissioner and later governor, escorted members of Boy Scout Troop 465 to the trial as a lesson in state government.)

State Police criminologist Michael Hurley testified that investigators found blood droplets widely scattered on the sidewalk, on the steps leading up to the porch, and on the porch itself. Ten days after the murder, he used a more advanced method of testing the scene for blood and found no blood in the area around Francke's car or within 100 yards of the car. Hurley noted the position of the body suggested that Francke had been on his knees with his fist through the window pane, and had fallen backward.

The defense argued the blood droplets and the arrangement of the body was evidence that Francke may have been killed elsewhere and then moved to the porch. Perhaps there had been two or more attackers. Or, possibly the first stab wound had been to the arm, accounting for the blood droplets on Francke's path to the porch and the assailant followed him there and stabbed him fatally on the porch. That might suggest that the goal of the evening was to kill Francke, not burglarize the car. If the goal was to kill Francke, others would have been involved, as Gable did not have a motive to want to kill Francke. If there were two attackers, this would conflict with the eyewitness testimony the prosecution planned to offer up.

State Medical Examiner Larry Lewman testified that Francke could have traveled the 100 feet from the car to the porch after being stabbed. In stabbing cases, it wasn't unusual to not find blood where the stabbing had occurred. The fatal stab wound to the heart was caused by a long, thin knife less than an inch wide, with one sharp edge. It had sunk five to seven inches deep into the chest, cutting into the main pumping chamber of the heart and cutting the artery that supplied the heart with blood. This caused massive bleeding into the chest area. Because most of the blood was flowing into the chest cavity, not out, clothing was soaking up blood—that would explain why there wasn't more blood at the scene of the stabbing, at the car.

Another stab wound, made by the same type of blade, was found in the victim's left biceps. The blade pierced business cards that were in Francke's left coat pocket, and nicked his chest a little more than an inch from the fatal stab wound. Francke may have had his left arm over his chest in a protective position at the time of the attack. Because the knife thrusts were oriented the same direction—horizontally—and went in at the same angle, Lewman concluded that they were the result from an attack by the same assailant with the same knife in quick succession.

Francke's right hand had cuts consistent with someone smashing through a window pane and not defensive wounds. In addition, there were scrapes near the hairline and around the left eye, likely caused by Francke's glasses. Lewman described these scrapes as not significant and he saw no evidence that Francke had been hit on the head with blunt force.

When the defense asked about other possible scenarios than the one laid out by prosecutors—multiple assailants, that Francke had been moved, that all the wounds to his hand had been caused by the broken window and not a defensive hand wound—a reportedly exasperated Lewman stated that anything was possible.

Police criminologist James Pex testified regarding the blood trail. The blood fell from Francke, and was not flicked or knocked off, indicating that he was moving slowly and steadily to the door, supporting the prosecution's theory of the crime. The drops began about ten feet south of the porch stairs and indicated that Francke had walked in one direction, toward the end of the porch where his body was found hours later. A bloody handprint to the left of the doorknob indicated that Francke had leaned against the wall.

The defense continued to challenge the state's version of events and questioned Pex why Francke hadn't continued straight up to the main doors, the doors that were more directly in line with his parked car and the door he used every day? Perhaps Francke had changed direction because someone had blocked his more direct route up the main steps.

Contamination of the crime scene was also a possibility argued the defense. Initially, police had only cordoned off the porch and the steps leading up to the porch. Later they expanded the area to include the grass and sidewalk in front of the steps. Still later the area was expanded to include Francke's car. Once Sgt. Karl Nelson arrived — a detective with 19 years' experience — the area was expanded still further to include the grounds around the building, agreeing with the defense that taping off the larger area would have been normal procedure.

Time of death was also an issue. The prosecution's case theorized that Francke had been stabbed at about 7:00 p.m. The defense raised the possibility that the death had occurred much later; and if it had occurred later, the damaging eyewitness testimony could be discredited. Body temperature would have been a key piece of evidence, as time of death can be more narrowly estimated with that information, but it was never taken that night.

Next came testimony about Francke's car alarm. Police testimony that day revealed that Francke's car was alarmed and working, but it was not known whether the alarm was turned on or off. The employee of Hear No Evil who had installed the alarm the month before Francke was killed testified that a siren would sound if the car was bumped, if someone opened the door, or if there was a voltage fluctuation in the car's electrical system.

Why hadn't it gone off if it was being burglarized? DA Moore had already established that Francke's car needed a new battery. Was that the reason? No. Both the installer and Pex stated the alarm was working; police had tested it a few days after the murder. There were three possible explanations.

The burglar could have deactivated the alarm with a device. Francke might not have turned on the alarm, something that his colleagues and family said would have been out of character, but was suggested by alarm technicians who testified that Francke was having electrical problems with the car. Or, Francke could have deactivated the alarm when he opened the car door himself and then was attacked. However, the last theory contradicted the eyewitness testimony of Cappie Harden who said that Gable was already in the car when Francke approached.

What about Francke's pager? The director of the State Police crime lab in Portland testified that he removed the pager from the body when he gathered Francke's clothes, keys, ring, watch, and wallet and turned those items over to police in Salem. Detective Terry Crawford had picked up Francke's personal effects, including the pager. He testified that it was off. It was the kind of pager that erased numbers once it was turned off. It was impossible to tell whether the pager was set to an audible or inaudible signal on the night of the murder. Francke's family contended that Francke never turned it off. Peterson, Francke's second-in-command said that he couldn't always connect with Francke using the pager.

The defense argued that despite claims that the evidence had been carefully collected and preserved, Francke's blood-covered pager was returned to Capital Paging a month following the murder, without investigation. Had it been turned on? If so, why had no one heard it going off if the body was so close to the building when his colleagues were paging him?

Elyse Clawson and Mary Blake testified how they had searched for Francke that night. Clawson testified that Francke wore his pager on vibration mode, so they wouldn't have been able to hear it when calls were placed.

Two state employees testified that they had seen Francke at his car twice earlier in the day and had not heard the chirping noise when the car alarm was activated or deactivated, suggesting that the alarm had not been set that day.

Second-in-command Richard Peterson testified that, upon being contacted about Francke being missing, he returned to the Dome Building about 8:45 p.m. to help with the search.

Peterson met with Dave Caulley, the department's financial officer, in Caulley's office. While Caulley kept trying to locate Francke by phone, Peterson searched the building.

Together, they unlocked Francke's office using Peterson's key and turned on the light. He and Peterson looked around, but did not see anything helpful and turned the light back off and re-locked the door. When asked later, they stated that they did not notice Francke's briefcase in the office.

Peterson testified that he checked two office doors in the room that led to the north porch. He didn't notice anything unusual, such as glass shards underfoot or cold air from a broken window. He looked at the door leading to the porch but couldn't see out because it was darker outside than inside and the glass created a mirror effect, hampering his ability to see out. However, this testimony raised doubts for some as to whether Francke had really been there at the time of the initial search.

Wayne Hunsaker worked at the State Hospital as a custodian and testified that he left the building at about 7:00 the evening of the murder. As he left the building from its north side, walking toward the North Parking Lot, he "heard some sound of somebody being hurt." He said it "Just—kind of like somebody had their breath knocked out. Kind of surprised. Kind of ugh, kind of a grunt sound." He turned toward the sound and saw two men facing each other a couple of feet apart about 40 feet from him. The two men separated, with one moving toward the Dome Building and one turning and running the opposite direction. The man walking toward the building was about six feet tall and was wearing a trench coat. He didn't see him stumble or stagger; that he was "walking like he was in a hurry. Like he was late for an appointment."[9] The other person was about six feet tall, 175 pounds, with short, dark hair, between 20 and 40 years old. He wore a knee length trench coat.

He ran at full speed until he got to the street, then disappeared behind a dumpster.

Cappie Harden testified that he witnessed the confrontation between the two men. He had met Gable before and recognized him. Hardin testified that Jodie Swearingen had called him asking him to pick her up near the Dome Building. He drove there and parked in the parking circle in front of the building. Swearingen got in the car, and then Harden noticed an interior car light come on. He saw Gable get into the car and decided to "stick around and see what [Gable] was up to."[10] Harden then saw another man approach the car. "He walked up to the car then and that's when I heard him yell, you know, 'Get out' and 'Hey, what are you doing in my car.' And he started running towards the car, and that's when I seen [Gable] come out of the car and stab the man one time in the chest. And that's all I seen." When asked why he didn't call police, Harden said, "I don't call the police because I'm not a rat."[11]

In response to defense counsel questions, Harden admitted his story had changed over time. At first he denied knowing anything about the murder. Then he said he'd heard about it on the streets. Then he said he heard about it from Swearingen and another street acquaintance. Harden had then accused John Bender, a local drug dealer, of the murder. He said Bender had given him a knife and that was probably the murder weapon. Defense counsel Storkel noted that back in November 1989, Harden had told police that he would need to see a photograph of Gable in order to remember him, suggesting that Harden hadn't really seen or recognized Gable the night of the murder. Harden denied that his testimony was traded for a softer sentence on his many crimes. The gun and delivery charges were dropped because they were weak, he contended. Although Harden was already on probation he was given probation yet again and allowed to attend a drug rehabilitation program.

Storkel asked Harden about a letter Harden had written to his nephew after his January 1990 arrest. In the letter, Harden wrote to his nephew that the police had given him a list of people who had snitched on him, and that police wanted him to testify against Frank Gable, who Harden considered a rat, and receive money and freedom in return. Harden explained that he was referring to reward money and he was lying to his nephew to explain why he was going to testify.

Earl Childers testified that as a condition of his parole, he attended Alcoholics Anonymous meetings. His usual meeting ended at 6:30 p.m. On his walk home, he would generally pass the Oregon State Hospital grounds at about 7:00 p.m. As he was walking home on January 17, 1989, he saw Gable driving away from the hospital grounds between 6:30 and 7:00 p.m. He tried to get Gable's attention and waved, yelled, and whistled at him, but Gable didn't stop.

A couple of months later, he was with Gable and the topic of the Francke killing arose. "And I asked him again if he did it and he told me he had done it. He said that he killed him. And I asked him, 'Well why?' And he said that he was burglarizing the car, going through some cars and he was in Francke's and he got caught and he ended up sticking the guy. And I told him, I said, 'You're shitting me, you stuck him over a car burglary?' He said, 'He was going to take me in and didn't want to go back to prison.'"[12]

Upon cross-examination, Childers agreed that when he had spoken to detectives on September 20, 1989, he denied that Gable had talked to him about the murder. He also admitted to having read news articles about Gable that labeled Gable a police informant. The defense suggested that Childers had cut a deal with prosecutors for a lighter sentence on his own crimes. Prosecutor Moore countered that Childers had been prosecuted for crimes following his cooperation and that the DA had recommended Childers remain in police custody at his parole hearing, for fear of his becoming involved in drugs again.

Mark Gesner, an associate of Gable's, testified that on the night of the murder, Gable came to his house and asked if Gesner could get rid of something, "where no one else could find it." Gable then retrieved a plastic bag from his car. When Gesner asked what it was, Gable said, "Don't worry about it. I'll tell you later." But after learning of Francke's death and knowing Gable picked up his wife near the area, he thought Gable's nervous attitude might be connected. The bag felt like cloth and he decided to throw it in the river. At the river, he opened the bag to put some rocks in it, and while he didn't inspect the contents of the bag, it felt like cloth wrapped around a hard, cylindrical object.

Gesner later asked Gable about the bag contents. "He said it was the stuff that I was wearing the night of the murder. And I said, 'What murder?' And he said, 'The Michael Francke murder.'"[13]

Gesner said he hadn't come forward right away because he didn't want to be a snitch. Once he found himself in Washington charged with gun and drug law violations he decided to talk to police. Gesner admitted telling a Washington Corrections official that he was going to change his story and testify against Gable because it would mean the difference between 15 years or a few months in jail.

Janyne Vierra Gable testified she worked as a nurse at OSH and Gable drove her to and from work each day. She testified that Gable was not home the night of the murder and didn't return until about 6:25 a.m. the next morning. She had not seen Gable since about 1:00 p.m. the day before. When he drove her work on the 18th and they saw the police around the Dome Building, he got nervous.

About a month before the murder, Gable gave her a list of names and asked her to access the computer system to determine whether they were informants or otherwise identified. She gave up when she saw the security system on the computer. She also testified that Gable frequently carried knives and she had given him a six-inch Chicago Cutlery knife in December 1988 and had not seen it since.

Linda Perkins, the mother of Gable's friend Theresa Ross, testified that Gable arrived at Ross's apartment the morning of January 18 and appeared very nervous. His appearance was atypical; he was dirty and unshaven. "He kept looking out the window like every sound he heard or even in between sounds that he heard, he kept looking out the window as if—I got the impression he was afraid someone was chasing him or following him." She had asked him what was wrong and Gable said, "I fucked up ... I fucked up big time this time." When she asked him what he meant by that, he said, "Well, I'll put it to you like this, you will be reading about it in the papers." A week to ten days later, she testified that Gable, "told me that if I opened my mouth I was a dead motherfucker."[14]

John Kevin Walker testified that Gable had called him on January 18, and Walker went to Gable's apartment to sell him some meth. Gable asked had I heard the news. And I said what news? And he said, "About that guy over there at the State Hospital grounds." And I said, "Yeah, he got shot or something." And Gable said, "Well, that's not exactly what happened, but it's close enough. I stuck him." And then later he said, "I'm sorry, you, if you tell on me, I'm going to have to kill you and kill your family."[15]

Daniel Patrick Walsh testified that in February or March of 1989, Gable came over to the apartment complex where Walsh shared an apartment with Studer and Ross. Walsh was sticking a knife in a tree and Gable asked him where he got the knife. Walsh told him that Jerry Paul Baker had given it to him. Gable then told him that Gable had given Baker the knife and "that was the knife that he used to kill Michael Francke."[16]

Walsh said he didn't take the comment very seriously at the time. Later that summer, he said that Gable had told him about the murder. "He had said that he had been jock-boxing and the car had the car door open, and that he was laying across the seat and that Mr. Francke come up along to—up on him, and he had lunged out into Mr. Francke. Didn't say whether he was out of the car or in the car, lunged into his body and stuff stabbing him repeatedly and that he had fled across the parking lot." [17]

When contacted by police nine months after the murder, Walsh admitted he had denied knowing anything about it, due to Gable's threats and because he was dealing drugs at the time. He was also afraid police would find his fingerprints on the knife and accuse him. He swore he had received nothing from prosecutors in return for his testimony.

The jury also heard from the detectives who had interrogated Gable on September 15-16, November 3, and December

22, 1989. On September 15, 1989, at about 5 p.m., detectives Paul Bain and Fred Ackom picked up Frank Gable from Gable's foster father's house in Coos Bay and brought him to the Coos County patrol office. They questioned him most of the night, together and separately.

Gable's alibi for that night was sketchy. First he said he was home with his wife. Then he said he was having a drug party of 20-30 people the night of the murder, but couldn't recall who was at the party. Later he claimed he was with a friend that night. Then he said he wasn't sure.

Ackom testified that Gable had told him that part of his mind told him that he did the murder, but another part said he didn't, but Gable continued to deny killing Francke. Gable admitted that he had made statements that might have been misinterpreted by some. When asked if he murdered Francke, Gable had replied, "It doesn't matter if I said yes I did it or no, I didn't. They're going to fry me for this."[18]

Ackom asked Francke how God would view the murder. Gable replied that God would forgive the murderer adding, "Yeah, but I'm not saying I did it. I'll go to the end of the trial saying that, Fred. There are only two people who know who killed Michael Francke—Michael Francke and God." Ackom then told him that Francke was dead, and Gable looked puzzled and said, "Well, there are only two people who know Francke—yeah, me and God. Yeah, yeah. Me and God."[19]

When Ackom told Gable he had made a Freudian slip, Gable disagreed and stated, "I'm going to the end of the trial saying I didn't do this. I'll be talking to God all the way. I'll go to heaven saying it and all those mother fuckers will go to hell for lying."[20]

Detective Daryl Berning had also questioned Gable. Gable had worked around the building as an inmate and was familiar with the grounds. Berning showed Gable an aerial photograph of the Dome Building and adjacent grounds. He asked Gable to show him on the photo where he thought Francke had been found. He pointed to the south porch instead of the north. He also pointed to the wrong parking lot. Upon cross-examination, Berning admitted Gable denied killing Michael

Francke.

The interview ended about 3:20 a.m., once Gable asked for a lawyer. The defense suggested that Gable was tired and confused and may have not known what he was saying. Ackom agreed with the defense who pointed out that Gable had consistently denied having anything to do with the murder.

During the November 3 questioning, Gable denied confessing to Mike Keerins. He denied he had told friends he had killed Francke, but admitted, "I might have made some stupid statements."[21]

The prosecution asked police detectives about Jodie Swearingen and how Frank Gable had reacted to her name in interviews. When shown pictures of various people, Gable stared at Detective Ackom without reacting but when he saw a photo of Swearingen, he said. "That Jodie gal, the bitch is saying she saw me run from the scene, isn't she?"[22]

Swearingen, 19, had testified to the grand jury in April 1990 that she saw Gable running from the murder scene. Detective Fred Ackom testified that Gable had denied knowing Swearingen until Ackom showed him a picture of her. Then Gable told detectives that he had met her in July, 1989. When asked if it was possible Swearingen had seen Gable near the Dome Building that night, Gable repeated that he wasn't near the building that night. Detectives had told Gable that he had been seen, but did not tell him who had seen him. Detectives found Gable's statement significant.

Gable's attorneys did not. Under cross-examination, Abel got Ackom to agree that detectives had shown Gable Swearingen's photo and had asked about her repeatedly. She was the only one of Gable's associates for which that was done. Might it not be a reasonable assumption that she had been the accuser? Ackom reluctantly agreed. The prosecution focused on the fact that hers was the only name to which Gable had reacted.

Detective Loren Glover took the stand and recounted the interviews with Gable while transporting Gable from the Coos County jail to the Lane County jail in Springfield. Gable had continued to plead his innocence, but had volunteered that it was likely Earl Childers who had told police that Gable was at the scene of the crime.

The prosecution surprised everyone by resting its case without calling three material witnesses: Jodie Swearingen, Randall Studer, and Michael Keerins.

Swearingen had recanted her testimony, saying she had lied about seeing Gable at the scene to protect her boyfriend Timothy Natividad. She contended that police had coached her in her testimony and had allowed her to meet with Cappie Harden prior to their grand jury testimony to get their stories straight. Her attorney argued that the DA had been holding Swearingen since the prior fall to pressure her in testifying their way.

Randall Studer had also recanted, saying he had lied to the grand jury. Studer had initially denied knowing anything about the murder, but two weeks after pleading guilty to sexually abusing a boy, Studer reported to police that Gable had told him he had killed someone at the state hospital in January 1989. He had also informed police that a month prior to the murder, Gable had talked about killing an unnamed official.

Keerins had been the first of the eight witnesses to implicate Gable. When first questioned by police in May 1989, Keerins had said nothing about a Gable confession. In September of that year, Keerins told police from his Idaho jail cell that Gable had admitted to killing Francke while they were both locked up in the Marion County jail in June 1989. In return, Keerins was transferred back to Oregon.

•••••

The defense opened its case on the eighteenth day of the trial on June 5, 1991. The thrust of the defense was that witnesses had lied about seeing Gable at the murder scene and lied about hearing Gable's many confessions. Throughout the defense portion of the case momentum was difficult to create as witnesses often showed up late, when they showed up at all. They also sought to introduce the murder confessions of Johnny Crouse.

The defense questioned the tactics used when police took 28 hours to transport Gable from Coos County to Salem, interrogating him the whole time about the murder in an attempt to get him to confess or otherwise implicate himself. The defense also called a number of people who were in the area about the time of the murder who testified that they had not seen anything, again trying to plant doubt about the time of the murder.

Oregonian columnist Phil Stanford was asked about his May 3, 1991 column concerning a conversation Stanford had with Mark Gesner in the autumn of 1989. Gesner had told Stanford that he had denied to police that Gable had told him anything about the murder but that his lawyer was encouraging him to give the state what it wanted and implicate Gable. At the time, Gesner was facing 15 years imprisonment on gun charges.

Pam Winn, Gesner's ex-wife, testified that she didn't think Gesner and Gable were particularly close friends. She added that Gesner was a habitual liar.

Cheryl Lowery, Mark Walsh's former girlfriend, said Walsh had did not seem afraid of Gable and had not told her that Gable had threatened to harm her or her children if Walsh went to police with Gable's confession. She said Gable had treated her kids better than their dad (Walsh) did. Gable and his wife had lived with Lowery and Walsh for a month in 1989.

The next day the court saw another sampling of Salem's criminal element take the stand. Inmate Mark Davis testified that John Kevin Walker had told him in June 1990 that he wasn't really going to testify against Gable, but he wanted the DA to drop some of the criminal charges against him. Walker told Davis that he had made up the story about Gable to get even for a bad drug deal. Walker had earlier testified that he served his full sentence and had not cut a deal for his testimony.

Ex-con Patrick Boggs testified that Shorty Harden told him that he had lied about Gable's involvement with the Francke killing and hoped to make some money off the testimony.

Inmate Dewayne Christiansen testified that Harden said

he would be paid for his testimony. Harden said Gable didn't know anything about the murder adding that he was surprised that Harden had gotten rehab given his record, suggesting that he had gotten something in return for his testimony.

Ken Beeler, a former prisoner, testified that Harden told him, too, that he would be splitting the reward fund with seven other witnesses; he had to help the police or face a stiff sentence on his pending charges.

Vicki Boyd, an acquaintance of Gable's, testified that Gable had spoken with her around the time of the murder, after 6:30 and before 7:00 p.m. She was at the house of her friend Shelli Thomas. Gable had called Thomas.

Scott Hedlund, another friend of Gable's, testified that he had driven by the murder scene with Gable about a month after the killing and Gable didn't seem to know much about the murder and wasn't nervous talking about it.

Gable's former landlady testified that she gave Frank and Janyne an eviction notice the morning of January 18, 1989, the morning after the murder. Neighbors had complained about a loud party the night before.

Dennis Gause testified that he had the cell next to Shorty Harden's at the Marion County jail. Harden told Gause that he kept changing his story because police lie detector tests indicated that he was lying. Harden had talked about getting the $30,000 reward. Both Harden and Keerins had talked about book rights. Gause admitted that he had suggested to his jailed friend Bill Storm, that Storm tell police that Gable had confessed to him, but police didn't believe him, indicating that police were scrutinizing the alleged confessions. Gause stated that John Kevin Walker had told him that he didn't know anything about the murder but he was tired of the police bothering him.

Frank Gable's ex-mother-in-law and ex-sister-in-law testified that ex-wife Janyne was not a truthful person, casting doubt on her testimony about the missing knife and that Gable had been nervous when he drove her near the murder scene the next day.

The next day, Marvin and Rosella Tooker testified that they had driven down Center Street at about 6:55 p.m. the night of the murder and that three men ran across Center Street toward the Dome Building. They had almost hit them. The man in the lead was about six feet tall, had long blond hair and was wearing a knee-length coat. The other two were shorter, dark-haired, and wearing dark clothing. Custodian Hunsaker had testified that the man he saw running away was wearing a knee-length tan coat.

Marvin Tooker had retired from the Dallas police force ten years earlier. When he heard about the murder, he reported what he had seen to police. The police report, however, was wrong. The police report placed the men two blocks further east and running away from the Dome Building. Tooker learned of the mistakes and called police requesting that the record be corrected. Following the request, he and his wife began receiving threatening phone calls. Tooker testified that he received two such calls and a number of hang up calls

The defense was still trying to cast doubt about the time of Francke's killing, and therefore, Cappie Harden's eyewitness testimony. The defense called a number of people to the stand who testified they were at the crime scene about 7:00 p.m. but hadn't seen Harden's car or anything unusual.

The timeline at the crime scene was laid out.

• 6:50 p.m.: Francke tells Dave Caulley he is going back to his office to call his wife. Caulley leaves the Dome Building, walks past Francke's car, and does not notice anything unusual. Cappie Harden claims to be parked at the far end of the parking lot at this time, but Caulley does not notice the car.

• 6:50 – 7:00 p.m.: Three men are seen running toward the Dome Building.

• 7:03 p.m.: Custodian Wayne Hunsaker hears a "surprise, hurt" sound and sees two men facing each other in the parking lot.

• 7:04 p.m.: Diana Long, another Corrections official, exits the Dome Building at 7:04 p.m. and does not notice anything unusual as she walks to her car.

- 7:05 p.m.: Jim and Marsha Haskins, who work with Hunsaker, agree that Hunsaker leaves at about 7:03 p.m., and they soon follow him out.
- 7:05 – 7:10 p.m.: Four hospital patients walking down the street just north of the Dome Building to a Narcotics Anonymous meeting notice Francke's car door open. They also see a heavyset man, believed to be Wayne Hunsaker, walking away, north of them. One of the men thinks he sees a Datsun 280z or a Toyota Celica parked where Harden said he was parked. Former suspect Timothy Natividad drove a 280z.

•••••

The defense brought back Wayne Hunsaker to highlight inconsistencies between what Hunsaker and Harden saw. The prosecution argued, and Harden testified, that Gable was in Francke's car. Francke reached across Gable. Gable slashed Francke across the left arm and coat sleeve. Then Gable came out of the car and stabbed Francke once through the left bicep and once in the chest.

Hunsaker testified that after exiting the building and crossing the street, he heard a "surprise, hurt" sound and turned toward the noise. He saw two men facing each other less than two feet apart, on the driveway at the edge of the grassy area, about 40 feet away. Both men had their arms down and seemed to be having a normal conversation. They faced each other for only a moment before the taller man turned around and ran away from the Dome Building. The other man turned and walked toward the Dome Building. Defense attorney Abel pointed out that Francke, at 6'3" was actually taller than 5'11" Gable. Prosecutor Moore noted that Hunsaker only saw the men briefly.

The next day, the defense called Jodie Swearingen to the stand. She denied having called Harden from the hospital; the closest phone was blocks away, on 25th and State. She only said she had seen Gable kill Francke when pressured by police to back up Harden's story. Prosecutor Moore asked if Swearingen recalled saying that she had seen Gable and Francke scuffle, saw Francke fall, and Gable turn around with a bloody knife in his hand. She agreed she had, but said it wasn't true. She acknowledged that she could go to jail for lying to the grand jury and denied that she was changing her story to avoid being labeled a snitch and alienating her meth crowd. On cross-examination, however, Swearingen admitted that she had told two juvenile court counselors that she was either an accomplice or an accessory to a murder. She had also hired an attorney and had an immunity agreement in place that protected her from being charged with a crime connected to the killing. Prosecutor Moore challenged the jury as to why someone would need immunity for something they didn't do and something they didn't see.

Johnny Crouse, who had confessed to killing Francke and then recanted, decided to take the fifth and not testify about his earlier confessions.

(At a hearing outside the jury's presence, Crouse forgot to invoke for the first question. He replied, "No," when asked if he had killed Francke. The defense wanted his earlier confessions on the record. The prosecution did not. Judge West ruled that Crouse was an unavailable witness.)

Francke's widow Bingta testified that her husband was extremely security conscious. For example, he would lock his car in a locked garage and put his German shepherd in there as well. They had moved to Scotts Mills in October 1988 in part because of security concerns. She said that when someone escaped from one of the prisons, Francke would call her and tell her to lock the house, bring in the dog, and get out his Colt .45 semi-automatic handgun. After Diane Downs escaped, Francke had a police riot shotgun issued to him. When Bingta returned to Salem to pick out a suit for Francke's burial, she found more ammunition in the house than normal.

According to stipulated testimony, Francke had requested more ammunition in December 1988 and was issued 300 shells.

Francke had also pulled out a chair from the den into the

kitchen to better see if anyone was coming up the walk to their home. He was always careful about locking his car and setting the alarm.

Bingta also testified that her husband was concerned about some of the Corrections officers and was under pressure from the Governor's Office to fire some of them.

The last witness of the trial was Werner Spitz, an expert pathologist who testified he had participated in 50,000-60,000 autopsies and had served on the 1978 Kennedy assassination congressional investigation, the assassination of Martin Luther King, and investigated the drowning of Mary Jo Kopechne.

(Later he would testify at the trials of O.J. Simpson, Phil Spector, and Casey Anthony and consult on the JonBenet Ramsey investigation.)

In his opinion, the Chicago Cutlery knife had not been the murder weapon. The murder weapon had some kind of handle or structure at the hilt of the blade that had caused a small, half-moon bruise around the cut. Such structures were common on folding knives, but not kitchen knives.

Also, the kitchen knife was not the right thickness. Rather than a five to seven-inch knife, the wound could have been made by a three to four-inch blade. Spitz also pointed out a number of deficiencies in the investigation. The wound had not been properly measured. The core body temperature should have been taken at the scene to narrow down the time of death. The autopsy report neglected to mention some things clearly visible in photographs, such as bruising. Spitz did rule out a knife owned by Natividad as the murder weapon.

A blow to the defense was Judge West's decision to exclude testimony about Johnny Crouse and his confession as an alternate theory of the crime.

Closing arguments took about three hours for each side. Both questioned the credibility of each other's witnesses. The prosecution argued that Gable was looking for names of prison snitches when he was surprised by Francke; he stabbed him because he didn't want to return to prison. The defense argued that the case had many unanswered questions and that the evidence did not conclusively prove that Gable was the killer; many of the witnesses were punishing Gable for his work as a snitch for the Keizer police.

After less than 24 hours of deliberation, the jury returned its verdict: Guilty on all six counts of aggravated murder and one count of murder. The defense team was stunned. Defense investigator Tom McCallum described Gable as very upset that some things were not brought out at trial and that he had not taken the stand to explain the statements he made to police.

Gable refused to speak to his lawyers following the verdict and complained to the judge about his attorneys. He claimed his lawyers were not prepared, didn't allow him to participate in his defense; they were given discovery documents late; that certain defense witnesses were not allowed to testify; and essential evidence was not presented.

The Francke family was surprised by the verdict also, and vowed to continue the investigation.

The same jury would also sentence Gable. During the penalty phase of the trial, the jury would need to address four questions: Did the killer deliberately act with the reasonable assurance that his act would cause the death of Francke? Does the killer constitute a continuing threat of violence? Was the killer's act unreasonable in light of provocation, if any, by the victim? Should the accused be sentenced to die? There were two sentencing options at the time of the crime: the death penalty (which required a unanimous vote) or life in prison with the possibility of parole. An amendment to the death penalty law had occurred after the date of Francke's murder: life in prison without the possibility of parole. The application of that sentence could have been challenged by Gable's attorneys, but was not. The jury considered all three.

During the sentencing period, the jury heard the good, the bad, and the ugly about Frank Gable's life. Prosecutor Tom Bostwick told jurors that Gable was clearly a dangerous man who should be put to death. Gable's ex-wife testified to the domestic abuse.

During a morning recess on July 10, from the third row

bench, Rev. Bob Biggs startled those in the courtroom by intoning the words of a wedding ceremony. Biggs pointed to Gable sitting 20 feet away and asked whether Gable took attorney Karen Steele to be his wife. Gable nodded and said, "I do" and Steele answered similarly. The accomplished defense attorney and small time criminal were married. They would divorce six years later.

A psychiatrist testified that early abuse in Gable's life probably led to his anti-social personality disorder and that such a disorder was not treatable. Another psychiatrist agreed, but thought that future violence could be contained in a controlled environment. Gable's sister testified that their parents were alcoholics, that their mother would physically abuse them, and that "foster father" Les Gederos sexually abused Frank and his brother Syd.

On July 11, 1991, the jury sentenced Frank Gable to life in prison without the possibility of parole. Two jurors opposed giving him the death penalty.

Aftermath

In September, following the murder sentencing, Gable was given an additional eight-year federal sentence for being an armed career criminal, stemming from his arrest in 1989 for having been found with a short-barreled, pistol-grip shotgun.

Gable was transferred from Salem to a series of out-of-state prisons.

After all the costs were added up, the defense had billed the indigent defense fund over $1 million, a record-setting sum. It cost the state police another $1 million to investigate the crime. DA Penn estimated it cost his office $105,000 in salaries and expenses to prosecute the case.

Dale Penn, citing issues in working together, asked the two Gable prosecutors to resign.

A month after Gable was found guilty, 14 prisoners were tossed into segregation on contraband charges, suggesting the smuggling of prohibited items into the prison continued.

Following his conviction, Gable appealed multiple times citing inadequate trial counsel and that the sentence of life without parole should not have been a sentencing option. He was denied relief in all cases until his final appeal.

The amount and content of the press coverage of the murder and trial was controversial. Some believed that Steven Jackson's coverage for the Salem *Statesman Journal* did not appropriately cover the prosecution's case. Phil Stanford, who wrote a column for *The Oregonian*, provided a platform for those involved and who raised doubt about the prosecution case. *Willamette Week* also questioned the prosecution's dismissal of a possible conspiracy.

In 2005, *The Oregonian* assigned two investigative reporters—Noelle Crombie and Les Zaitz—to review thousands of pages of documents, interview key players, and run down Gable's possible alibis, which he claimed were never fully explored. The reporters found no evidence of a conspiracy and found holes in Gable's alibis and that despite claims that the prosecution was based on unreliable testimony from drug-addicted criminals with motives to lie, Gable had made plenty of incriminating statements to police and to his ex-wife, all of whom stood by their stories.

Kevin Francke offered the theory that Scott McAlister had arranged for Francke's murder. McAlister's motive was to keep secret some kind financial kickback he was getting from the prison, or to get Francke's job, or revenge. Francke thought something had happened between the two men on a trip to Reno. Francke contended that Michael had cut short the trip and flew home early to escape McAlister. However, records uncovered by *The Oregonian* investigation found Francke had canceled his flight and had driven back with McAlister, undercutting the theory that something had happened between the two men.

On the website freefrankgable.com,[15] an uncorroborated story was posted by the Corrections employee responsible for the high speed copier in the Dome Building. She reported that the man who appeared to repair the copier the day of the murder at 4:00 p.m. was not the regular repairman, but resembled the sketch of the olive-skinned man in the pin-striped suit seen at the Dome Building. The unknown repairman told her that he would need more time with the copier and would need to stay after hours, an unprecedented occurrence. When the Corrections employee returned to work the day after the murder, the copy machine was in pieces, and the repair call had not been logged in, as per procedure. She called for a repairman, and the regular technician showed up and had the machine fixed inside of 30 minutes. The employee later read in a news article that she had identified the regular copy repairman as the man who had been there that day, which she disputed.

In late 2014, Gable filed another appeal with the assistance of federal public defenders. The Oregon Innocence Project filed a friend of court brief, as well. The appeal in federal court based on a number of issues, including flaws in the use of polygraphs in his case, the inability to include evidence of third-party guilt (Johnny Crouse) and the recantations from trial witnesses:

In an affidavit for Gable's federal appeals team, Greg Johnson, an ex-con and associate of Natividad's, claimed that around dusk on the night of the murder Natividad asked Johnson to drive him to the Dome Building. He watched Natividad walking toward the building steps as he drove away. Sometime later, Natividad called him to be picked up at the doctors' offices west of the Dome Building. He appeared out of breath and told Johnson, "it's not my blood," referring to his wet gloves. He put a briefcase in the back seat and they went to a bar. He did not tell Johnson what had happened but said that it will be "all over the news tomorrow"[23] and to keep his mouth shut. A few days later, Johnson stated he accompanied Natividad for a $20,000 payoff from two Corrections officials.

Elizabeth Godlove told Gable's defense team that Natividad had come home late one night in mid-January 1989 with wounds on his leg and head, and a few days later during a fight where he was threatening her, told he had killed a man. He had also shown her large sums of cash.

Mike Keerins, who had told police Gable confessed to

him, stated he did so in exchange for a transfer back to Oregon from an out-of-state prison, to deflect suspicion away from his family, and because Gable had been a snitch for the Keizer police.

Cappie Harden, who told police he had witnessed the murder, said he was not at the Dome Building that night and had lied because police had threatened him and his family and told him that Gable had informed against him previously.

Jodie Swearingen recanted her testimony of witnessing the murder with Harden, stating she was coerced by police who told her that her testimony had to jive with Harden's.

John Kevin Walker recanted his testimony that Gable had confessed to him and said he had lied because police led him to believe he was being investigated as a possible accomplice to the murder and because he believed Gable had snitched on him to police. When first polygraphed, Walker said he had told the truth. But polygrapher was coercive and said he had been lying and "if you don't start cooperating … you're going to be standing on the curb with Frank … Get on the bus now, or stand on the curb with Frank, and you can go down with him."[24]

Daniel Walsh stated he had lied about Gable confessing to the crime due to police pressure to incriminate Gable and in exchange pending Ohio charges were dismissed and he was given immunity for past and present crimes. Walsh's ex-wife added that Walsh was angry at Gable for taking advantage of him.

Earl Childers testified that he had seen Gable near the scene of the crime and that Gable had confessed to him but later said that Gable had never confessed to him and he wasn't sure it was Gable's car that he saw. He lied when police became angry with him for not telling the story they wanted to hear and because Gable owed him money.

Randy Studer stated that he had told police Gable never confessed to him but was pressured by police to confirm Linda Perkins' story of a Gable confession and police subsequently dropped a criminal charge against him that carried a ten-year sentence.

Teresa Ross, daughter of Linda Perkins, stated she had never heard Gable confess and didn't believe her mother had heard him do so, either. She concocted the Gable confession after police implicated her in a sexual abuse case involving a minor.

In an affidavit for Gable's appeal, Janyne stated that had she seen the January 18 eviction notice, she would have testified that Frank was home that night and that phone records established he was home.

On April 18, 2019, U.S. Magistrate Judge John Acosta ruled that the trial court had erred in excluding evidence of third-party guilt (Johnny Crouse) and that trial counsel provided ineffective assistance in failing to assert Gable's federal due process rights in the face of the trial court's error.

Acosta wrote, "Thus, the state's evidence at trial centered on eyewitness testimony, circumstantial evidence, Gable's statements to police, and Gable's statements to several acquaintances, all of whom were part of a loose network of people who used or sold methamphetamine in the Salem area."[25]

He wrote that, "Although the evidence presented at trial in 1991 resulted in a guilty verdict, the court concludes that it is more likely than not that no reasonable juror would find Gable guilty in light of the totality of all of the evidence uncovered since that time, particularly the newly presented evidence of witness recantations."[26]

The judge ordered Gable be retried within 90 days or released from prison. Oregon appealed the decision and requested a stay on the order he be released or retried. Gable was released under supervision pending the outcome of the decision on June 28, 2019, having served 30 years in prison. As of publication, that appeal is still pending.

While in prison, Gable changed his name to Franke J. Different Cloud.

Who killed Michael Francke? Frank Gable? Rooster Natividad? Johnny Crouse? Was the murder the result of a routine car burglary gone wrong? Or a well-planed conspiracy gone right? Was the burglar after guns? The names of snitches?

Information about corrupt government officials who were going to be named the next day's legislative hearing?

We will probably never know the answer with any certainty. Both Crouse and Natividad are dead. Uncorroborated stories by those in the underworld are viewed skeptically. When looking for explanations for an unfortunate event and the choice is between stupid people making mistakes or clever people devising a complicated plan, nine times out of ten, stupid is to blame. But is this case the one in ten where there actually was a conspiracy? When powerful people are murdered there will always be those who question easy answers and lone gunmen. The skeptics may ultimately be wrong, but are right to raise issues and question authority—especially when that authority has a history of corruption.

Benjamin Franklin is reported to have said, "Justice will not be served until those who are unaffected are as outraged as those who are." A cornerstone of democracy is a justice system that metes out justice blindly, based on evidence. Ensuring that one exists should be the priority of its citizens—all of them.

Chapter 1

[1] Painter, John. Brudos Family Members Said Hiding to Avoid Subpoenas by Grand Jury. *The Oregonian.* June 7, 1969, p. 7.

Chapter 3

[1] Sheriff Censures West's Leniency. *The Morning Oregonian.* June 21, 1911, p. 2.

[2] Mob Rule is Feared. *Sunday Oregonian.* July 28, 1912, p. 12.

[3] https://digital.osl.state.or.us/islandora/object/osl%3A16830

[4] Withycombe Busy With Job Hunters. *The Morning Oregonian.* November 21, 1914, p. 9.

[5] Harry Minto to be Penitentiary Head. *The Morning Oregonian,* March 4, 1915, p. 6.

[6] Folder 1, Box 1. Carl Panzram Papers, p. 5. Special Collections and University Archives, Library and Information Access, San Diego State University. The Collection was donated by Henry Lesser.

[7] Folder 1, Box 1. Carl Panzram Papers, p. 5. Special Collections and University Archives, Library and Information Access, San Diego State University. The Collection was donated

by Henry Lesser.

[8] Folder 3, Box 1. Carl Panzram Papers, p. 24. Special Collections and University Archives, Library and Information Access, San Diego State University. The Collection was donated by Henry Lesser.

[9] Prisoner No. 6435, *The Oregon Penitentiary*, p. 1.

[10] Woodford-Beals and Carl Beals. Oregon State Prison Superintendents; *The Shepherds of State Street*. Airy Woods Publishing Co. 2009, p. 15.

[11] Webb, Jesse, aka Prisoner 6435. *The Oregon Penitentiary*.

[12] Folder 3, Box 1. Carl Panzram Papers, p. 24-25. Special Collections and University Archives, Library and Information Access, San Diego State University. The Collection was donated by Henry Lesser.

[13] Hooker Lies in Morgue At State Prison. *The Oregon Statesman*. September 30, 1915, p. 1, 5.

[14] Folder 5, Box 1, Carl Panzram Papers, p. 33. Special Collections and University Archives, Library and Information Access, San Diego State University. The Collection was donated by Henry Lesser.

[15] Minto Resigns at Demand of Board. *The Morning Oregonian*. November 16, 1916.

[16] Serious Condition Face at Prison. *The Morning Oregonian*. November 19, 1916, p. 10.

[17] Folder 5, Box 1, Carl Panzram Papers, p. 33. Special Collections and University Archives, Library and Information Access, San Diego State University. The Collection was donated by Henry Lesser.

[18] Folder 5, Box 1, Carl Panzram Papers, p. 33. Special Collections and University Archives, Library and Information Access, San Diego State University. The Collection was donated by Henry Lesser.

[19] *Oregon Commission to Investigate State Penitentiary*. Report. 1917. 76 p.

[20] Folder 5, Box 1, Carl Panzram Papers, p. 33. Special Collections and University Archives, Library and Information Access, San Diego State University. The Collection was donated by Henry Lesser.

Chapter 5

[1] Chemawa Man Slain. *Capital Journal*. September 5, 1921, p. 1.

[2] Ibid.

[3] Official Report of the Nineteenth Annual Conference of Charities and Correction (1892), p. 46. Reprinted in Richard H. Pratt, "The Advantages of Mingling Indians with Whites," Americanizing the American Indians: Writings by the "Friends of the Indian" 1880-1900. Cambridge , Mass: Harvard University Press, 1973.

[4] Chemawa Man Slain. *Capital Journal*. September 5, 1921, p. 1.

[5] Ibid.

[6] Woman Slays Her Husband. *The Oregon Statesman.* September 6, 1921, p. 8.

[7] Chemawa Man Slain. *Capital Journal.* September 5, 1921, p. 1.

[8] Ibid.

[9] Ibid.

[10] Ibid.

[11] Ibid.

[12] Ibid.

[13] Ibid.

[14] Murderess Arraigned. *Capital Journal.* September 6, 1921, p.1.

[15] Chemawa Man Slain. *Capital Journal.* September 5, 1921, p. 1.

[16] Murder Not Yet Fully Explained. *Capital Journal.* September 10, 1921, p. 1.

[17] Ibid.

[18] Ibid.

[19] Ibid.

[20] Anger Is Denied By Husband-Killer. *The Morning Oregonian.* September 10, 1921, p. 1.

[21] Insanity to be Defense. *Capital Journal.* September 9, 1921, p. 1.

[22] Ibid.

[23] Ibid.

[24] Anger Is Denied By Husband-Killer. *The Morning Oregonian.* September 10, 1921, p. 1.

[25] Insanity to be Defense. *Capital Journal.* September 9, 1921, p. 1.

[26] Woman Slays Her Husband. *The Oregon Statesman.* September 6, 1921, p. 1, 8.

[27] Ibid.

[28] Insanity to be Defense. *Capital Journal.* September 9, 1921, p. 1.

[29] Murderess Arraigned. *Capitol Journal.* Sept. 6, p. 1.

[30] Ibid.

[31] Ibid.

[32] Ibid.

[33] Wife's Friend, Of Whom Murdered Man Became Jealous, Former Convict. *Capitol Journal.* September 8, 1921, p. 1.

[34] US v. Wurtzbarger. (D.C. Or) *753. 276 Federal Reporter.* November 14, 1921.

[35] Mrs. Wurtzbarger Brooding In Cell. *The Sunday Oregonian.* September 11, 1921, p. 1.

[36] Anger Is Denied By Husband-Killer. *The Morning Oregonian.* September 10, 1921, p. 1.

[37] Ibid.

[38] Murder No Yet Fully Explained. *Capital Journal.* September 10, 1921, p. 1.

[39] Mrs. Wurtzbarger Brooding In Cell. *The Sunday Oregonian.* September 11, 1921, p. 1.

[40] Anger Is Denied By Husband-Killer. *The Morning Oregonian.* September 10, 1921, p. 1.

[41] Ibid.

[42] Murder No Yet Fully Explained. *Capital Journal.* September 10, 1921, p. 1.

[43] Mrs. Wurtzbarger Gets Ten Years In Government Jail. *Statesman Journal.* January 8, 1922, p. 1, 2.

[44] Ibid.

[45] Ibid.

[46] Mrs. Wurtzbarger To Be Imprisoned In Oregon Bastille. *The Oregonian.* March 4, 1922, p. 1.

[47] Women Prisoners Are Restricted. *The Oregonian.* March 15, 1924, p. 1.

Chapter 7

[1] Dullenty, Jim. Harry Tracy: The Last Desperado. Kendall/Hunt Publishing Co. 1989. P. 8.

[2] Wake of Death; Convicts Slay Guards and Escape; Victims Number Three; Prisoners Intervenes and Is Shot in the Leg. Desperate Foray Succeeds. Fugitives Tracy and Merrill Are Still at Large – State Penitentiary Scene of a Daring and Bloody Outbreak. *Morning Oregonian.* June 10, 1902, p. 1, 3.

[3] Ibid.

[4] Ibid.

[5] Kelley, Buncko. *Thirteen Years in the Oregon Penitentiary,* p. 6.

[6] Kelley, Buncko. *Thirteen Years in the Oregon Penitentiary,* p. 104.

[7] Ibid.

[8] Kelley, Buncko. *Thirteen Years in the Oregon Penitentiary,* p. 111.

[9] Trap for Posse. *The Morning Oregonian.* June 12, 1902, p. 1.

[10] Trap for Posse. *The Morning Oregonian.* June 12, 1902, p. 1.

[11] Trap for Posse. *The Morning Oregonian.* June 12, 1902, p. 1.

[12] Kelley, Buncko. *Thirteen years in the Oregon Penitentiary.* P. 120.

[13] Tracy on Water. *The Morning Oregonian.* July 3, 1902, p. 1, 3.

[14] Tracy on Water. *The Morning Oregonian.* July 3, 1902, p. 1, 3.

Chapter 9

[1] Poisoning from Frozen Canned Eggs Held Cause. *The Oregonian.* November 19, 1942, p. 13.

[2] Nokes, Richard. Victim Tells How Poison Meal Brought Paralysis. *The Oregonian.* November 20, 1942 p.14.

[3] Nokes, Richard. Victim Tells How Poison Meal Brought Paralysis. *The Oregonian.* November 20, 1942 p.14.

[4] Death List of Poisoned Eggs at Hospital 47. *Capital Journal.* November 20, 1942, p. 1.

[5] Poisoning from Frozen Canned Eggs Held Cause. *The Oregonian.* November 19, 1942, p. 13.

[6] Death List of Poisoned Eggs at Hospital 47. *Capital Journal*. November 20, 1942, p. 1.

[7] Poison Deaths at Hospital Probed. *Capital Journal*. November 21, 1942, p. 1, 9.

[8] Poison Deaths at Hospital Probed. *Capital Journal*. November 21, 1942, p. 1, 9.

[9] Hospital Poison Mistaken for Dried Milk. *Oregon Statesman*. November 22, 1942, p. 1.

[10] Hospital Cook Arraigned for Manslaughter. *Capital Journal*. November 23, 1942, p. 1.

[11] Hospital Cook Arraigned for Manslaughter. Capital Journal. November 23, 1942, p. 1.

[12] Gustafson, Alan. Blame stayed with patient after deaths. *The Statesman Journal*. November 18, 1992, p. 1C, 3C.

[13] Gustafson, Alan. Blame stayed with patient after deaths. *The Statesman Journal*. November 18, 1992, p. 1C, 3C.

Chapter 10

[1] Mosey, Ed. Wampler convicted, draws life sentence. *The Oregonian*. March 24, 1976, p. 1.

[2] Stone, Jerry. Groener Ruled Guilty of Speeding. *Oregon Statesman*. October 17, 1958, p. 1.

[3] Eden, Melina. Ex-Wife Asserts Wampler Never Got Over Being Fired. Oregon Statesman. March 10, 1975, p. 1.

[4] Mosey, Ed. Wampler convicted, draws life sentence. *The Oregonian*. March 24, 1976, p. 1.

[5] Mosey, Ed. Wampler convicted, draws life sentence. *The Oregonian*. March 24, 1976, p. 1.

Chapter 11

[1] Pitiful End of a Brave Struggle. *Daily Capitol Journal*. March 11, 1912, p. 3.

[2] Ibid.

[3] Ibid.

[4] Ibid.

Chapter 12

[1] *Gable v Williams*, No. 3:07-cv-00413-AC (D. Or) April 18, 2019, p. 38.

[2] *Gable v Williams*, No. 3:07-cv-00413-AC (D. Or) April 18, 2019, p. 38.

[3] *Gable v Williams*, No. 3:07-cv-00413-AC (D. Or) April 18, 2019, p. 40.

[4] *Gable v. Williams*, No. 3:07-cv-00413-AC.Brief in Support of Amended Petition for Writ of Habeas Corpus Brief in Support of Amended Petition for Writ of Habeas Corpus. P. 130. http://media.oregonlive.com/pacific-northwest-news/other/Nell.Brown.brief.gable10.14.2014.pdf

[5] Streisinger, Cory. Interoffice memo to Neil Goldschmidt. August 22, 1989.

[6] Jackson, Steven P. Gable's ex tells about inquiries. *Statesman Journal*. October 22, 1990, p. 1A.

[7] Warden, Judge John C. Report to Governor Neil Goldschmidt of Judge John C. Warden's

Corrections Investigation. December 14, 1989, p. 2.

8 Warden, Judge John C. Report to Governor Neil Goldschmidt of Judge John C. Warden's Corrections Investigation. December 14, 1989, p. 3.

9 *Gable v Williams*, No. 3:07-cv-00413-AC (D. Or) April 18, 2019, 4/18/19, p.8.

10 *Gable v Williams*, No. 3:07-cv-00413-AC (D. Or) April 18, 2019, 4/18/19, p. 9.

11 *Gable v Williams*, No. 3:07-cv-00413-AC (D. Or) April 18, 2019, 4/18/19, p. 10

12 *Gable v Williams*, , No. 3:07-cv-00413-AC (D. Or) April 18, 2019, 4/18/19, p. 20.

13 *Gable v Williams*, , No. 3:07-cv-00413-AC (D. Or) April 18, 2019, 4/18/19, p. 21.

14 *Gable v Williams*, , No. 3:07-cv-00413-AC (D. Or) April 18, 2019, 4/18/19, p.16.

15 *Gable v Williams*, , No. 3:07-cv-00413-AC (D. Or) April 18, 2019, 4/18/19, p.17.

16 *Gable v Williams*, , No. 3:07-cv-00413-AC (D. Or) April 18, 2019, 4/18/19, p. 18.

17 *Gable v Williams*, , No. 3:07-cv-00413-AC (D. Or) April 18, 2019, 4/18/19, p. 18.

18 *Gable v Williams*, , No. 3:07-cv-00413-AC (D. Or) April 18, 2019, p. 25

19 *Gable v Williams*, , No. 3:07-cv-00413-AC (D. Or) April 18, 2019, p.26.

20 *Gable v Williams*, , No. 3:07-cv-00413-AC (D. Or) April 18, 2019, p. 26..

21 *Gable v Williams*, No. 3:07-cv-00413-AC (D. Or) April 18, 2019, p. 28.

22 *Gable v Williams*, , No. 3:07-cv-00413-AC (D. Or) April 18, 2019.

23 *Gable v Williams*, No. 3:07-cv-00413-AC.Brief in Support of Amended Petition for Writ of Habeas Corpus P. 139. http://media.oregonlive.com/pacific-northwest-news/other/Nell.Brown.brief.gable10.14.2014.pdf

24 *Gable v Williams*, , No. 3:07-cv-00413-AC.Brief in Support of Amended Petition for Writ of Habeas Corpus. P. 70. http://media.oregonlive.com/pacific-northwest-news/other/Nell.Brown.brief.gable10.14.2014.pdf

25 *Gable v Williams*, , No. 3:07-cv-00413-AC (D. Or) April 18, 2019, p. 7.

26 *Gable v Williams*, , No. 3:07-cv-00413-AC (D. Or) April 18, 2019, p. 58.